Common Knowledge

CRPYK

Knowledge

The development of understanding
in the classroom

Common Knowledge

The development of understanding in the classroom

DEREK EDWARDS
and NEIL MERCER

London and New York

First published in 1987 by
Methuen & Co. Ltd

Published in the USA by
Methuen & Co.
in association with Methuen, Inc.

Reprinted in 1993 by
Routledge
11 New Fetter Lane, London EC4P 4EE
29 West 35th Street, New York, NY 10001

© 1987 Derek Edwards and Neil Mercer
Appendix © Janet Maybin

Photoset by Rowland Phototypesetting Ltd
Bury St Edmunds, Suffolk
Printed in Great Britain at
the University Press, Cambridge

British Library Cataloguing in Publication Data

Edwards, Derek
Common knowledge: the development
of understanding in the classroom.
1. Educational psychology
I. Title   II. Mercer, Neil
370.15   LB1051

Library of Congress Cataloging in Publication Data

Edwards, Derek
Common knowledge.

Bibliography: p.
Includes index.
1. Communication in education – Great Britain.
2. Interaction analysis in education.
3. Comprehension.
I. Mercer, Neil.   II. Title.
LB1033.E33   1987   371.1'02   87-1738

ISBN 0-415-043085

Contents

Preface and Acknowledgements

The research and theory that are the basis of this book are the outcome of a collaborative project on the nature of classroom education that has been in progress since about 1982, conducted in and between our host institutions at Loughborough University and the Open University. Many people have helped us in all stages of the work, from the initial formulation and conduct of the research, through to the critical reading of parts of the manuscript. We should like to thank the following people in particular.

The Education and Human Development Committee of the ESRC provided essential funding between 1984 and 1986 (award ref. no. C00232236). The funded project team consisted of the authors, together with Janet Maybin, project officer, who arranged visits to schools, conducted some of the data transcriptions, helped in the analysis of recordings, read the entire manuscript and wrote the appendix. Janet's influence is felt throughout the book, in the ideas developed in it as well as in the fact that the research got done. The fourth member of the team was our invaluable project secretary, Pat Stroud, located at the Loughborough end. Pat's work in transcribing video and audio recordings, apart from many other tasks willingly undertaken, surpassed what anyone could reasonably expect of a secretarial assistant. Others who have been of direct help in the general conduct of the research include Sue

Sheldon, who conducted some of the interviews with pupils, and Pam Powter, secretary in the School of Education at the Open University, who has provided such excellent secretarial support for our research since it began. We should also like to thank the ILEA Schools Television Unit for allowing us to use their materials, and the Audio-Visual Services at the Open University for their expertise in making our own video recordings.

Friends and colleagues who have read parts of the manuscript and provided useful comments include the following: Michael Billig, David Middleton, Douglas Barnes and Martyn Hammersley. Our thanks to them, and to the others whose views have shaped what is written here. Finally, we offer our heartfelt thanks to the teachers and children in London and Buckinghamshire who took part in this research.

Key to
data transcriptions

Several of the chapters present sequences of classroom dialogue, together with contextual information, printed to the right of the speech, concerning what the teacher and pupils were doing at the time they were talking. The names of the children have been altered to protect their identity, and the teachers are identified by the single letter 'T'. Our aim has been to present these sequences of talk as accurately as possible, using some conventions for the transcription of discourse, but at the same time ensuring that they remain easily readable and comprehensible. Our purpose has not been to produce an analysis of linguistic structure, but to provide the sort of information that is useful in analysing how people reach common understandings with each other of what they are talking about. So, while commas are avoided, and certain conventions are used to indicate such things as pauses and simultaneous speech, we have retained the normal written uses of capital letters and full stops (periods) to mark the start and end of sentences.

Transcription conventions

(. . .)   Words undeciphered

.
.   Omitted discourse which is irrelevant to the issue being
.   discussed

. . .   Sequence starts or ends within a speaker's turn

/   Pause of less than 2 seconds

//   Pause of greater than 2 seconds

Bold type Emphatic speech

[Simultaneous or interrupted speech

Example:
SPEAKER 1: . . . that's very ⌈ interesting isn't it?
SPEAKER 2:   ⌊ Say if the string's . . .

(&)   Continuing speech, separated in the transcript by an interrupting speaker

Example: speaker 1 continues talking without a pause, despite interruption:
SPEAKER 1: You think even if you stuck a ton on
                       ⌈ it wouldn't make any difference a ton?
                       │ (&)
SPEAKER 2:   ⌊ No/ no/ not even a ton.
SPEAKER 1: (&) it would still be about ten seconds . . .

1
Introduction

This book is about education as a communicative process. The research it describes is not about classroom language as such, and so cannot be called research in linguistics. Nor is it really about the nature and functioning of the education system, as might be the case for a piece of sociological research. And, although our research is probably best described as 'psychological', we are not concerned with the intellectual development or attainment of individual children, as are many psychological researchers.

The research is about the ways in which knowledge (and, principally, that knowledge which forms the content of school curricula) is presented, received, shared, controlled, negotiated, understood and misunderstood by teachers and children in the classroom. We are interested in what that knowledge means to people, and in how and to what extent it becomes part of their common knowledge, their joint understanding. The whole of our enquiry is based on the belief that all education is essentially about the development of some shared understanding, some mutuality of perspectives. Much goes on in classrooms besides education, and there is more to education than the sharing of knowledge. But, where and when education *is* taking place, then mutuality is always an issue. This is true for all styles and philosophies of teaching.

Now this may seem a contentious assertion. It might be objected that

the most formal, traditional and didactic styles of teaching, which emphasize the acquisition of factual knowledge, accurate recall and 'right-
answerism' (Holt 1969), are concerned not with developing a mutuality of
perspectives but with imposing the teacher's knowledge on the blank
slates of the pupils' minds. Like Mr Gradgrind in Dickens's *Hard Times*,
some teachers may see children as 'little pitchers . . . to be filled so full of
facts'. But even Gradgrinds pursue the goal of common knowledge. It is
simply that the nature and scope of that knowledge is not negotiable, or
open to question by the pupils. The intended end-product of the process
is the pupils' acceptance and understanding of what their teacher already
knows. On the other hand, a more progressive educational approach
might well offer more opportunities for pupils and teachers to negotiate
common curriculum goals, or at least for teachers to incorporate pupils'
wider experience and interests into what is taught. But whether such
opportunities are taken up, and whether they are successfully incorporated into teaching and learning, can be discovered only by observing
what goes on in actual classrooms. The pursuit of shared understanding
is problematical under any educational ethos, and we are not suggesting
that it is easily, or often, achieved. We are suggesting that to look at how
shared understanding is pursued, achieved, lost or even avoided in the
everyday classroom talk of teachers and pupils will tell us more, not only
about classroom education, but also about the communication of knowledge in a much broader sense. Indeed, we were surprised at the extent to
which the relatively 'progressive' sorts of teaching that we examined
were characterized by the overwhelming dominance of the teacher over
all that was done, said and understood to be correct.

Schools serve many social and cultural purposes, from child-minding
to the transmission of moral values; but their institutional *raison d'être* is
always their function of passing on a part of the accumulated knowledge
of a society, and evaluating children's success in acquiring this knowledge. Educational knowledge, as represented by the school curriculum,
is a selection from all the knowledge of a particular culture. As Douglas
Barnes (1982) reminds us, it is possibly never more than 'an arbitrary
selection, sanctioned only by convenience and tradition' (p. 101). But it
consists of much more than given 'facts'; it includes ways of operating on
the world, and of making judgements. At best, it embodies useful ways of
evaluating given information, of generating new information and creating new ways of thinking about, and acting upon, the world. At worst, it
excludes much 'worldly' knowledge, practical skills and commonsense
understandings, in such a way that it remains for ever peripheral, and in
the great part dispensable, to most of the people to whom it is offered.
Although educational knowledge has no well-defined boundaries, and
merges with other kinds of social understanding and experience that
children acquire during their school years, any analysis of educational

practice would not benefit from leaving it embedded in its broader cultural context. The boundaries of educational knowledge are continuously marked out, and reinforced, in classroom discourse. Schools have their own epistemological culture, and it is with the perpetuation of this culture that we are concerned here.

Sharing knowledge

What is the essence of the act of sharing knowledge? What are the minimum requirements of an interaction, which would allow it to be so described? Consider the proposition that such an act is 'that two people now know what only one knew before'. This minimal statement, in its apparent simplicity, conceals more than it reveals about a feature of human life which, perhaps more than any other, distinguishes us from other animals. It is now fully appreciated that the dominance of our species is largely due to our unique ability to avoid the 'genetic bottleneck' which restricts the quantity and quality of information that even the most intelligent of other species are able to pass on from one generation to another. Apes and monkeys pass on information and learn habits through observing each other's actions; what they do not do is share knowledge by symbolizing it out of context. They do not discuss, compare notes, exchange views or negotiate understandings of what they have done or seen. When two people communicate, there is a real possibility that by pooling their experiences they achieve a new level of understanding beyond that which either had before.

There is another flaw in our minimal statement. Two people may both come to know something, but not communicate it. They may both learn that the king is dead, but not appreciate that this knowledge is mutual. This is no philosophical pedantry; the roots of a serious misunderstanding, or the reasons for a choice of an inappropriate style of communication, are often to be found in speakers' misconceptions about what the other already knows.

'Sharing knowledge', in the sense we mean here, is an activity which pervades the whole of human social life. When people are not intent on communicating information to others, they are often intent on preventing it being shared too widely. People share knowledge in many places other than in school, and we might well have chosen to study the phenomenon in one or more of those other locations where it has prime significance: in the mass media, counselling and other client–professional relationships, in business organizations, or even in the everyday conversational exchange of memories (see Edwards and Middleton 1986). We have more than one reason for having chosen to study it initially within the education system. One is simply that it was through our own involvement with education that our curiosity about these matters was aroused. We spent our 15,000 hours of childhood in compulsory schooling, and quite a few hours more as volunteers. In adulthood, teaching and learning have long been part of our daily occupations, and we have spent some of this time teaching other teachers. We wanted to know more ourselves about what we had been doing, and why it had succeeded or failed. Secondly, as psychologists specializing in the study of language, we have inevitably been intrigued by the many profound, and still largely unresolved, issues involved in understanding the relation between language and learning in children. Moreover, these issues are often at the heart of pedagogy; one of the ways in which teaching methods vary is in their typification of the child as learner, and another is in their conception of the most effective ways for teachers and learners to communicate. Unresolved conflicts between different teaching styles and methods represent, to some extent, our lack of knowledge about such matters. There was thus the attractive possibility that our research might yield findings of practical educational value.

Given these various factors, and all the other practical considerations which constrain researchers, it seemed appropriate to limit ourselves in our empirical research to observing one age group in one educational setting. We therefore chose 8–10-year-olds in mainstream junior schools in England. This age group falls within that slightly broader band which has been given particular attention by developmental cognitive psychologists, and so we have the opportunity to relate and compare our findings to an existing body of research (albeit one largely based on a different, experimentalist tradition). It also comprises children who have been in the school system long enough to have acquired some general understanding of how schools work, in terms both of their function as social institutions and of the nature of particular educational activities. They are children who are not naïve about school, and most of them will have acquired basic skills in literacy and numeracy. However, they still have much to learn about matters that educated adults will normally take for granted. Finally, British junior schools were attractive to us as locations for this research because of their freedom from the constraints of examination syllabuses which, coupled with their generally 'progressive' ethos, allows teachers and children good opportunity for varied styles of interaction, some negotiation of curriculum content, and some flexibility in the rate at which it is tackled. It is perhaps important to emphasize that it was the variety of styles of interaction, rather than the opportunity to observe any particular style of teaching, which appealed to us. Moreover, we wanted to observe experienced teachers who were confident in what they did and who felt that they could carry on teaching while being recorded. Unlike some other observers of classroom processes, we were not planning a taxonomy of discourse structures (see Sinclair and Coulthard 1975), nor conducting a survey of teaching styles and ways of organizing classrooms (see, for example, Galton, Simon and Croll 1980; Bennett 1976), and this freed us from some of the sampling constraints that they would encounter.

Furthermore, we felt that any attempt to code and categorize the phenomena that we were interested in would subvert one of the most important points we wished to make. Coding and counting schemes rely on the assumption that particular categories of speech mean the same thing each time they occur. In chapter 5 we discuss the notions of 'context' and 'continuity', which involve a process whereby the meanings and the communicated content of what people say inevitably change as they proceed. Things said at the ends of lessons carry a wealth of shared and implicit understanding, established during the lesson, that they could not carry at the start. And, since the raw data of speech are lost in the process of coding, it then becomes impossible to reconstruct the way in which that 'common knowledge' was created.

Discourse and the development of shared understanding

Although most substantial examples and illustrations will be drawn from observations of junior classrooms, we do not wish our consideration of the development of common knowledge to begin and end there. As we have at least partly explained above, those classrooms represent one of many possible locations for exploring such matters, and the nature of some of the issues involved may be best understood by stepping out of the classroom and considering other kinds of social setting, and the dialogue that takes place there.

Take, for example, the idea that (as it is sometimes put) Britain and the USA are two nations divided by a common language. An American says, 'I'm mad about my flat', and means that they are furious about their punctured tyre. An English person (southern, upper-middle-class varie- ty) might well use the same phrase to mean they adore their new apartment. These two hypothetical individuals might thus seem to be bound to misunderstand each other's use of this particular phrase. But, in reality, how likely would such a misunderstanding be? To know this, we would need some additional information. Are the talkers aware of each other's nationalities, and so perhaps sensitive to each other's variety of English? Do they know each other well (do they know, for example, that one of them is particularly inept with automobiles, or that the other has recently moved house)? Is this phrase being used within a continuing conversation which has already established the matters under dis- cussion? It would seem that, the more relevant common knowledge these two people have, the less probable it is that they will misunderstand one another.

But there are yet more eventualities. Perhaps because the speakers do know each other so well, they erroneously assume that some things are common knowledge. It may be, for example, that the English person thinks that she has previously mentioned moving house, but has not. Or she did, but the American was temporarily distracted. They may clarify any misunderstanding immediately, by asking a couple of questions. Or they may not. The plots of many successful farces, and of more serious dramatic works, have revolved around persistent, unresolved misunderstandings arising in the course of ordinary conversations. The establishment of mutual understanding is an everyday matter; but so too is the creation of misunderstanding.

That people recognize the importance of establishing communication on the basis of shared experience is without question. We will all have noticed how, even in relatively superficial social encounters, people quickly use effective heuristic techniques to discover if they have friends, family background, occupational interests, etc., in common. Moreover, people are able to demonstrate their mutuality in ways other than by direct and explicit reference to factual information. We may refer an acquaintance to a shared area of experience by modifying our speech to include more technical terms, jargon or slang expressions, or by a choice of dialect, accent or language. We may also, of course, demonstrate it in non-linguistic ways, by visibly performing some action.

There are some basic elements of the process of establishing a shared understanding, of building an ever-expanding foundation of shared knowledge which will carry the weight of future discourse. These are the offering of new information, reference to existing past experience, requests for information, and tests or 'checks' on the validity of interpretations of information offered. It would be misleading to represent these in some 'ideal type' model of the process (as is sometimes done for more general 'models of communication'), for they follow no necessary sequence, and their relative occurrence is strongly influenced by the particular kind of discourse in which they are used.

By the use of these elements, or mechanisms, two or more people can construct through discourse a continuity of experience which is itself greater than their individual experience. Its existence as a referential framework may become taken for granted by the participants, so that they do not strive to be as explicit as they might for an uninitiated newcomer. They may construct it well, or badly. They may use this mutual knowledge to good effect, or squander it. Later in this book, we may learn from the examples of the teachers and pupils we observed.

The themes of the book

There are six main themes in the book, each of which could in itself provide a good starting point for a discussion of the development of common knowledge. Each is like a sketch, from one particular perspective, of a partially glimpsed object. These sketches, or themes, relate and overlap. But they are not reducible to a single perspective view. And, although, when combined, they offer the beginnings of a three-dimensional description, our knowledge of the whole is still so incomplete that constructing a model must involve a good deal of speculation.

These themes are: (1) educational ideology and practice; (2) educational ground-rules; (3) context and continuity; (4) principled and ritual knowledge; (5) the control of knowledge by teachers; and (6) the handover of competence to children. The meanings and implications of these themes will become clearer as each is developed. Each of the first five themes has a chapter to itself, while the sixth recurs throughout. But the chapters are not self-contained. Each takes as its focus a different aspect of the same whole process. Each draws upon the same essential phenomenon – the development of shared understandings in a series of video-recorded classroom lessons. The major source of data, though supplemented by interviews and other researchers' work, is the set of transcripts of talk and action taken from those video recordings.

In chapter 2 we discuss the range of contexts that have informed our own theoretical perspectives – including linguistic, psychological, sociological and anthropological approaches to discourse, shared knowledge and education. Chapter 3 examines the particular educational ideology that appeared to be the basis of all of our teachers' approaches to their job: an ideology of essentially 'progressive' education based on the value of 'learning by doing', learning through activity and experience rather than from didactic instruction. Chapters 4–7 then take up the remaining themes of the book: the foundation of shared understanding in a set of implicit understandings (ground-rules) about the nature of classroom talk and of educational knowledge; the importance of context and continuity in the development of shared knowledge; the distinction between procedural ('ritual') and principled knowledge, and the ways in which the former is created through characteristics of classroom talk; and the nature and implications of the teacher's control of the discourse, and of what comes to count as common knowledge. Chapter 8 summarizes the earlier ones and attempts to draw together their overall implications. The appendix, written by Janet Maybin, provides information about our research project, and especially the recorded lessons and interviews which are the main empirical basis for the ideas developed in the book.

2
Approaches to classroom knowledge and talk

A multidisciplinary army of researchers has gathered data in schools over the years. Represented in its ranks are not only teachers and other educationalists (i.e. researchers with a practical interest in curriculum content and teaching methods) but also anthropologists, psychologists, linguists, and researchers from a number of different schools of socio-logical thought. Despite all this activity, however, until recently, little interest was shown in the observation and analysis of classroom talk. The 1960s ended with very little being known about the particular and peculiar characteristics of educational discourse.

Since then, different groups of social researchers have become involved with classroom talk for a variety of reasons, not all of which are relevant to our concerns here. We shall consider these different disciplinary approaches in turn, to the extent that they inform our basic concern with the establishment of common knowledge. In doing so, we knowingly take the risk of oversimplifying a complex area of research, and of 'pigeon-holing' researchers too neatly as 'linguists', 'psychologists', and so on. Many research endeavours in this field are characterized by a genuinely interdisciplinary perspective, and by a combination of both 'pure' and 'applied' interests. Moreover, different methodologies are used within particular disciplines. Nevertheless, disciplinary traditions – which are still an important influence on researchers – do embody certain perspectives, with the attribution of greater importance to some questions than to others, which make them useful for our own interdisciplinary purposes.

Linguistic approaches

The field of linguistic research most relevant to our interests here is *discourse analysis*. To many people in the field of educational language research – in Britain, at least – the words 'discourse analysis' are firmly attached to the names of Sinclair and Coulthard. This is due to the impact of their book, published in 1975, in which they set out a scheme for analysing and categorizing the structure of the talk of teaching and learning in secondary classrooms. They showed, especially, that the formal social order of a typical secondary classroom is embodied in a linguistic order, a patterning of talk which represents how education is pursued in such settings. Their scheme offers a way of categorizing classroom talk under the hierarchical headings 'Lesson', 'Transaction', 'Exchange', 'Move' and 'Act'. Thus a lesson consists of one or more transactions, which in turn consist of one or more exchanges, and so on. The strength of this scheme (which is well explained, both in rationale and procedure, in Stubbs and Robinson (1979)) is that *all* of the talk in any lesson can be ascribed to one of a finite number of categories; no data are left out. Moreover, the various categories have a functional relevance, a meaningful quality such that even a casual involvement with this analytic procedure can yield new insights into the nature of classroom language. The basic 'I–R–F' exchange structure they identified – an *initiation* by a teacher, which elicits a *response* from a pupil, followed by an evaluative comment or *feedback* from the teacher – is, once seen, impossible to ignore in any observed classroom talk.

Although Sinclair and Coulthard's data were recordings of classroom talk, their primary interest was not educational. They were linguists, exploring language beyond the well-charted lands of sentence grammar into the relatively unknown waters of textual cohesion (how language is organized in units larger than the sentence). The classroom was for them simply a convenient setting for this research. Elsewhere, however, linguists with a more 'applied' interest in education were in need of a methodology. Dissatisfied with the inherent subjectivity and lack of rigour which they saw in much contemporary research into classroom talk (for instance, the 'insightful observation' approach of Douglas Barnes (1976), of which more later), they took up discourse analysis with enthusiasm. Two such influential exponents of the application of Sinclair and Coulthard's methods to educational research are Michael Stubbs and Mary Willes. Stubbs (1981) goes so far as to argue that those methods provide the *only* satisfactory basis for a systematic analysis of classroom talk; without them, researchers will be doomed to merely 'scratching the surface' of their data. His argument is that, 'by studying discourse sequencing, one can study in empirical detail: how teachers can select bits of knowledge to present to pupils; how they break up topics and order their presentation – how these discrete items of knowledge are linked . . . [etc.]' (Stubbs 1981, p. 128).

There is no doubt that the analysis of discourse structures can highlight interesting and important features of educational communication. For example, Willes (1979, 1983) has shown that structures which typified the talk in secondary classrooms analysed by Sinclair and Coulthard can be seen emerging in the talk of infant classrooms, with the implication that children are very quickly socialized into fairly rigid pupil roles which they act out for the rest of their school careers. We shall be drawing on the results of this kind of research, where appropriate, in the analysis of our own data. But as a self-contained approach to the study of classroom communication, of what teachers and pupils say, formal discourse analysis has some limitations. Because it was devised to reveal linguistic structures, not educational or cognitive processes, it deals most explicitly with the *form* of what is said, rather than with its content. So those matters quite rightly identified by Stubbs as important – the spoken presentation of curriculum content as 'bits of knowledge', 'items of knowledge' or 'topics' – actually lie outside the domain of discourse analysis and its underlying theory. For psychologists interested in cognitive and educational processes, and particularly those whose research incorporates a developmental perspective, it is arguably discourse analysis which 'scratches the surface'.

Our concern is more with content than with form. That is, we are interested in what people say to each other, what they talk about, what words they use, what understandings they convey, and with the problematics of how these understandings are established and built upon as the discourse proceeds. This means that we are concerned not only with the discourse itself, but also with those non-linguistic activities and settings that are the context within which the discourse takes place. And we shall be looking for continuities of talk and of shared experience that transcend the moment-to-moment flow of talk, the alternation of turns at speaking and listening that are the principal object of Sinclair and Coulthard's analysis. It may be thought that a concern with the content of talk rather than with its form, and with interpreting people's meanings rather than coding their turns at speaking, is an altogether less rigorous and objective way of dealing with discourse. We offer three justifications:

1 We have little choice in the matter. Formal discourse analysis is not designed to answer the questions that we want to ask. We have to be concerned with content, meaning and context if we are to examine how

common knowledge is established, rather than how people manage to engage in sequential dialogue.

2 When we come to present and interpret our data, we shall do so by presenting substantial excerpts of situated classroom talk, transcriptions of more or less raw speech with information about contextual activity. Our analyses will be accountable in terms of the data, which the reader can examine with us. One of the disadvantages of some formal procedures for analysing discourse (but not that of Sinclair and Coulthard) is that one is often presented with a coded and/or quantified analysis as a *fait accompli*, the original discourse having been lost at some earlier stage of the process. The section below on 'educational research' provides some further discussion of these approaches.

3 It is also important to realize that discourse analysis, and other formal approaches to natural conversation, are not simply alternatives to more qualitative treatments that deal with content and meaning. Interpreting what people mean by what they say, and what they are trying to achieve in what they say, and what assumptions they appear to be operating with, are in any case all prerequisite to making a formal analysis. Take the IRF structure, for example. In order to be able to classify an utterance as initiation, response or feedback, the analyst must be able to interpret the talk in terms of the speakers' intended meanings. This stage of the procedure is not itself formal. It is not like the standard linguistic process of deriving grammatical classes (verbs, nouns, adjectives, etc.) from the positional occurrences of words in sentences. Discourse analysis necessarily proceeds on the basis of the investigator's interpretations of what is said. This is strikingly revealed in the definition of 'feedback': 'Note that whatever the teacher says after a pupil's utterance is almost certain to be interpreted as evaluative, hence [it is coded] F not R' (Stubbs and Robinson 1979, p. 44). Since some sort of interpretative analysis, based on no more than the investigator's own understanding of the discourse as a vicarious participant, is necessary to the formal analysis of conversation, then there is clearly no inherent gain in objectivity or rigour (though there may be other gains) achieved by taking that anaiysis further and building upon it some system of codings and categories.

The latter point is a significant one, so we shall dwell on it a little longer. One of the key features of discourse analysis in general (including analyses other than that of Sinclair and Coulthard, and including the work of psychologists as well as linguists) is the notion of *given* and *new information*. These are particularly relevant concepts for us, since they concern the business of common knowledge, and have a direct relationship to content. They concern the ways in which the information provided by a speaker is assumed to be already known to the hearer (given), or else is assumed to be unknown to the hearer (new).

Linguistic treatments of given and new information have concentrated on identifying how they are marked by features of grammar and intonation (e.g. Halliday 1967; Prince 1981; see Brown and Yule 1983, for a useful discussion). For example, given information may be marked by the use of pronouns and proper names (these depend on the hearer's prior knowledge of whom and what they refer to), while new information is marked by the use of special stress or emphasis on certain words when speaking, or by grammatical and rhetorical devices, as in the following sentences 1–3 (where the new information is italicized):

1 John paid for the meal *with his credit card*.
2 *It was John* who paid for the meal.
3 *Was it John* who paid for the meal?

The norm is for given information to precede new information, as in sentence 1. The assumption there is that speaker and hearer already share knowledge about the contextual persons and events (John, payments, meals, etc.), but that the speaker is assuming that the hearer did not know that John used his credit card. This normal interpretation could be overridden by placing the stress elsewhere in the sentence, such as on 'John'. Then the interpretation would be as for sentence 2, where the new information concerns not the method of payment but the identity of the person who paid. In sentence 3, the speaker uses a similar grammatical device to request information. This is far from an exhaustive account of these phenomena, but hopefully it conveys the sort of thing that linguistic analyses are trying to achieve.

However, there are serious problems in the attempt to identify given and new information in terms of the linguistic features that carry them. Brown and Yule (1983, p. 218) provide an example from some actual recorded dialogue:

> there was nine – ten – eleven in the family altogether – two girls – and nine boys – and she lost eight sons one after the other.

The pronoun 'she' refers to nobody that had been mentioned or was present. But, as we have said, pronouns are used to invoke 'given' information. So how do we make the likely interpretation that 'she' refers to the mother of the family? Lacking sufficient linguistic information, we presumably make such an inference on the basis of common knowledge – it is something we know about the world, not about language, that families and children involve relations with persons called mothers. Once again, as with the analysis of IRF structures, we find that sensible interpretation is the prerequisite, rather than the product, of the analysis of discourse.

The value of formal analyses of discourse is not that they help us to make sense of what is said, but rather that they attempt to explicate the basis on which such sense is made. They reveal the structures and properties of talk and text that we use in interpreting it. The limitation of such approaches is that our sense-making procedures for dealing with discourse are not ones that deal exclusively with language. Apart from simply hearing and processing the words said, we make sense of discourse primarily and overridingly in terms of our understanding of the persons speaking, the setting, their likely communicative purposes, the unwritten ground-rules of conversation, both general (Grice 1975) and specific (we shall look at some educational ones in chapter 4), and, of course, in terms of the general and specific common knowledge that holds, or is assumed to hold, between speaker and hearer.

We can illustrate the point with a brief return to the notions of given and new information. In a television interview shortly after the American bombing of Colonel Ghadaffi's headquarters in Tripoli (ITV, *Weekend World*, 20 April 1986), the Foreign Secretary Sir Geoffrey Howe carefully informed us that 'American presidents are presidents of the United States. French presidents are presidents of France.' How do we analyse this in terms of given and new information? It is difficult to see how the latter part of each sentence adds anything to the first part: the sentences are tautologies. And in terms of assumed shared knowledge it is unlikely, whatever we think of politicians' estimations of the intellect of the electorate, that Sir Geoffrey thought he was telling anyone anything new. In fact, in the context of the interview, it was clear that Sir Geoffrey was trying to convey something about the different styles of leadership that the British must learn to expect from the heads of state of two such different nations.

In Grice's (1975) terms, the apparent breaking of the maxim of 'quantity' (i.e. informativeness – we are being informed of something we obviously already know) leads us to seek to interpret Sir Geoffrey's utterance as informative, as not really breaking a rule. In terms of given and new information, we have an interesting phenomenon. Information can be presented linguistically as new when in fact (cognitively) it is known, or, indeed, presented as given when in fact it is new. The latter would be an effective means of persuasion, useful in indoctrination or advertising, as well as in ordinary conversation and in the classroom; we shall encounter the phenomenon in chapter 7. The point to be made here is that given and new information are not phenomena that reside simply in discourse, awaiting linguistic analysis. There are indeed linguistic devices that are used in *presenting* information as either given or new, but these do not map in any simple way on to what speakers and hearers actually do know, nor even on to what they assume each other to know. Rather, they are devices available for use in the construction of common knowledge, in agreement and disagreement, in persuasion and rhetoric, in winning arguments, or whatever other purposes speakers may have in saying what they do.

In our treatment of classroom discourse in later chapters, linguistic notions such as those of given and new information, and of IRF sequences in the flow of talk, have influenced our perspective, and are referred to in the course of our analyses. But we have made no attempt to present the data systematically in terms of these sorts of features. We are interested more in the relations between discourse and the sharing of knowledge than in linguistic devices and structures themselves.

Sociological and anthropological approaches

By the middle of the 1960s there had been a distinctive 'sociology of education' in Britain for about ten years. Very little of it, however, involved research within schools, and even less within classrooms. It was essentially social science at the 'macro' level; researchers were concerned with 'input' and 'output' characteristics of the education system, such as the relation between pupils' social-class backgrounds and their eventual levels of achievement and occupational destinations. At the end of the sixties, however, this and most other branches of sociology suffered what is now commonly referred to as a 'crisis', and so began a period of internal upheaval and dramatic change. This crisis was in fact one of confidence in what was then the dominant theoretical approach in modern sociology, 'structural functionalism'. Its disestablishment led to the emergence of what one sociologist of education, Martyn Hammersley (1980), has rightly called 'a bewildering variety of alternative approaches; inter-actionism, phenomenology, ethnomethodology and various kinds of Marxism'. One of the main criticisms of structural functionalism had been its exclusively 'macro' focus, with people represented only as the passive pawns in society's game. As one critic, Harold Garfinkel (1967), summed it up, they were treated as 'cultural dopes', robots who daily acted out their socialized roles. Although divergent in many respects, the new approaches unanimously rejected this view, and insisted that sociology must recognize that human beings play an active role in creating, inter-preting, and recreating their social world. There was thus a keen interest in how people interacted in particular social settings, and also in what they, the 'actors', thought of what they did. For sociologists of education, this meant a belated discovery of the classroom. As Hammersley puts it:

> Apparently lying at the heart of the education system, classrooms were an obvious setting in which to begin to apply these new ideas. . . .
> Previous work in the field was largely rejected on the grounds that it treated the classroom as a black box, simply measuring the inputs and outputs and ignoring what went on inside. (1980, p. 48)

This shift in focus demanded new research methods. One of the methods taken up by sociologists was *ethnography*, a method originally used by anthropologists to describe and understand other cultures. There had already been some anthropological studies of schools, in which a dominant theme was the relation between the cultures and social practices of school and those of the communities in which the schools were set. More recently, anthropological work has also focused upon the classroom, but still relating what goes on there to local cultures. A good example is Philips's (1970) studies of American Indian children, which showed that there was conflict between the interactional norms of the classroom and those of their home community, and explains why such children behaved in ways considered inappropriate by their (white) teachers. This line of educational anthropology continues, being well represented by the research described in Shirley Brice Heath's book *Ways with Words* (1983).

The ethnographic approach requires researchers to make detailed observations of what is said and done, and, more problematically, to suspend their own 'commonsense' interpretations of what is going on when making an analysis. The aim is to avoid making the false assumption that what seems commonsensical to the researcher is seen in the same way by the participants. In contrast, participants' own interpretations of what they are doing, and why, are sought and may be used as data. Classroom talk is thus analysed not for its linguistic structure, but for what its content (what people talked about) and patterning (who talks to whom) may reveal about social order in this microcosm.

The establishment of the 'new sociology of education' is often linked with the publication, in 1971, of Michael Young's *Knowledge and Control*. 'Control' is, perhaps, the key concept in this approach, not least in those studies particularly concerned with discourse. Thus A. D. Edwards (1980) begins a chapter on classroom talk with the assertion 'Classroom talk is organized for the controlled transmission of knowledge.' Researchers attempted to describe the strategies that teachers use to control what pupils learn and do. There were also attempts to show how classroom life embodies the power relations of wider society. In the same article, Edwards quotes Anthony Giddens, one of the principal theorists of modern, reconstituted sociology:

> Analysis of classroom discourse makes it possible to show at the 'local' level how 'social structures are both constituted by human agency and yet at the same time are the very medium of this constitution', and perhaps to show that middle-class children have greater access to 'privileged' forms of discourse. (Edwards 1980, p. 249)

For Edwards, the predominant uses of language in classrooms are to 'focus and filter' children's experience in a way which both reflects and reproduces the social order of wider society. The following example, from a secondary classroom, illustrates the nature of this analysis. It was selected by Edwards to show how teachers inform pupils of what has 'really' been learnt in a lesson, in contrast to what pupils might themselves think were the relevant issues.

T: Right, do you notice what we've done? We started off saying we're going to look at ideas about the world, how people long ago explained the world. But what else – and this is very important – what else have we also done?

P: Saw how men looked at women.

T: We saw how men looked at women – you're nearly there. What exactly do you mean? Can you say – tell us a bit more, go on.

P: How he doesn't like her, and how he thinks she's weak.

T: Yeah (*tentatively*) – so we've also looked then – anybody else before I say it, anybody else have any ideas? He's on the right track there. He said we've also looked at how man looked at woman. What else have we looked at here?

P: God.

T: No, not to do with God.

P: How they lived.

T: How they lived! In other words the ideas they had about themselves and how they lived. So from a story long ago we've used that story to work out how people thought about themselves, how they lived, as well as looking at their stories about the world we've used the stories to work out something about them. Let's go on because this is *very* important, because all the time you're in Humanities you'll be doing this. You'll be looking at what people have said about themselves long ago, and trying to work out how they lived, and we call that something you look for *evidence*. (Edwards 1980, p. 245)

Because of their choice of data, and their 'micro' level of analysis, some of these sociological studies have a superficial similarity to other more linguistic, educational and psychological research into classroom talk. Moreover, some of these studies – for example, Edwards and Furlong (1978) and Mehan (1979) – offer insights which are essentially social-psychological. This superficial impression of similarity is, however, misleading in that it ignores the true scope and aim of the best of this research, which is to understand schools as part of society. As Olive Banks (1978) comments, the enduring task facing this research is to 'build bridges' between sociological understanding about society as a whole (the macro level of social structure) and what is observed to go on in particular social settings (the micro level). Although we are not directly concerned with this macro–micro relationship here, it is nevertheless the case that the establishment of joint understandings takes place in the context of a power relationship between teacher and pupils, with the teacher representing and providing for the pupils an accepted wider culture of educational ideology, knowledge and practice. These will be important issues for our examination (in chapters 6 and 7 especially) of the nature and problems of how common knowledge is created in the classroom.

Psychological approaches

Of all social scientists, psychologists are the most recent to have become involved in the study of classroom discourse, and even now such studies are few. To an outsider, this may seem surprising, given psychology's central concern with the behaviour of individual people, and the existence of a group of professionals called 'educational psychologists'. The reasons are, in the Kuhnian sense, paradigmatic: the history of psychology is a story of the increasing dominance of experimental, laboratory-based research over more 'naturalistic', observational kinds of enquiry. In the particular case of educational psychology, this paradigm has been translated into an overwhelming concern with *measurement* – making accurate assessments of individual abilities, aptitudes and attitudes. Hudson (1972) has suggested that educational psychologists' preference for 'hard', quantitative methodologies rather than those of 'soft', qualitative analysis reflects their insecure professional status in relation to other psychologists and to teachers. Thus research in educational psychology has typically meant either designing and using psychological tests, or reducing features of educational life to quantified measures which are then statistically compared and contrasted (e.g. Rutter, Maugham, Mortimore and Ouston 1979).

There are also a number of 'mainstream' psychologists, influential in their own field of experimental research, who have had a great deal to say about 'learning' and how teachers should be able to promote it. Desforges (1985) names a few such prominent historical figures – Bain (1879); James (1899); Gagné (1965); Skinner (1968); Piaget (1971); Broadbent (1975) – and points out that none of their advice was based on the observation and analysis of what goes on in classrooms. This has led to the underemphasis in psychology of one of the most characteristic features of the educational process – its mutuality, that it is made up of the interactions between teachers and children. Desforges comments:

> Prescriptions for the design of ideal learning environments often contain detailed analyses of the performance limitations of learners but take no account whatsoever of the performance characteristics of teachers. This is akin to designing aeroplanes on sound aerodynamic principles but in ignorance of the forces of gravity. (Desforges 1985, p. 121)

There *is* an established strand of educational psychological research concerned with classroom interaction (e.g. Merrett and Wheldall 1978), but it is entirely behaviourist, concerned only with the identification and modification of particular patterns of action. A favoured theme in such research, for example, is the development of more efficient ways to control disruptive or nonconforming behaviour in school and, through 'positive reinforcement' (i.e. the use of some reward system), to direct or 'shape' the actions of children towards more acceptable goals. Discourse processes and the development of knowledge are outside its field of interest.

Generally speaking, then, most educational psychology has been the study and measurement of individual attributes and behaviours. One has only to look at even recently published textbooks on educational psychology to see the stamp of history displayed. In Kagan and Lang's (1978) *Psychology and Education: An Introduction* the dominant themes are those of an exclusively individualistic psychology – personality, learning, motives, intelligence – and in all of its 606 pages there is only one 'tidied-up' example of a piece of sustained discourse from a real lesson. We cannot turn to educational psychology for an understanding of the development of common knowledge.

A less individualistic, more interactional analysis of the process of teaching and learning has been emerging recently in developmental psychology, a field which has been dominated for the last twenty or so years by the theoretical influence of Jean Piaget. (We might note too at this point that his theory also provides the rationale for the current post-Plowden style of British primary school teaching – a matter we shall take up again later). According to Piaget, the natural progressive development of children's thinking, from the most primitive early stages in the first years of life through to the emergence of such sophisticated abilities as the capacity to make logical deductions, to formulate and test hypotheses, and generally to reason abstractly, is first and foremost a consequence of children's direct involvement with physical reality. The development of the intellect is an adaptive process in which an intelligent organism comes to terms with a complex environment. As Bruner (1985, p. 26) puts it, 'in the Piagetian model . . . a lone child struggles single handed to strike some equilibrium between assimilating the world to himself or himself to the world.' Language – and hence discourse – is not give particular weight in this account. Action is primary, with language abilities and other ways of using symbols (as in play activities) following on from the development of more general, underlying cognitive structures.

The extended series of experiments into children's reasoning abilities carried out by Piaget and his associates (e.g. Sinclair 1969) confirmed their belief that thought preceded language and was not determined by it. The evidence provided by these imaginative, careful studies was seen as convincing by many other developmentalists. Conflicting evidence, showing the influence of language use on early thought, was offered by some researchers, but though debate continued about the role of language there seemed no alternative theoretical framework worthy of serious consideration. None, that is, apart from Bruner's (1964) continued insistence on the importance of language in cognitive development, and the more recent rediscovery of the work of the Russian developmental psychologist L. S. Vygotsky, who, along with Piaget, had been a formative influence in the development of Bruner's psychology (Bruner 1983b).

When Vygotsky died in 1934 at the age of 37, his ideas had already had a profound influence on those working with him (see Wertsch 1985). However, these ideas were apparently so much at odds with the dominant 'connectionist' school of Pavlovian psychology (and the 'tightening party control over the soft fringes of culture and science' (Kozulin 1986)) that his publications were, for a couple of decades, officially banned (see Kozulin (1986) and Luria (1979) for fascinating accounts of that period). This meant that, although Vygotsky's work continued to influence that of Luria, Leontiev and others in the Soviet Union, it had little impact on western psychology until its republication in 1956 (and the subsequent translation in 1962 of *Thought and Language*). Even then, the piecemeal fashion in which his research was communicated to the west, the almost unassailable dominance of Piaget's theory, and, perhaps, the unreceptiveness of American and European psychologists to ideas emanating from the Soviet Union, have meant that his theories have yet to be properly evaluated. Thanks largely to the efforts of Michael Cole, James Wertsch and a few others, these works are now becoming more readily available.

Like Piaget, Vygotsky studied the development of cognitive processes. He also agreed that reasoning could develop independently of language, with language and thought having their own, separate mental origins. But, in strong contrast to Piaget, he proposed that language and thought come together, that they are combined to create a cognitive 'tool' for human development, such that 'Children solve practical tasks with the help of their speech, as well as their eyes and hands' (Vygotsky 1978, p. 26). Moreover, for Vygotsky the child was not the 'lone organism' of Piaget, with each new generation acting out its rediscovery of knowledge. Instead, 'Human learning presupposes a specific social nature and a process by which children grow into the intellectual life of those around them' (1978, p. 89). In other words – and, on the face of it, this may seem a surprising issue to be contentious – Vygotsky was attempting to provide a theory of intellectual development which acknowledged that children undergo quite profound changes in their understanding by engaging in joint activity and conversation with other people.

The role of language in the development of understanding is thus characterized in two ways. First, it provides a medium for teaching and learning. Second, it is one of the materials from which the child constructs a way of thinking. The medium of social interaction is taken over and *internalized* by the child, whose thought processes are drastically reorganized as a consequence. So Vygotsky was proposing that children's understanding is shaped not only through adaptive encounters with the physical world but through interactions between people in relation to that world – a world not merely physical and apprehended by the senses, but cultural, meaningful and significant, and made so principally by language. Human knowledge and thought are themselves therefore fundamentally cultural, deriving their distinctive properties from the nature of social activity, of language, discourse and other cultural forms.

It is only a short inferential leap from the ideas in the last paragraph to the following conclusion: Vygotsky's theory – unlike that of Piaget, which has been so widely taken up by educationists – has a place in it for the role of the teacher as a language user. The teacher can be accommodated into a Piagetian framework, but only in a peripheral manner, as provider of a suitable environment in which the child can learn, and as monitor and assessor of children's cognitive progress. Piaget acknowledged that 'educative and social transmission (linguistic, etc.) plays an evident role' in cognitive development, but insisted that, 'in order to understand the adult and his language, the child needs means of assimilation which are formed through structures preliminary to the social transmission itself' (1969, p. 274). That is, the child must already have a basic non-linguistic understanding of what is being talked about. In contrast, according to Vygotsky's theory, teachers may well lead children on to new levels of conceptual understanding by interacting and talking with them.

Valerie Walkerdine (1982, 1984) offers a critique of Piagetian theory and its educational applications in which, like Piaget himself, she is concerned with how children acquire the capacity for logical reasoning and mathematical thought. Her analysis is clearly more consonant with Vygotsky's approach than with Piaget's. According to Piaget, the origins of logical reasoning are not to be found in discourse, as others have thought, but in action. Piaget's argument can be illustrated by a brief examination of Plato's famous syllogism about the mortality of Socrates:

All men are mortal.
Socrates is a man.
Therefore Socrates is mortal.

We may begin by agreeing that the syllogism is logically valid. But what makes it so? Arguably not the language that expresses it. No rule of grammar or of cohesion would prevent the last sentence from being 'Therefore Socrates is immortal.' The notion that the logic of the argument resides in what Piaget termed 'internalized action' might run as follows. The statement 'All men are mortal' says that all men belong in the category 'mortal'. It is rather like saying that all of a set of beads are in a particular box. We can imagine this as physically real – we have a lot of beads in a box. If we then assert that 'Socrates is a man', this is like saying that one of the beads is called Socrates. Having already understood that all of the beads are in the box, we have little trouble finding Socrates! In other words, the essential logic that forces us to the conclusion 'Therefore Socrates is mortal' is nothing other than the logic of objects, actions and places. We understand the syllogism because it is based on a much older and more basic logic, a logic derived from our actions and experiences with the physical world. The same case can be made for mathematics: the rules of arithmetic are essentially an abstract version of the rules that govern physical transactions.

Piaget's theory is plausible and attractive, but the evidence for it is problematical. Whatever else is involved, the ways in which both children and adults appear to reason about things has been shown to be closely bound up with the nature of the social transaction and discourse within which the reasoning is done (Donaldson 1978; Labov 1972; Cole, Gay, Glick and Sharp 1971). Logic and mathematics are not merely mental activities performed in some abstract domain of disembedded thought, but types of discourse which have recognizable forms, contexts and rules of interpretation (we shall take up this issue in chapter 4). According to Walkerdine, logical and mathematical reasoning not only occur in discursive and communicative contexts, but are themselves forms of discourse, relations between statements, deriving not from actions and things, as Piaget has it, but rather from language itself:

> in formal reasoning truth is determined in terms of the internal relations of the statement itself . . . the basis of formal reasoning need not be sought as an essential quality inside the mind, the result of the internalization of structures of action. Rather, we can see that the lingusitic system itself provides the tools necessary to formal reasoning. (Walkerdine 1982, p. 138)

Despite her opposition to Piaget, Walkerdine is in pursuit of the same goal, an explanation of the development of abstract, formal reasoning. She presents a detailed argument in support of her case, and uses examples of classroom discourse to demonstrate its force. Consider the following nursery school example (т = teacher, c = child).

The teacher begins:

т: . . . and I know Debbie did so we're just going to go over what you did at home and what you started before. How many's there?
c: Two.

T: How many's there? There? How many's there? Two and put them all together. How many have we got already?

She puts the blocks in two piles on the table, and as she says 'put them all together' she moves them together with her hands. . . . The task is practised a second time and then the teacher makes an interesting move in the discourse:

T: Good boy, let's count them all together. One–two–three–four–five–six–seven. So Nicola had four, Debbie had three, so three and four make . . . (*She puts the blocks together.*)
C: Seven.

She repeats the same exercise of putting the blocks together, but this time the phrase that she uses refers to the blocks *implicitly* but makes no reference in language to them, so that she introduces the children in this way to the 'disembedded' form of the statement: 'three and four make . . .' . . . the teacher's next move is to take the children from utterance to the first stage of written representation. (Walkerdine 1982, p. 146)

The sequence that Walkerdine captures in a single classroom lesson is one that represents a long-term and fundamental development of thought. Mathematics begins as a relationship between discourse and practical actions: the teacher counts the number of objects aloud as she physically groups the objects together. She then moves on to the use of numbers without naming the objects, effectively disembedding the arithmetic in discourse, while the physical objects and actions have now become its unspoken context. Finally, Walkerdine notes how the process is taken further, into written representation: the teacher goes on to write out the sum. The point to note here is that the acquisition of mathematical concepts is presented not simply as the translation of action into numbers, but as a process of being guided by an adult into a particular form of discourse which has a developmental sequence of its own, moving from an embeddedness in practical actions towards an abstract and apparently self-contained disembeddedness. The value of Walkerdine's analysis is that it demonstrates the essentially social and discursive basis of learning mathematics (and, in a similar vein, logical reasoning), while retaining the importance of practical actions.

We would argue that Walkerdine's analysis contextualizes rather than replaces Piaget's. Piaget's action basis of logic remains convincing, but it is an account of logicality itself, of why arguments are logical rather than of how people learn to engage in logical reasoning. Learning to reason according to the laws of logic must involve learning to operate within a specialized form of discourse. Syllogisms are not simply descriptions of actions. Children learn how to recognize and participate in logical reasoning within the same sorts of social transactions through which they learn to talk and think about everything else. And, within even the narrow world of formal education, syllogistic logic is overshadowed in importance by rhetorical argument, scientific method, narrative forms of representation and the sheer content of shared knowledge. It is with these more substantive sorts of 'common knowledge' that we shall be concerned in this book.

Consistent with Walkerdine's analysis, and in contrast to Piaget, Vygotsky did not offer a conception of human development as something that we can study by observation and experiment with individual children and then apply to education as a set of principles for teachers to follow. For Vygotsky and his followers, human development is intrinsically social and educational – using the term 'education' in a broad sense, to include more than formal schooling. Development is to a significant extent a product, not a prerequisite, of education. It is the acquisition of culture, including the practices and symbol systems of culture, that makes possible creative thought and activity.

The educational basis of development is captured in what Vygotsky called the *zone of proximal development*, defined as 'the distance between the actual developmental level as determined by independent problem solving and the level of potential development as determined through problem solving under adult guidance or in collaboration with more capable peers' (1978, p. 86). Jerome Bruner offers a useful summary of the concept:

> If the child is enabled to advance by being under the tutelage of an adult or a more competent peer, then the tutor or the aiding peer serves the learner as a vicarious form of consciousness until such a time as the learner is able to master his own action through his own consciousness and control. When the child achieves that conscious control over a new function or conceptual system, it is then that he is able to use it as a tool. Up to that point, the tutor in effect performs the critical function of 'scaffolding' the learning task to make it possible for the child, in Vygotsky's word, to internalize external knowledge and convert it into a tool for conscious control. (Bruner 1985, pp. 24–5)

These notions of 'scaffolding' (see Wood, Bruner and Ross 1976) and of the 'zone of proximal development' contain a particularly important notion for our analysis of classroom education – that is, if we may borrow a term from Bruner's (1983a) account of how children learn to talk, the notion of *handover*. The essence of the process is that learners do not remain for ever propped up by the scaffolding of adult assistance, but come to take control of the process for themselves. Language learners and craft apprentices become masters of the art. It is here that we find one of the most problematical aspects of formal education: where is the handover? Why do many pupils apparently fail to achieve the competence of teachers? Are they really meant to? What are they supposed to be learning – how to become teachers themselves? The problematics of handover will be one of our major concerns in later chapters.

Although Vygotsky's work was supported by his own experimentation, it is interesting and surprising to see that his posthumous impact on developmental psychology has not been achieved through the revelation of hitherto unfamiliar experimental findings. It has been much more to do with the persuasive nature of his analysis of the relationship between factors that appear to influence young children's learning – an analysis which can help modern researchers make sense of observations that a Piagetian framework cannot handle. It is for this reason that Vygotsky has been drawn on in recent critical reinterpretations of Piagetian 'conservation' experiments, notably Donaldson's (1978). But the most striking influence he has had on research into cognitive development is that this now includes the study of joint activity, tutoring and discourse. These are the aspects we shall be examining.

Educational research

In one sense, any research which looks at classroom communication might be described as 'educational'. But under this heading we mean here to restrict ourselves to research that has arisen directly from questions about curriculum and pedagogy, and whose aim is primarily to inform educational policy or practice. There has been quite a lot of research of this kind which uses observations of classroom interaction as data, but which nevertheless does not deal with discourse as such. Sometimes called 'systematic observation' or 'interaction analysis', this kind of research grew mainly out of methods developed by the American social psychologist Bales in the 1950s for studying group processes in business meetings. In its early stages, the work in school classrooms is well represented by the work of Flanders (1970). More recently, it has been used in the ORACLE survey of sixty British primary classrooms (Galton, Simon and Croll 1980).

Essentially, this approach involves the use of some coding scheme by the observer, who assigns the interactions observed to take place to one of a set of previously defined categories. That is, discourse itself is not recorded for subsequent analysis; decisions about what is going on are made on the spot by the observer, so that the quality of the data gathered depends heavily on the adequacy of the categorical scheme and the observer's skill in applying it. Typically, this kind of research provides findings in terms of the relative frequency of occurrence of different interactions or speech behaviours.

The Flanders Interactional Analysis Categories System (FIAC; Flanders

1970) allows a researcher to reduce classroom interaction to ten coded categories, each of which represents a class of events such as 'praises or encourages' or 'gives directions' (categories of teacher talk), and 're- sponse' or 'silence and confusion' (categories of pupil talk). This system is responsible for revealing the famous 'two-thirds rule': across a wide range of teachers, classrooms and even countries, it has been observed that

(a) for about two-thirds of the time someone is talking;
(b) about two-thirds of this talk is the teacher's;
(c) about two-thirds of the teacher's talk consists of lecturing or asking questions.

In the ORACLE study, whose concerns have more apparent relevance to ours here, this approach was used to describe 'some of the richness and variety of what goes on in a modern primary classoom' (Galton, Simon and Croll 1980). More interestingly, perhaps, the researchers also wished to identify patterns within this richness which would 'help explain why certain teachers do one thing while others do something else'. One must note, however, that the *only* research instruments used by the ORACLE researchers to investigate these matters were their own observational category schemes for coding teacher and pupil behaviour, supplemented by short 'descriptive accounts' in which observers commented on the perceived style of teachers and on other features of classroom life con- sidered relevant. No attempt was made to ask teachers why they were going to do or why they had done what they did, and pupils' views of the lesson were likewise left unsought. The kind of data obtained from systematic observation studies does not allow researchers to reconstruct the course of any given lesson; the only information available about the course of events after the lesson has finished is in the form of numerical frequency codings. One feels, therefore, that there was surprisingly little of the right kind of information available to researchers wishing to explain why teachers did one thing rather than another, or why certain patterns of classroom interaction seemed to work better in the teaching of some topics rather than others.

ORACLE is on safer ground in its descriptions and analyses of patterns of classroom management. They note, for example, that, while children were often placed in small groups around tables (the usual practice in British primary schools), they *worked* almost entirely as individuals. In this respect, as in several others, ORACLE found a disparity between the 'Plowden philosophy' of progressive education espoused by the teachers in the study and what the teachers actually did (we shall be discussing this philosophy in the next chapter). Thus they conclude: 'There is no clear evidence that co-operative group work of the investigating, problem- solving, discovery kind which Plowden held that all children should experience, features more than sparsely in our primary schools' (p. 159). Moreover, the 'individualized' teaching that they observed did not fit Plowden's essentially Piagetian emphasis on the teacher's stimulating the child's self-discovery of knowledge, 'leading the child from behind' as it were. Instead, they found that, when children were given individual attention, this was usually so that the teacher could transmit information and control behaviour. This disparity they attribute to the sheer impossibility of practising Plowden-style education with classes of around thirty young children. When teachers did use the probing, guiding style of interaction associated with progressive education, this was usually done with the whole class.

Despite a shared interest in primary classrooms, then, the aims, methods and scope of the ORACLE research are very different from our own. The most relevant implication of their findings is perhaps to remind us and our readers that there is no good reason to think that the interactions we selected for analysis – between a teacher and a small group of children – are in the normative sense 'typical' of most everyday classroom life (and even that of the children and teachers we observed). This is, however, an intentional consequence of our research design. We did not intend a survey of styles of classroom management, or a study of how overstretched teachers cope with too many children. Teachers have to do many things other than teach, and they are often unable to give the job the attention they would wish even when they are teaching. We explicitly wished to avoid observing circumstances in which practical issues such as shortage of time, limited resources and large numbers of children force teachers to compromise, or even abandon, their educational ideals and pedagogic intentions. Because of our interest in one particular aspect of teaching – the development of shared understanding – our intention was rather to see how teachers would use fairly favourable conditions to teach in the ways they thought best.

There is another kind of educational research concerned with classroom communication, very different from 'systematic observation', which shares more of our interests and also uses methods more similar to ours. Sometimes called 'insightful observation', it is best represented by the work of Douglas Barnes (e.g. 1971, 1976). Barnes is a former secondary school teacher (of English), and it is perhaps for that reason that his research shows a direct concern with the quality of educational communications which is uncommon in the work of more detached social scientists. His general intention is to relate observed features of classroom discourse to pupils' learning processes. He does this by observing, and tape-recording, stretches of talk in lessons (mostly in secondary schools), and then commenting on what appears to be taking place. Barnes gives ultimate priority to the language of lessons because 'The major means by which children in our schools formulate knowledge and relate it to their own purposes and view of the world are speech and writing' (1976, p. 19). He does not, however, underestimate the importance of the teacher's role in this process, since 'Classroom learning can best be seen as an interaction between the teacher's meanings, and those of his pupils, so that what they take away is partly shared and partly unique to each of them' (1976, p. 22).

Below is an example of Barnes's analysis. He uses extracts from a science lesson in which a teacher is working with a group of three children aged 12–13 on a series of practical activities to do with air pressure. The children were required to use various kinds of apparatus in performing these activities, to observe what took place and to explain their findings. These activities include drinking milk through a straw, blowing between two apples suspended about an inch apart on long strings, and blowing into a stoppered jar of liquid, making it spurt out like a fountain. He uses the examples to show how teachers ask questions which (1) sometimes require pupils to give more explicit accounts and explanations, (2) sometimes require pupils to make more systematic analyses of their experience, and (3) try to get pupils to use language 'as an instrument to break down and restructure' their experiences (in ways relevant to the curriculum).

TEACHER: Well, we blew into it, and what happened?
PUPIL F: All the water came out of the straw.
PUPIL P: The water came out of the s-top.
TEACHER: All came out! Now why? Come on! This one's easy.
PUPIL F: 'Cos when you were blowing bubbles in, all the . . . air came up the straw . . . and the water with it.
TEACHER: Ooh no! I don't think that's quite right. When we blew air through here . . . where did it go?
PUPILS (*together*): Into the bottle.
TEACHER: Into the bottle! So was there more air in here or less air?
PUPILS (*together*): More.
TEACHER: More air, wasn't there? There was a lot more air in here. Now this air . . . wanted to do what?
PUPILS: (*clash of voices*) Get out
                          Push water . . . push water outside to get room
                          for itself.
TEACHER: Yes, ah. That's a very good answer.

(Barnes 1976, pp. 73–4)

Sometimes Barnes's analysis is more dynamic, more concerned with the flow of discourse. He presents this by giving a kind of 'running commentary' on what is said: for example, the following interaction between two girls, Betty (B) and Teresa (T), and their teacher (T, bracketed speech) during a lesson on Saxon settlements.

Dialogue	Commentary
B: The Saxons used er used timber didn't they to . . .	*Betty begins the sequence with what appears to be a statement. It functions however as a*
(T: Yes)	*hypothesis inviting further*
B: . . . build houses?	*exploration. (Implicitly: How should we take this into consideration in choosing a site for the village?)*
T: They cleared a . . . Say they found a forest and you know they're probably all forests near the . . . [inaudible]	*Theresa takes up the implicit suggestion of the need for a site with a plentiful supply of timber. The 'Say' formula and the 'probably' invite the others to regard this contribution not as final but as open to qualification.*
B: Yes. They cleared it all away . . . and then built all the little huts . . .	*Betty accepts the invitation and develops the idea further.*

(Barnes 1976, p. 54)

In our own presentations of discourse in later chapters, we too provide a column of comments to be read in parallel with the talk. Barnes's commentary does not, however, serve the same function as ours. While our 'context notes' merely provide a record of physical props, movements, activities and gestures which are necessary for understanding what went on and what people were talking about, Barnes's commentaries represent *the analysis itself*. They embody his reflective interpretation of the significance of the dialogue.

It is at least partly due to this early intrusion of the subjective observer into the analysis of what is said and done, as well as the disregard of any formal linguistic conventions for transcribing speech, that some linguists – notably Michael Stubbs (e.g. Stubbs and Robinson 1979) – express a basic dissatisfaction with Barnes's methods. For such critics, his methods lack rigour and his analysis defies replication; the approach seems altogether too subjective, involving unsystematic 'interpretative leaps' from data to conclusions. Barnes himself (Barnes and Todd 1977) has acknowledged the difficulty of objectifying his analysis. But, as we commented earlier (p. 10), the more rigorous methods of discourse analysis advocated by Stubbs only carry observers to a certain vantage point, an interpretative threshold beyond which subjective insights must serve them too if they are to *make sense* of their data. Indeed, we also argued that making informal sense of what is said in the dialogue (though not necessarily the sort of interpretation done by Barnes) is in any case an essential and prerequisite part of the formal analysis of discourse.

Barnes's approach may not be highly systematic, but it is not atheoretical. Most explicitly stated in *From Communication to Curriculum* (1976), the theory of educational language which informs his analyses is imaginative and eclectic. Despite acknowledgements to Piaget, Vygotsky's legacy is more apparent – as in such remarks as 'Talk and writing provide means by which children are able to reflect upon the bases upon which they are interpreting reality, and thereby change them' (1976, pp. 30–1) and 'Classroom learning can best be seen as an interaction between the teacher's meanings, and those of his pupils, so that what they take away is partly shared and partly unique to each of them' (p. 22). A teacher is not, for Barnes, a mere provider of 'learning environments' in which children may explore and extend their conceptions of reality. The relationship is more dialectical, even confrontational: dialogue between pupil and teacher may reveal to children disjunctions between their implicit beliefs and those offered by the teacher. If suitably motivated, children may then focus on parts of their world-view which they had not considered problematic, and so go on to recode their experience and to reconstruct their understanding of it. In Vygotskyan terms, the teacher can use discourse to lead children through new zones of proximal development. Children must be encouraged to use language to give form to their understanding, because 'by formulating knowledge for oneself one gains access to the principles upon which it is based' (Barnes 1976, p. 115).

Barnes is thus looking at classroom talk for evidence of such mutual endeavours, in which teachers and children establish what they both know and understand and then move on into new realms of knowledge and understanding. What he finds, however, rarely matches up to this ideal. Instead, pupils and teacher seem to spend much of their time playing the roles of competitors and question master in an ill-defined, hastily conceived quiz:

> Much teaching leaves the pupils dependent not on publicly established systems of knowledge (if such exist) but on quite trivial preconceptions set up arbitrarily either on the spur of the moment, or when the teacher planned the lesson during the previous evening. This reduces the part played by the pupils to a kind of guesswork in which they try to home in upon the teacher's signals about what kind of answer is acceptable. (1976, p. 179)

He illustrates this well with the following piece of dialogue, in which a teacher is talking to some 11-year-olds about deserts and how they are formed by the disintegration of rock into sand. She asks them: 'Now if you think of the seaside and it's been a windy day, and you've been on the beach what can you tell me about the sand?' (P = a pupil, T = the teacher):

Dialogue	Commentary
P: It starts to fly about.	
T: Mm and something else about it when it starts flying around.	*The teacher indicates that the pupil has not grasped the precise aspect of sand she has in mind.*
P: It gets in your eyes	
T: Yes it gets in your eyes.	*This non-committal reply indicates that while this is true it is not the required answer.*
P: It slaps against your face.	
T: It slaps against your face or against your . . . the backs of your legs. That's what I was thinking of . . . it stings.	*None of the replies contains the required idea so the teacher supplies it herself – the abrasive effect of sand.*

(Barnes 1976, p. 180)

Barnes is not critical of the teacher's (unsuccessful) attempt to relate classroom knowledge to out-of-school experience. His criticism is that this quite admirable aim is subverted by the form of the discourse through which it is pursued, which appears to allow the pupils no opportunity for asking their own questions, to formulate hypotheses, or to make intelligent responses other than those predetermined by the teacher's own, implicit, associations of thought and frames of reference. As later chapters show, we also frequently observed this kind of constraint on interaction. Barnes attributes the prevalence of this kind of talk to teachers' attempts to maintain control – an explanation similar to that of Edwards and Furlong (1978), which sees much classroom dialogue as being primarily concerned with the teacher's need to maintain control of the content and destination of any discussion, a need which is the classroom embodiment of a wider social order. This explanation is probably true, so far as it goes; it is hard to conceive of a school system which does otherwise, and there is substantial body of research which shows how teachers' actions represent institutional norms and imperatives (e.g. Keddie 1973; Denscombe 1985). But it is almost certainly not a complete explanation. There are other ways of controlling knowledge, and children, besides involving them in these kinds of guessing games. One can ask more direct questions, for example, or insist on the silent attentiveness and recitation rituals of the Victorian schoolroom. Teachers may all be obliged to control classes and lessons, but they choose particular strategies for doing so. This is a matter of pedagogic ideology; a belief in the effectiveness of a particular style of teaching and learning will make teachers choose one strategy rather than another. However, there has been hardly any research on teachers' purposes in asking questions, and on why they choose to play guessing games.

Hammersley and Woods (1986) suggest that this whole issue is so embedded in our educational tradition that those involved in education are barely conscious of its problematic nature. They comment that asking teachers why they ask the questions they do 'often seems to strike teachers as, to put it politely, strange or naïve'. Moreover, this common-sensical attitude is shared by most educational researchers:

> Virtually the whole tradition of research on teachers' questions is based on the assumption that inference-type questions generate more effective learning than do recall questions, and this assumption is also found in the range of manuals that have been published for teachers about how to ask questions. (Hammersley and Woods 1986, p. 89)

The kinds of questions teachers ask, the kinds of dialogue they strive for, cannot be entirely explained either in terms of the deterministic influence of a social order or by appeals to 'common sense'. These matters can be understood only by trying to take account, as well as possible, of different levels of constraint and influence on classroom communication, including:

1 the responsibilities of teachers as representatives of a culture, and as agents of society;
2 the immediate, practical difficulties facing an adult with limited re-sources in charge of a group of young children;
3 teachers' implicit beliefs about how children learn, and how they can best be helped to do so.

The latter point is one where we have available to us the things that teachers said in interviews, as well as what can be inferred from their talk and practices in the recorded lessons. But we also have something rather unique in research of this sort; we have a written manifesto of educational theory and assumption, the Plowden Report, in which many of the assumptions and principles held by our teachers were made explicit. It is these ideological assumptions underlying educational practice that we shall examine in the next chapter.

3
An ideology of teaching

If we are to make sense of what goes on in any conversation, we need to have some idea of what people are trying to achieve. This includes not only the particular outcomes they hope will be achieved by the particular interaction, but also how they construe the activity they are engaged in, and how they think such activities should be carried out. One important source of reference for the meaning of any social activity is culture, and culture also provides guidelines for how to behave appropriately in particular contexts; the activity, or conversation, is defined as a particular kind of event, such as 'making friends', 'buying and selling', 'teaching and learning', and so on, and pursued accordingly. The importance of such matters has long been recognized by anthropologists but, as we noted in chapter 2, only recently by sociologists of education, some of whom consequently adopted anthropologists' ethnographic methods of enquiry. Some psychologists concerned with educational issues have also given particular attention to cultural meanings. A good example of this kind of research is that of Michael Cole and his associates (e.g. Cole and Scribner 1974; Scribner and Cole 1981), in their investigations of educational problem-solving and literacy. Unlike the microsociologists, however, psychologists engaged in classroom research have not given much attention to cultural definitions of teaching and learning. In this chapter, we try to provide some cultural context for the teaching-and-learning activities that we observed.

There were obvious differences in style and temperament between the teachers we observed, and between the children in the groups being taught. Each of the lessons observed also had its own curriculum topic or theme, and this too created diversity in the types of interaction between children and teachers. But, in some quite striking ways, the lessons we observed were similar. And, what is more, they were similar in ways that are relevant to our interest in how knowledge is shared.

The teachers used a range of teaching activities, and a variety of styles of talk and action to communicate with their children. In doing so, however, they appeared continually to emphasize the need for certain kinds of contribution from children, to accord more significance to certain kinds of interactions than others, and to reward children differentially for their responses, not purely out of expediency. In other words, there seemed good reason to think that these teachers shared some beliefs or assumptions about what constituted good teaching practice; or even that they were trying to put into practice the same basic pedagogy. Moreover, these same pedagogic elements often surfaced in our interviews with the teachers when we asked them about what they were going to do, or had done, in a lesson. These themes are summarized below, illustrated wherever possible either with direct quotations from the teachers in interviews after the lessons, or with reported speech taken mainly from notes made at the pre-lesson discussion of the work to be covered.

1 Setting up conditions which they believed would allow children to discover things for themselves:

> Given sufficient time and resources, I [the teacher] feel that the best learning experience is one where children work things out for themselves.

> I didn't want to tie them down to a heavily structured procedure because it might kill the possibility of children making their own observations and conclusions.

2 Planning their teaching to include activities which would give children direct, concrete experience, and which would require them to act, not just listen, read or write:

> [The teacher] said that in the practical work, where children were much more interested, they would obviously acquire and retain more knowledge. Children learn mainly from doing, at this stage, rather than from a discussion of principles, etc., and [the teacher] feels that practical activities are a very productive way of working.

If you draw it on the blackboard, you know, however clever you are you can never reproduce in the child's mind the same picture that the concrete thing would give them.

3 Attempting to refer to children's wider, out-of-school experience when explaining curriculum topics (in the sense of 'general knowledge', but hardly ever by reference to the particular life experience of any one child in the group):

[The teacher] plans to introduce the session [the first pendulums lesson] with a story about Galileo in church. Then she'll try to get the children to identify pendulums in the world around them, and describe the properties of a pendulum.

4 By the use of techniques like the 'guessing game' question-and-answer sessions described in the previous chapter, to elicit 'key' ideas from children rather than informing them of these directly:

[The teacher] has gone over the procedures with the children in the previous lesson, asking 'leading questions' to which, in the main, they gave the answers she wanted.

5 Never defining (for the children) the full agenda of any activity or lesson in advance. Although such curricular agendas were always invoked implicitly by teachers in the ways in which they structured lessons, and in their choice of questions to children, they clearly felt dissatisfied if, on reflection, they considered that this implicit agenda had limited the lesson's possibilities for children to make their own discoveries:

The children will realize the principles behind the work mainly through doing it. Sometimes the variables involved are very complicated and you would not expect a primary child to understand them.

[The teacher] felt unhappy about the session because he felt he was manœuvring the children too much in the discussion.

6 Not defining explicitly (for the children) the criteria for successful learning which would eventually be applied to what they had done:

[The teacher] said that he would not have questioned the children's conclusions [about the results they had obtained in an experiment] at this stage. He believes that each stage of science work involves acquiring a model for understanding something, and that model is often shattered when one goes on to a further stage.

Just as every researcher has a theoretical stance of some kind which, however implicitly, shapes their research (strictly speaking, there can be no 'atheoretical' research, but only researchers who are more, or less, aware of using theory), so too every teacher relies at some level of self-justification on a set of beliefs about how teaching should be done. The common philosophy we attribute to the teachers we observed is a version of what is popularly called 'progressive' – an approach normally contrasted with the 'traditional' one, which relies heavily on didactic methods and formal procedures. In Britain, the kind of teaching we observed – and the cultural definition of teaching and learning that we were offered by teachers – has its antecedents clearly documented in a government-backed policy statement called the Plowden Report.

In America in the 1970s there was a similar and related movement towards the implementation of a more progressive approach in elementary education. This is often called 'open' education, and, though it shows some differences from the British Plowden variety, there is, as Bennett (1976) and others have pointed out, a great deal of overlap between the two in ideology and practice. Moreover, the later American developments were much influenced by the 'Plowden revolution'; in 1967 Featherstone wrote that 'the American interest in British primary schools is one distinct and powerful stream in a growing, turbulent movement for open informal schools', and by the early seventies Leese (1973) wrote of 'droves of Americans' descending on British primary schools in the years following the Plowden report in search of inspiration and support for their own 'open' approach. There appeared a series of American publications eulogizing British primary practice (e.g. Rogers 1970; Fisher 1972; Howe 1974). Stephens (1974) describes the American style of 'open education' as follows:

> Open education is an approach to education that is open to change, to new ideas, to curriculum, to scheduling, to use of space, to honest expressions of feeling between teacher and pupil and between pupil and pupil, and open to children's participation in significant decision-making in the classroom.
>
> Open education is characterized by a classroom environment in which there is a minimum of teaching to the class as a whole, in which provision is made for children to pursue individual interests and to be actively involved with materials, and in which children are trusted to direct many aspects of their own learning. (Stephens 1974; cited in Bennett 1976, p. 8)

There is little reason to believe, therefore, that the ideology of teaching espoused by the teachers we observed is purely a local cultural phenomenon. The central tenets of that ideology are those of 'progressive' or 'open' education, wherever it is practised. And, as we shall see, those tenets embody some particular, and questionable, psychological assumptions.

  It is probably worth stressing at this point in the book that we shall not be using any critique of progressive education to argue for a return to traditional, didactic methods. The progressive movement was right to argue for the importance of children's active engagement in their own education. What we shall advocate is a third step, towards a cultural-communicative model of education. In rejecting the traditional model and in emphasizing children's cognitive growth, the progressive movement lost sight of the importance of cultural transmission. What we need is an understanding of education as a process in which children are helped and guided into an active, creative participation in their culture. The traditional ideology was all about teaching, and the progressive ideology is all about learning. What is needed is a new synthesis, in which education is seen as the development of joint understanding.

The Plowden ideology

In a scene set by the cumulative influence of economic expansion, population growth and the liberal political climate of the 1960s, the Plowden Report – *Children and their Primary Schools* (Central Advisory Council for Education 1967) – wrote the agenda for the future development of primary education in England and Wales (schools in Scotland and Northern Ireland have always maintained some distinctive features). It was the report of an Advisory Council for Education (chaired by Lady Plowden) which was commissioned by the government, and, although any document from such an authoritative source always commands attention, the Plowden Report received more than usual attention and made an enormous impact on policy in the primary sector. We do not intend to make a proper political and historical analysis of it as a piece of educational policy-making; our sole interest is with its explicit, authoritative, socially legitimized rationale for the kinds of teaching we encountered. Of particular interest to us also was the relationship of this teaching philosophy to Piagetian child psychology. As psychologists, it seemed to us that teachers viewed children's learning from a perspective that owed much to Piaget. Yet Piaget never directly addressed British primary school teachers, and cannot be held responsible for one particular, and yet surprisingly widespread, transformation of his ideas into classroom practice. Walkerdine (1984) has shown that the Nuffield Mathematics Project, which she calls 'the first and most influential curriculum intervention into primary school mathematics in the 1960s', embodies essentially the same pedagogy based on Piagetian psychology. Thus its teachers' guide begins with the quotation:

I hear and I forget
I see and I remember
I do and I understand.

In Piaget's own words, 'Each time one prematurely teaches a child something he could have discovered himself, the child is kept from inventing it and consequently from understanding it completely' (1970, p. 715).

The Plowden committee explicitly espoused Piagetian theory:

Piaget's explanations appear to most educationalists in this country to fit the observed facts of children's learning more satisfactorily than any other. It is in accord with previous research by genetic psychologists and with what is generally regarded as the most effective primary school practice, as it has been worked out empirically. The main implications of that practice are described in the following paragraphs and, where relevant, reference is made to the support given them by the Piagetian school of thought. (Plowden Report, para. 522)

Contrary to popular belief in Britain, the report did not uncritically endorse 'discovery learning'; the committee in fact commented upon its widespread misapplication, and advised caution in its use. But, as is often the case, cautionary comments do little to dampen the resonance of a text's major themes. The child is the agent of his or her own learning, said Plowden, and examples of 'good practice' were included to illustrate what this meant. In the section on science teaching, for instance, the following advice was offered to teachers:

The treatment of the subject matter may be summarized in the phrase 'learning by discovery'. . . . Initial curiosity, often stimulated by the environment the teacher provides, leads to questions and to a consideration of what questions it is sensible to ask and how to find the answers. This involves a great exercise of judgement on the part of the teacher. *He will miss the whole point if he tells the children the answers or indicates too readily and completely how the answers may be found,* but he must not let them flounder too long or helplessly, *and can often come to the rescue by asking another question. . . . Essential elements are enquiry, exploration, and first hand experience.* (para. 669; our italics)

In a section on general aspects of children's learning, the committee wrote:

Verbal explanation, in advance of understanding based on experience, *may be an obstacle to learning*, and children's knowledge of the right words may conceal from teachers their lack of understanding. (para. 535; our italics)

The idealized model of learning is one in which children's natural curiosity about 'real problems' motivates their exploration of educational knowledge, and wherein existing and new knowledge are synthesized in the act of discovery. This is clearly what the committee hoped to illustrate by including anecdotes such as the following:

> A top junior class became interested in the problem of measuring the area of an awkwardly shaped field at the back of the school. The problem stimulated much learning about surveying and triangles. From surveying, interest passed to navigation; for the more difficult aspects of the work, co-operation between members of staff as well as pupils was needed. (para. 542)

Following Piaget, exploratory activity by children was identified with 'play':

> Adults who criticize teachers for allowing children to play are unaware that play is the principal means of learning in childhood. (para. 523)

Piaget's influence was particularly apparent in the Plowden Report's emphasis on children's reaching *states of readiness* to learn: teachers must only try to move children on when they are standing firmly on one step of the Piagetian staircase of cognitive development, with their resources gathered to make the next step upwards. Discovery, play, firsthand experience, 'real problems', acting rather than listening (for children), eliciting rather than telling (for teachers), steps – or, rather, plateaux – of learning which children reach and rest on before moving upwards: these are the Plowden Report's main themes, to be orchestrated and conducted by a teacher 'leading from behind'. The model of the child learner implicit in this pedagogy is that of a psychological individual, a 'lone organism' (Bruner 1985) more than a cultural participant. Not only is this educational philosophy, and the practice it generates, *informed* by Piagetian theory; as Walkerdine (1984) points out, the status of this psychological theory *legitimized* the pedagogy.

In interview, the teachers we observed often identified themselves with this pedagogy (unfortunately, explicit statements of pedagogic principles by British primary teachers outside our study are few and far between). The teacher in the 'pendulums' lessons, which figure largely in chapters 6 and 7, explicitly contrasted her own experience of schooling with what she offered children today:

I used to go to an old convent school and we weren't allowed to touch bunsen burners. The teacher did it and we watched, as much as we'd have liked to have done something. Last year, we were doing field studies, so what we did was we built an environment in the classroom. Dirt, we grew a plant, grass from seed. We went out and collected all sorts of creatures and then we spent weeks finding out what the ants eat and how many leaves the caterpillars ate. They loved it and that's far better than saying to them 'I'll draw an ant', 'I'll draw a caterpillar', 'Draw the leaves that they eat'. (Interviewer: You think they learn more in fact?) Of course they do.

Children are the agents of their own learning, and so must be given the opportunity to make their own discoveries. However, this does not mean that these teachers abdicate their responsibility for what is done or learnt. What we see in their practice is a Plowdenesque compromise between allowing children scope for exploration, discovery and self-definition of problems, and maintaining the teacher's control of the class in the pursuit of predetermined curricular goals. They construct dialogues and contexts to enable this compromise, as we shall see.

Finally, we must address a question about the embodiment of Plowden philosophy in teaching styles which has been raised by other classroom researchers. The ORACLE project was discussed in chapter 2. Using systematic-observation methods, its researchers (Galton, Simon and Croll 1980) drew the conclusion that the Plowden approach was *not* alive and well and living in British primary classrooms. They found that none of those teachers whom they identified as having consistent, stable teaching styles seemed to embody the Plowden ideals. What is at issue here is the Plowden Report's suggestion that classes of children should be organized into subgroups working together in some co-operative manner. ORACLE found that, although children were seated around tables in small groups, they still usually worked (under the teacher's direction) on their own. What is more, teachers tended to use the probing, eliciting and more cognitively demanding kinds of questions only with whole classes (something discouraged by Plowden), and to interact with individuals mainly to provide information and correction. We do not dispute these findings; any apparent conflict between ORACLE's findings and our own is resolved by considering – as we did in chapter 2 – the very different nature and purposes of the two studies.

The direct relevance of ORACLE's findings to our interests is, therefore, slight. However, there is a danger that such findings are interpreted as showing that teachers do not practise what they preach. That would not only be an unjust criticism of English primary teachers; it would also amount to a gross oversimplification of the relationship between philosophy (or ideology) and practice. Largely through the efforts of their trade unions, it is now widely appreciated that most teachers in state schools are overstretched and under-resourced. The ORACLE teachers may have achieved little success in embodying Plowden ideals within the greater part of their activities during normal schools days (as revealed by the relative frequency of the appropriately coded observations made by the ORACLE researchers). But systematic-observation methods do not provide data about ideologies or intentions, only about behaviour. (A systematic observer watching a series of nil–nil draws in World Cup football would be foolish to infer that scoring goals was a matter of little importance in the game!) One cannot conclude that primary teachers are not able to put their ideals into practice *given the right conditions*. One can agree with ORACLE that teachers' working conditions in schools may often make Plowden an impractical philosophy, but it is nevertheless the philosophy that predominates. As Walkerdine (1984) has argued, the standards for good pedagogy which are to be seen everywhere in the 'apparatus' of primary schooling – the content of teacher-training courses, the work cards and record sheets, the use of resources and the classroom layout – are unmistakably drawn from an interpretation of Piagetian psychology represented by the Plowden Report. Without its rationale, its legitimizing ideology, primary teachers would have no basis for their professional practice other than trial and error and 'common sense'.

Some further issues of ideology and practice

There are, of course, important aspects of the ideology of teaching which can be traced to other sources, but which we do not consider here because they have less relevance to our present interests. Examples would be: the 'nature versus nurture' controversy in the psychological study of intelligence, and its influence on teachers' attitudes about children's learning potential; and the 'difference versus deprivation' debate in the study of language use, social class and educational achievement, and its influence on teachers' evaluation of the talk of children from different social backgrounds. Here, instead, we will point to two issues which arise out of the discussion of educational ideology in this chapter, and which will figure in the content of later chapters. First, the practice of education occurs in a cultural and ideological context such that the criteria which define good teaching and successful learning are likely to be embodied in lessons in an implicit way, though teachers and pupils may to some extent be able to articulate them if asked to do so. Second, there is, within educational ideology, a tension between the notions of education as a 'drawing out' of the potential and ability of children, and, on the other hand, a requirement to inculcate pupils into a pre-existing culture of educated knowledge, thought and practice. We shall look at some ways in

which teachers and pupils handle the dilemma of achieving these conflicting aims.

In the next chapter, we shall take up the notion that there is an implicit
basis to being competent in educational discourse.

4
Ground-rules of educational discourse

Classroom talk is one instance of talk in general, one kind of social interaction, and so has properties which are common to all conversations and interactions. Before we deal with specifically educational matters, then, we shall deal briefly with the more general business of how people share understandings through conversation. This will not be about the psychology of language comprehension, of how people analyse and interpret sounds, words, sentences and texts. Our interest is in the more general 'pragmatic' rules that speakers and hearers must in some sense know and abide by in order to engage in conversation. The notion of *ground-rules* refers to a set of implicit understandings that participants in conversations need to possess, over and above any strictly linguistic knowledge, in order to make proper sense of what each other is trying to say, or trying to achieve in saying something. We have encountered an instance in chapter 2, the notions of 'given' and 'new' information. We shall now put those notions into a larger frame.

A useful and influential treatment of the general ground-rules of conversation has been offered by the philosopher Paul Grice (1975). According to Grice, conversations are generally conducted on the basis of a *co-operative principle*, which is defined as a rule that people expect each other to follow: 'Make your contribution such as is required, at the stage at which it occurs, by the accepted purpose or direction of the talk exchange in which you are engaged.' The co-operative principle breaks down into a set of four 'maxims', as follows:

1 *The maxim of quality (truth)*
   Try to make your contribution one that is true, and specifically:
   (a) do not say what you believe to be false;
   (b) do not say that for which you lack adequate evidence.

2 *The maxim of quantity (informativeness)*
   (a) make your contribution as informative as is required for the current purposes of the exchange;
   (b) do not make your contribution more informative than is required.

3 *The maxim of relevance*
   Make your contributions relevant.

4 *The maxim of manner (intelligibility)*
   Be perspicuous, and specifically:
   (a) avoid obscurity;
   (b) avoid ambiguity;
   (c) be brief;
   (d) be orderly.

The maxim of quantity, or informativeness, clearly relates to the notions of given and new information. But here, rather than appearing as characteristics of language itself, we have what is obviously a social norm, an understanding expected of each other by participants in a conversation. If, in polite conversation, we express some bewilderment about the changeable weather, we do not expect to receive in exchange a detailed exposition of the nature, causes and predictability of climatic variation. But, of course, given some other 'purposes of the exchange' – as in, say, an oral examination in climatology – such an exposition may well be exactly what is required. The maxims are sensitive to particular social settings and purposes.

While Grice's maxims may readily be perceived as appropriate descriptions of an idealized conversation, it may be objected that many conversations are not so straightforward. People are not always so co-operative, so truthful and informative, so relevant and clear. In fact, however, it is in dealing with such exceptions, where the maxims appear to have been broken or ignored, that they are shown at their most powerful. What happens is that, faced with an apparent exception to the normal flow of co-operative conversation, our first reaction is to strive to make sense of what is said on the basis that it does in fact conform to co-operative expectations. We construct a 'reading' of it that makes sense. Indeed, this process of trying to make co-operative sense of anything said to us before rejecting it as meaningless can be shown to be an essential feature of all normal conversation. This is what we did in chapter 2 with Sir Geoffrey Howe's statement about the status of American presidents as presidents of America; on the assumption that the informativeness norm was, despite appearances, being upheld, we were able to give the utterance a co-operative interpretation.

Consider the following exchanges (taken from Labov (1972), pp. 122–3):

1   A: Are you going to work tomorrow?
    B: I'm on jury duty.
    A: Couldn't you get out of it?
    B: We tried everything.

2   LINUS: Do you want to play with me, Violet?
    VIOLET: You're younger than me. (*Shuts the door.*)
    LINUS: (*puzzled*) She didn't answer my question.

Items 1 and 2 both represent sequences of talk which apparently break Grice's rules, but which nevertheless make obvious sense. Labov treats the problem as one of having to find the missing propositions that make the necessary connections: 'When A hears B say "I'm on jury duty", he searches for the proposition B is asserting; in this case, he locates "If someone is on jury duty, he cannot go to work." B's answer is then heard as "I'm not going to work tomorrow"' (1972, p. 122). Similarly, sequence 2 (from the cartoon *Peanuts*) entails a missing proposition: 'The missing proposition being asserted here by Violet is presumed to be part of the communal *shared knowledge*, but it has not in fact reached Linus yet' (1972, p. 124). Grice's maxims are an attempt to specify the rules by which people supply the missing propositions and shared knowledge necessary to understand the dialogue as something coherent and sensible.

In fact, as we argued in chapter 2, the communal shared knowledge within which discourse makes sense is not necessarily a matter of language alone – of 'missing propositions'. It includes all sorts of non-linguistic shared experience, assumptions, perceptions and understandings that may not be easily stated linguistically. Grice's rules are not merely rules of language, but are rules that govern any sort of coherent social transaction. Stephen Levinson offers the following observation:

> Consider, for example, a situation in which A and B are fixing a car. If the maxim of Quality is interpreted as the injunction to produce non-spurious or sincere acts (a move we need to make anyway to extend the maxim to questions, promises, invitations, etc.), B would fail to comply with this if, when asked for brake fluid, he knowingly passes A the oil. . . . Similarly, A would fail to observe the maxim of Quantity, the injunction to make one's contribution in the right proportion, if, when B needs three bolts, he purposely passes him only one, or

alternatively passes him 300. Likewise with Relevance: if B wants three bolts he wants them *now* not half an hour later. Finally, B would fail to comply with the maxim of Manner, enjoining clarity of purpose, if, when A needs a bolt of size 8, B passes him the bolt in a box that usually contains bolts of size 10. In each of these cases the behaviour . . . violates one or another of the non-verbal analogues of the maxims of conversation. (Levinson 1983, p. 103)

Conversation is a species of social interaction; many of its properties are ones that pertain to social interaction generally, and not only to linguistic exchanges. At the same time, conversations, like all other social inter-actions, take place in real social settings, where the participants share understandings of the nature and purposes of the transaction, the significance of persons, place and time, and (usually) cultural knowledge, which is the essential backdrop to all that happens at the level of overt talk and action. School classrooms are a subset of those social settings. They are characterized by local versions of the ground-rules of conversation and of social activity, and the local shared knowledge and experience of the participants. These 'local' characteristics also range widely in their generality, from general properties of educational talk and text, to very specific things that a particular teacher and pupils have done and said a few moments earlier. We shall remain mostly at the general level in this chapter, and look at more specific features in chapter 5.

Making sense of classroom talk

Although we have so far stressed the common properties of all conver-sations, it is also quite clear that classroom talk has special properties that distinguish it from talk in other settings. Indeed, the same can be said of talk in other settings – high street shops, doctors' surgeries and lawcourts all have their own forms of discourse. Many of the special properties of classroom discourse have been revealed by the sorts of research that we outlined in the previous chapter – such as IRF (initiation–response–feedback) structures, and the remarkable dominance of classroom discourse by the teacher's questions. What concerns us here is not so much the patterning of the discourse itself, but rather the understandings that participants must possess in order to be able to take part. There are three such understandings that we shall deal with here:

1 It is the teacher who asks the questions.
2 The teacher knows the answers.
3 Repeated questions imply wrong answers.

On the face of it, item 1 is a little puzzling, especially given item 2. One would be forgiven for assuming that the essential situation is one in which the teacher knows everything and the pupils have everything to learn. A natural pattern of discourse in such circumstances might be that the pupils ask all the questions and the teacher answers them. But this is not the case. As we noted in chapter 2, the 'two-thirds rule' assigns most of classroom talk to teachers, and much of that talk to asking questions.

Dillon (1982) quotes Mishler's findings that, in 85 per cent of exchanges observed in primary classrooms, teachers put a further question after pupils had responded; in 67 per cent of the classes, they replied to a pupil's question by asking another one. Traditionally, questions have been used to check pupils' attention and to assess rote learning. Progressive teaching makes even greater claims on the importance of questions, seeing them as vital to stimulate pupils' thought and discussion. Dillon argues that they represent teachers' predominant technique for initiating, extending and controlling classroom conversation. He suggests, however, that there is actually no firm research evidence to prove that teachers' use of questions does 'stimulate thought and discussion'. Indeed, turning to other fields of enquiry and looking at the theoretical analysis of questions in logic, linguistics and philosophy, the practical use of questions in opinion-polling and cross-examination, and the tactical avoidance of questions in personnel interviewing, psychotherapy and group discussion, Dillon finds that in no enterprise other than education is it held that questions stimulate and enhance thought. Interviewers, therapists, barristers and others whose job it is to ask questions are typically advised that asking strings of direct questions is the surest means of shutting the interviewee up! Silences, declarative statements and other less direct prompts are apparently more effective in getting people to talk. The prevalence of direct questions in teacher talk would on the face of it appear to be counter-productive to the aim of getting pupils to articulate their thoughts. The likelihood is that teachers' questions, and IRF discourse structures in general, serve other, less obvious purposes.

Of course, when teachers ask questions of pupils we are dealing with a phenomenon quite different from what is happening when pupils ask questions of teachers. While pupils may be seeking information, guidance or permission to do something, the teacher is checking that pupils know what they are supposed to, testing their knowledge, checking whether they have been paying attention, defining the agenda for thought, action and discussion. Most of the questions that teachers ask do not, in the most straightforward sense, seek information. They are part of the discursive weaponry available to teachers for controlling topics of discussion, directing pupils' thought and action, and establishing the extent of shared attention, joint activity and common knowledge (see Edwards and Furlong 1978; Hammersley 1977; Mehan 1979; MacLure and French 1980).

Because most of the teacher's questions are ones to which everyone supposes that the teacher knows the answer, the status of any answer offered by a pupil is also affected by the nature of the exchange. The teacher is understood to be in a position to evaluate any such response (the feedback part of the IRF), and so the teacher's next move will be taken as evaluative. So, if what the teacher does is to pose the same question again, the implication is that whatever answer was received was evaluated as incorrect, and an alternative is now requested. Silence on the teacher's part may imply the same thing; the earlier question remains 'on the table'. If the teacher ignores a question put by a pupil, we may expect the opposite interpretation – the question has failed to be put on the agenda. In other words, the teacher is in a position to control the discourse, to define what are appropriate things to talk about, and may act as the arbiter of valid knowledge. We shall examine this process and its implications for the creation of shared understandings in chapter 7.

The important point to note here about these rules of classroom talk is that they are rules of interpretation, rules that have to be understood and acted on by the participants, rather than simply characteristics of recorded talk. And they are implicit rather than explicit: like the rules of grammar and of social interaction that govern talk and behaviour in the classroom, they are not rules that the participants will necessarily be aware of knowing. They can act upon them without being able to articulate them in the way we are doing here. In this respect, these rules of classroom talk are part of a more general set of unwritten rules of interpretation which underlie successful participation in educational discourse. They include rules about how to deal with the content or subject matter of the lesson – such as that teachers' test questions need to be answered with a degree of explicitness and formality that would not be required in ordinary conversation. 'Not bad' would, in the classroom, probably be an unacceptable answer to a question about the quality of Henry VIII's foreign policy.

We have called these implicit rules of educational talk and practice *educational ground-rules* (Mercer and Edwards 1981). They extend beyond gross understandings about classroom talk and the explicitness of answers, to the special domains of particular curriculum subjects and topics. There are special ways of dealing with problems posed in mathematics, in English, or with particular teachers or in specific settings. The question arises, then: what happens when pupils fail to recognize these different sorts of discourse, and the appropriate ways of responding to them? Given that the rules are generally implicit and that (as we suggested in the previous chapter) teachers' understanding of the learning process is usually based on individual mental abilities, the obvious danger is that such pupils may be inappropriately labelled as unintelligent or backward. And, although this is not something that we have investigated directly, it is likely to be a problem especially for pupils who do not share with the teacher a background of cultural experience that might make such implicit rules more easily recognized or learned. A further question, to which we shall return at the end of this chapter, is whether or not normal educational practice *precludes* the mutual exploration of this rule system by teachers and pupils.

Ground-rules and misunderstandings

When we began our research into classroom knowledge and talk, one of our first interests was with the misunderstandings that arise in communications between teachers and children in school. We had observed some instances of misunderstandings, or had them reported to us, in visits to classrooms and in other contacts with teachers, and they also are referred to here and there in the research literature. Some of these – the most obvious kind – were about the specific subject matter of lessons, but others were more to do with the purposes or goals of activities, and the criteria for success that children were being judged against. What they had in common was that they were all illustrations of the failure of educational communication; although engaged together in classroom talk and activities, teachers and children had not achieved a shared understanding of what was going on. Especially interesting were situations where such misunderstandings had been unapparent to the teacher or the child, or to both, and so had persisted, unresolved, for some time, despite continued contact between the two. With the co-operation of some teachers, we investigated this in a fairly informal way by (1) asking some 10-year-old children what they thought was the purpose of certain things they did in class, and (2) asking them to mark pieces of writing by other children, to see what criteria they applied. This research is discussed briefly in Mercer (1980), and drawn on in our later publications (Mercer and Edwards 1981; Mercer 1985). Essentially, we found no consensus among the children about why they did things in class, and there was marked divergence by some of the child markers from the criteria for success applied by their teachers.

Some surprising and bizarre examples of classroom misunderstandings have been recorded by teachers. For example, Powell (1976) found that pupils who had been achieving quite acceptable standards in her secondary science lessons thought that 'evaporation' meant making milk thicker, and that liquids were by definition thick and sticky (like the various 'liquid' detergents that are used for washing dishes). Hull (1985) noted the following misunderstandings among a group of 14- and 15-year-old boys:

> 'Animals harbour insects' meant they ate them. 'The lowest bridge-town' was a slum on a bridge. 'Flushing (22,000)' meant they caught 22,000 fish there. Expressions such as 'molten iron', 'physical feature',

'factor', 'western leader' were often insuperable obstacles to comprehension. (p. xi)

Traditionally, divergences on the part of children from the 'correct', normative understandings have been interpreted by researchers and teachers as some kind of individual failure. The blame is usually attributed to the child (insufficient effort to listen, learn or concentrate on their part, or perhaps the limitations of their intelligence or cognitive development); but, if not, it will probably be attributed to the teacher ('poor teaching' of one kind or another). More unusually, the problem may be identified as inherent in 'the language' of school itself, which is seen as a problematic medium through which teachers and children swim with difficulty (Creber 1972; Hull 1985). Investigators rarely dig for the roots of misunderstanding in the communicative processes of education, in the meeting of two minds which education is contrived to achieve. John Holt's *Why Children Fail* (1969) does address this issue, but his explanation is not grounded in the analysis of interactions between particular children and teachers. The same can be said of Basil Bernstein (1971), whose very useful discussion of the 'classification and framing' of curriculum knowledge never comes to grips with classroom processes. On the other hand, many of those researchers who have analysed classroom communications, from the 'systematic observers' (e.g. Galton, Simon and Croll 1980) to the 'discourse analysts' (e.g. Sinclair and Coulthard 1975), do not show any particular interest in mutual understandings or misunderstandings. They are more concerned with identifying regularities and typical features in the stretches of interaction they observe. Much of this research into classroom communications has had little to say about what the pupils actually learn. An exception to all this is the work of Edwards and Furlong (1978), Barnes (e.g. 1976) and Mehan (1979), all of whom have treated knowledge as something socially constructed and have investigated links between what is actually said and the prior and subsequent understandings of participants in education.

One of the purposes of classroom communications, albeit one often diverted or thwarted by other objectives, is to further the knowledge and understanding of children about topics which, however implicitly stated and ill defined, constitute the curriculum. For this to occur at all, a child and teacher must mutually establish a universe of discourse. For children, this amounts to more than learning how to take part in linguistic rituals, playing 'teachers and pupils', which (as Willes (1979) and others have shown) very young children do within months of entering school. As Moffett says, 'we have to distinguish . . . between the capacity to produce a given discourse and the capacity to receive and understand it' (1968, p. 31). That infants quickly learn how to dramatize scenarios for 'teachers and pupils', 'cowboys and Indians' or 'police and thieves' is interesting in itself. However, it is not the essence of education, ethnic relations or law enforcement that is captured in those games, but only the superficial characteristics of discourse, the histrionics.

The universe of educational discourse must be distinguished from that of everyday life outside school. Indeed, one of the skills most required of children in school is an ability to recognize when the hypothetical 'what if . . . ?' universe has been entered and everyday life left behind. For an educated adult, this transition will normally present few problems; different rules apply, as any biologist well knows when he or she enters a building labelled 'No Animals Allowed'. For children, the transition may be problematical, and a source of misunderstandings. Teachers lead children into this universe through talk, and it is one in which familiar things may adopt new, unfamiliar guises.

In the example below, a teacher uses the popular method of elicitation through questioning to try to draw a group of 7- and 8-year-olds away from their recent, concrete experiences in a simulation exercise into the educational realm of generalizations. As part of a social studies project intended to help them understand social relationships, they had pretended that they were stranded on a desert island, and had to organize themselves as castaways would. (Some further information about this project and the lesson are given in the appendix.) The teacher's aim in the discussion that followed was to get the children to consider how rules and laws may be altered by mutual decision within a community. She wished to draw this generalization from their reflections on their own experiences in the activity, when they had done this very thing.

Sequence 4.1   Compulsory schooling

T: Can we now leave the island for a moment and come back home. In this country there is a law that says that all children when they reach the age of five must attend school. How could you change that law? What could you do? Angelina?.

ANGELINA: You could say your child was a younger age.

T: Well/ if you were eleven Angelina for example/ thinking about some of the people who are eleven/ do you think you could get away with pretending that you are younger?

ANGELINA: No.

T: Why not Angelina?

ANGELINA: Because if you were eleven and you're about there and you went to go to school at five years old/ they'd easily know that you're not younger than five.

T: So you really couldn't trick someone that way could you? Jimmy?

JIMMY: Miss if we're on the island anyway miss/ you wouldn't get into trouble. There's no police or anything there.

T: Yes but Jimmy you will remember that I have said that we have now left the island and are back home. And there is this law that says you must attend school once you're five years old.

JIMMY: Miss we can just skive out of school Miss.

T: Well if you wanted to change the law what could you do? Adam?

ADAM: If you're a midget/ they'll never find out.

T: But you're not you see. Erm// Rosemary.

ROSEMARY: Miss if you pretend you're ill.

T: All the time?

ROSEMARY: Not all the time Miss.

T: So what would you do when you're not ill?

ROSEMARY: Miss only pretend that you're not ill at the weekend.

T: Yes but what about the times when you are well and you are over five and therefore should be in school?

ROSEMARY: Well Miss you could erm// go away and move to a different country and they wouldn't know how old you was.

T: Well if you went to a different country you might find that we have another law there's another law of the same kind. Sam?

SAM: I was going to say the same sort of thing Miss.

T: What could your mum and dad do about wanting to change this law about having to go to school at five? Gary?

GARY: They could teach you at home.

T: They could teach you at home.

DEAN: When my mum went to Jamaica 'cause my cousin couldn't// my cousin's mum went erm// had to go to school. So when my mum went there she teached my cousin.

T: That's the same idea as Gary's really isn't it? Erm// Angelina?

ANGELINA: Miss we can take// not so much as a real school but to a private school.

T: Yes.

DEAN: A private teacher of your own Miss.

T: At home. The same idea as Gary really. Have you got another idea Gary?

GARY: Yes Miss. Miss you could pretend you didn't exist.

T: Well how would you do that?

GARY: Miss make/ make pretend you did go to school Miss.

T: Well how would you pretend you did go to school?
 Who ⎡ might
GARY: ⎣ Just go out every day to a certain place.

T: Who might know that you're not actually going to school? Anita?

ANITA: The teacher.

T: How would the teacher know?

ANITA: She calls the register.

T: She calls the register. Now if you think this is a good law that you come to school when you are five years old put your hand up. Sixteen people believe that it is a good law. If you disagree with that law put your hand up. One/ two/ three/ four thank you. Now I'm going to ask you to very quietly get your diaries please.

(*Discussion ends.*)

In the best traditions of *e-ducare*, the teacher resisted telling the children what conclusions she was hoping to draw from their experience, and instead tried to elicit these from them. Having failed to do this, she eventually gave up and switched to the more reliable standby of 'diary work'. In the subsequent interview, the teacher expressed the belief that this discussion had been ill-timed, at the end of an hour's work when children were fidgety and unable to concentrate. She also thought that the level of the discussion might simply have been too difficult for most of the children, though she expected that some of them would make the links she intended. Her intention was to get the children to use their personal experience as a resource for educational debate. To do this, they would need to make a particular kind of interpretation of the questions she asked, and distil a particular essence from all that had occurred in their activity. Although there are many ways of drawing conclusions from experience – including the culturally specific modes of interpretation that Shirley Brice Heath (1983) calls 'ways of taking' – it is clear that only some of these ways are educationally appropriate.

Sequence 4.1 began with the teacher saying that they were all now going to leave their island and 'come back home' (she was obliged to remind Jimmy of this mental relocation later in the discussion). The children apparently interpreted this in a straightforward way: they were back home, where the rules of the world outside school would apply, and so they offered commonsensical, realistic strategies for avoiding school: 'Miss we can just skive out of school Miss'; 'Miss if you pretend you're ill.' Faced with the teacher's repeated appeals for a response – a feature of classroom discourse, as we noted earlier, that these pupils also have learnt means 'wrong answer, try again' – some children realize that the discussion was not actually located in the 'real' world, and so offered some imaginative alternatives: 'If you're a midget they'll never find out'; 'Miss you could pretend you didn't exist.' They know that, as Edwards and Furlong say, 'Being taught usually means suspending your own interpretation of the subject matter and seeking out what the teacher means' (1978, p. 104). However, none of their attempts is successful. What their teacher actually wanted was an abstract, generalized consideration of rules, laws and social consensus.

It is worth noting that, although the children did not enter the teacher's universe of discourse, they were perfectly able to participate in educational discourse in a more superficial sense – to fill response slots in IRF exchanges, to react appropriately to the teacher's repeated elicitations, and so on. What they and their teacher did not achieve was the construction of a shared frame of reference for their talk, a shared ground-rule; the pupils did not understand the implicit requirement for a particular sort of answer.

Being in school is a unique experience for children; they do things there that they would never do in the rest of their lives. School has its own rules for how they should talk and act – justifiable, to varying extents, in terms of the educational process – and very rarely are these rules, or the aims that underlie them, made explicit. Children will be taught how to do specific things, like how to perform long divisions, how to draw maps, and so on; but the underlying ground-rules are something they really have to try to work out for themselves. And their conception of what they are doing, and why, may differ considerably from that of their teachers.

The aims for the lessons based on the 'island' activity had been worked out by the teacher in conjunction with the local authority adviser responsible for the project. These made explicit the lessons' purpose of teaching children about society; they were to learn some sociology. Thus the adviser said that he hoped there would be

> discussion on the concepts of the *division of labour* (how we shared out the jobs), of *co-operation* and *interdependence* (we need someone to do this), of fairness (why shouldn't you help / what will you do instead). There should also be references to *conflict* and to *social control*, and these should be encouraged.

Before the lesson from which sequence 4.1 was taken, the teacher expressed her own main aims for the 'desert island' activity: to help the children to 'use their own experience as a source of knowledge about how their island society should operate' and 'use concepts of social control, co-operation, interdependence, division of labour and conflict to help them organize their description and management of the island.' She also specified some other aims for this lesson, to do with the development of children's communication skills. Thus the children should 'understand other people's points of view in the group'; 'use skills of operating in small group discussion, in arguing, conciliating and empathizing with others'; 'learn and practise a general range of oral language skills, in large and small groups, with and without the teacher's presence.'

After the lesson, we asked the children what they thought it had all been about, what they had learnt, and what they thought their teacher hoped they would get from what they had done. Here are the responses of one group who worked together.

ANGELINA (*after a few moments' hesitation*): I would think that I would learn that I would never go on a boat trip again.

JOANNE: It teaches you about what would really happen if you were on a desert island, what it's like on a desert island.

TARIQ: I never thought before about having to share things out like gold and food, 'cause food is usually easy to get in shops, but there are no shops on the island so you have to share it out. (Interviewer: How will that be useful to you? You're going to be somewhere near shops, aren't you?) If you go somewhere like Africa, there's not many shops there . . .

NEIL: Say if you were stuck on an island and you wouldn't know what to do so it gives you practice in that.

Our observation of the lesson leaves no doubt that the children did practise the communication skills mentioned in the teacher's aims above. They had found the activity interesting, and were enthusiastic for more of the same. All of this reflects the teacher's good organizational skills, and her excellent rapport with the children. But what was primarily intended to be an experiential lesson about a set of social science concepts appears to have been understood by the pupils themselves as some kind of training exercise in how to survive as a castaway. It is not that their classroom experiences would be of no value in forming an understanding of the social science concepts, but rather that the children were left to make the transition for themselves, and we have no evidence that they ever did so. We talked to the teacher about this, and asked why she had not explained the rationale for the activity to the children, or explicitly introduced sociological concepts into discussions. Her replies were suitably Plowdenesque. She did not feel she should constrain what the children might learn – the activity could provide a whole range of learning experiences besides those she had in mind – and she wished to avoid 'putting words into children's mouths'.

Understanding educational ground-rules

The special nature of educational discourse is not, as we have stressed, restricted to general properties of classroom talk. Particular subjects such as mathematics, science, history and English have discourse patterns, rules and characteristics of their own. Recognizing these characteristics, even if only unconsciously, is an essential part of dealing with them. The following problem (remembered from a secondary maths class years ago) illustrates this.

Suppose you are the conductor of a bus. The bus leaves the depot on its way towards the town centre. At the first stop it picks up 12 people. At the next stop another 11 get on. At the third stop 7 get off and 15 get on. At the fourth stop 21 people get off and 14 get on. The bus continues to the next stop where 7 people get off and a drunk climbs aboard. The conductor takes his fare, but the drunk is disruptive, and at the next stop 13 people complain to the conductor and get off the bus. The conductor tells the drunk to get off. The drunk does so reluctantly, after first asking the conductor's name.

Try to answer these questions before reading any further:

1 How many passengers are still on the bus?
2 What is the conductor's name?

People generally have no problem in dealing with the first question (the answer is 4) but baulk at the second, which seems to be a joke and impossible to answer. In the original maths class it was several minutes before the first few pupils' hands were raised to indicate that they had the solution, and twenty minutes later several pupils were still stuck. If you too are stuck, then read carefully the first sentence of the problem.

The bus conductor problem is of a recognizable sort. It has the superficial appearance of a brief narrative about a bus journey, but its real *raison d'être* is to embody a mathematical calculation. Our educational experience tells us that the narrative is more or less irrelevant, and that what we have to do is to extract the 'sum' that it contains, while discarding the text. The identity of the bus conductor is of no importance. Being able to recognize this sort of pseudo-narrative format for presenting mathematical problems is extremely useful in school, and the reason why the second question causes difficulty for many people is precisely because they have learnt this normally useful trick.[1] The last thing we expect of such a problem, presented to us as a mathematical one of a recognizable type, is that we should pay any attention to the narrative details of the story. Our eyes pass quickly over the first sentence, virtually discarding it as soon as it is read.

Participation in classroom education clearly requires familiarity and competence in dealing with a variety of special sorts of discourse. It is a key feature of this competence that it tends to be implicit rather than explicit. We took the notion of 'ground-rules' from Ulric Neisser's (1976)

---

[1] Terry Wrigley, a teacher in Yorkshire, provided us with the following account of his own experience with the 'bus conductor' problem which seems to fit our explanation of the trick:

> I tried your bus conductor problem on my 5-year-old daughter. She is very clever at manipulating numbers, but school has had little impact beyond simple recognition of figures. I turned the bus conductor into a bus driver (one-man buses here). She tried to interrupt me three times after the drunk got on. I blocked this. She correctly added the number of people on the bus at the end, and after only two seconds' hesitation with no prompting told me the driver's name was 'Kate, of course.' She then reinforced the point by reopening discussion of why the passengers had reacted as they did just because somebody had had too much to drink. Interestingly, she followed this by saying: 'Now it's my turn to ask you a question. You are a bus driver and five people get on your bus. How many people are there?' When I answered 'six', she replied (exact words), 'Oh, you knew it. You've heard that one before.' I interpret this as meaning that she had never made a distinction between mathematical puzzles and joke puzzles.

discussion of Michael Cole's studies of cognition and culture in Liberia. Those studies (reported in Cole, Gay, Glick and Sharp 1971), and Neisser's interpretation of them, stress the implicit cultural basis of educational thought.

> For some years Michael Cole and his associates . . . have been studying cognitive processes in a Liberian people called the Kpelle. They are an articulate people, debate and argument play an important role in their society. Many are entirely illiterate never having gone to school. Like members of traditional societies everywhere, unschooled Kpelle get poor scores on tests and problems that seem easy to people with some formal education. The following example gives some idea of the reason why:
>
> EXPERIMENTER: Flumo and Yakpalo always drink cane juice (rum) together. Flumo is drinking cane juice. Is Yakpalo drinking cane juice?
> SUBJECT: Flumo and Yakpalo drink cane juice together, but the time Flumo was drinking the first one Yakpalo was not there on that day.
> EXPERIMENTER: But I told you that Flumo and Yakpalo always drink cane juice together. One day Flumo was drinking cane juice. Was Yakpalo drinking cane juice that day?
> SUBJECT: The day Flumo was drinking cane juice Yakpalo was not there on that day.
> EXPERIMENTER: What is the reason?
> SUBJECT: The reason is that Yakpalo went to his farm that day and Flumo remained in town on that day . . .
>
> Such answers are by no means stupid. The difficulty is that they are not answers *to the questions*. The respondents do not accept a ground rule that is virtually automatic with us: 'Base your answer on the terms defined by the questioner'. People who go to school (in Kpelle-land or elsewhere) learn to work within the fixed limitations of this ground rule. . . . It is clear that (unschooled) subjects take their particular actual situation into account more fully than schooled people do, when they are presented with formal problems. This may seem a poor strategy, from the problem setter's point of view. In general, however, it is an extremely sensible course of action. In the affairs of daily life it matters who we are talking to, what we are measuring and where we are. . . . Intelligent behaviour in real settings often involves actions that satisfy a variety of motives at once – practical and interpersonal ones, for example. . . . All this is different in school. We are expected to leave our life situations at the door, as it were, and to solve problems that other people have set. (Neisser 1976, pp. 135–6)

There are obvious similarities between this example and the classroom discussion in sequence 4.1 above. Despite the experimenter's inclusion of culturally appropriate content ('drinking cane juice', etc.), the unschooled Kpelle do not deal with the problem in the intended way. Like the children in sequence 4.1, they treat it as a 'real-world' problem rather than a purely formal, educational one. And, like the children, their answers are not stupid, or wrong in any general sense. The answers are quite reasonable if one accepts that alternative ground-rules are being followed, whereby problems relate to real people and everyday life, or to imaginary people in a sensible story. It is all too easy to ignore the importance of social and situational factors in the use of language, and to treat those who are not familiar with some subtle aspects of educational discourse as lacking the linguistic or cognitive means for pursuing logical debate or rational enquiry. This is especially the case where such factors are part of the investigator's own cultural or educational experience, part of his or her own implicit knowledge.

Such social and situational factors have, until recently, been given little attention in studies of the development of children's thinking. Much of our understanding of the development of children's thought is derived from formal experiments in which they are asked to make judgements about various manipulated materials – for example, the relative length of two lines, or the amount of water in two jars. Recent research has suggested that these experimental studies – upon which the substantial edifice of Piagetian child psychology stands – may have misrepresented children's cognitive abilities. Take, for example, a classic Piagetian 'conservation' task. It is an obvious truth that if we roll out a ball of plasticine into a long sausage shape, say, or else pour water from one jar into another of a different shape and size, then we still have the same amount of water or plasticine that we had at the start. Only the shape or visual appearance has changed, not the quantity. That is to say, the quantity is 'conserved' through a change of shape. According to Piaget, there is a stage of development, which lasts up to about the age of 7 or 8, when children are unable to appreciate this. But what is the evidence for such an assertion?

The evidence is essentially a conversation between an adult and a child. Let us take conservation of length as an illustrative example (there are similar studies of conservation of number, volume, quantity, and weight). The following description is taken from Margaret Donaldson's influential book *Children's Minds*, which discusses these studies in more detail than we shall do here.

The test has three stages. First the child is shown two sticks of equal length placed thus:

in exact alignment. He is then asked whether they are the same length. It is essential that he should agree to equality of length at this stage, otherwise the test cannot legitimately proceed.

Next, one of the two sticks is moved (normally by the adult experimenter) so that the alignment is destroyed, thus:

The experimenter usually explicitly invites the child to pay attention to this transformation by saying, 'Now watch what I do'.

The third stage then consists simply in repeating the original question – 'Are they the same length?' or whatever was the precise wording – after the transformation of the second stage is complete.

. . . If, on the second questioning, the child still affirms the equality of the critical attribute then he is said to 'conserve' length or weight or whatever the attribute may be. Otherwise he is said to fail to conserve or to be a 'non-conserver'. (Donaldson 1978, pp. 61 and 62)

The traditional (Piagetian) conclusion is that 'non-conservers' fail to understand that the sticks are still the same length as they were before they were moved. But Donaldson shows that other conclusions are possible. If we take the situation as a whole, as summarized in the quotations above, then there is clearly much more going on than simply a child's judgements of the length of two lines. We have a piece of social interaction and conversation within which those judgements are elicited and expressed. An adult asks the question, the child answers, the adult then manipulates the materials and repeats the question. What is the child to make of this? Why would somebody ask the same question twice, if the same answer was required? (We have already noted that, in school, repeated questions imply a requirement for new answers.) Similarly, what is the significance of altering the materials in that way? What does the adult want the child to say? It is at least a possibility that the younger children could be swayed by such considerations into giving the answer that the situation and discourse contexts seem to demand – that is, the 'non-conservation' answer – especially if their grasp of what the word 'length' means is flexible enough to allow for the possibility that it refers to how some things protrude further than others.

There is good reason to believe that children are indeed swayed by these contextual features of the experiment, because altering some of these features leads to different experimental results. In one study (McGarrigle and Donaldson 1974), instead of the experimenter's moving the sticks, this was done by a mechanically operated 'naughty teddy' who would sweep down and mess things around. When asked again whether the sticks were the same length, far fewer children altered their answer to 'no'. In another variation (Rose and Blank 1974), which also obtains much-reduced levels of 'non-conservation', the question is asked only once, thus avoiding the possible effects of repeating a question that has already been answered.

Donaldson's main conclusion is that, when young children are asked these sorts of questions, they tend to answer them in terms of their understanding of the whole situation, the context in which they are embedded. She proposes that going to school involves learning to respond to language on its own terms, the words alone, 'disembedded' from the context in which they occur. We are back to the issues with which we began this chapter – misunderstandings, the relations between discourse, context and knowledge, and the particular 'ground-rules' which define these relations in educational settings. We shall take up the notion of 'disembeddedness', and consider its explanatory value, in chapter 5.

The implicit nature of ground-rules

It may appear from the above discussion that 'educational ground-rules' are simply arbitrary, implicit constraints imposed by educated adults upon the naïve, open-minded perspectives of the unschooled. This kind of imposition of world-view may in itself be taken as no more than another instance of the teacher as an agent of social control, the enforcer of conformity. Certainly ground-rules are imposed by teachers; but they are not all arbitrary, or trivial, for some represent important features of the world-view of the established academic community. They are aspects of culture, and as such are subject to the criticisms of cultural relativism; but this does not render their acquisition any less valuable, for it is through participation in schooling that children gain access to the 'cultural capital' of the classroom. And there is no reason why children's acquisition of the modes of discourse and thought required by education should entail their loss of other, 'real-world' perspectives. In their everyday lives, professional scientists, mathematicians, philosophers, and so on, cope quite satisfactorily by compartmentalizing their problem-solving strategies, drawing on whichever cognitive resources seem appropriate in a given context.

A more serious and problematical aspect of children's socialization into the educational universe of discourse is revealed by asking: why are these rules for successful participation in education normally kept so implicit? There seem to be three possible explanations, none of which necessarily denies the truth of the others. Indeed, they may all be true, but to varying extents in different sectors of education, in different classrooms and on different occasions. The *first* is that most educated adults, including teachers, tend to assume that the ground-rules are self-evident and unproblematical. They may not even be consciously aware of the implicit frames of reference they invoke and so would be unable to make these explicit. The *second* explanation is that teachers willingly restrict access to educational knowledge; they can maintain more control over the process of education, and hence their class, through the operation of a covert rule system. The teacher thus has a vested interest in maintaining the relative ignorance of the pupils. This kind of explanation, as offered by some sociologists (e.g. Hammersley 1977), suggests that this is also one way in which pupils are encouraged to associate 'knowledge' with 'authority'. The *third* explanation draws on our discussion of ideologies of teaching in chapter 3. Teachers may not be completely unaware of ground-rules, nor be keeping them tacit in order to maintain authority, but instead they believe that a good teacher *should not need to make such things explicit*, and will gain nothing by doing so. According to this ideology, successful teaching is the creation of successful learning environments; if tasks, activities and lessons are well conceived, then children will learn. What is more, they will learn as is appropriate to their developmental stage; the activities will 'bring out' what they have. Meta-level discussions of what is the purpose of it all, or in which specific concepts are abstractly defined, will constrain or distort children's learning experience, and probably confuse them. Such discussions might be just what the Plowden Report hoped to discourage by saying 'Verbal explanation, in advance of understanding based on experience, may be an obstacle to learning, and children's knowledge of the right words may conceal from teachers their lack of understanding' (para. 535).

One of the points at which education (teaching, learning, assessment) commonly fails is when incorrect assumptions are made about shared knowledge, meanings and interpretations. In the achievement of shared understandings between teachers and pupils, failure is at least as common as success. Misunderstandings are not confined to matters of content, what is overtly taught and learnt (facts, ideas, terminology, specific procedures, and so on). Indeed, these may be the most trivial kinds of misunderstanding, and the most easily recognized and resolved. The most profound and intransigent misunderstandings may be those about the underlying, implicit rules of interpretation, which define how particular bits of classroom speech, text or language are to be 'taken' and responded to. It is such things, after all, which distinguish education from mere experience. If, as we believe, there is an element of dominant teaching ideology which precludes the investigation of such matters by teachers and children together, this is serious indeed. A whole range of teachers' practices, including things like introducing new topics, leading discussions, designing worksheets and assessing children's knowledge, may be affected. And, of course, this issue may also be relevant to some of education's most enduring problems, notably the difficulty in achieving 'handover' of control of learning from teacher to pupil, and the seemingly inevitable reproduction of social inequalities through schooling. There may be many benefits, for both teachers and pupils, in finding out more about the ways in which, and the extent to which, children gain access to these implicit rules of interpretation in the classroom.

5
Context and continuity

The dependence of classroom talk on a given context of shared experience, activity, physical surroundings and talk itself is a common discovery in studies of classroom communication (e.g. Cooper 1976; Edwards and Furlong 1978; Mehan 1979). In all of our own samples of classroom talk, ranging through clay-modelling lessons, computer programming, science, social studies and mathematics, we found such talk to be heavily dependent on a context of physical props and activities. But this is not simply a discovery about classroom communication and language. It is a property of the educational process. As we emphasized in chapter 3, much of primary education (especially) in Britain since the 1960s has become systematically oriented towards practical activities – a development based on prevailing notions of the importance of individual activity and direct experience to the processes of learning and of cognitive development. The dependence of school language on context is therefore an inherent feature. This must create problems for analysts who focus on the linguistic properties of discourse (e.g. Sinclair and Coulthard 1975; Stubbs 1976), and for those who have argued for the inherent 'context-disembeddedness' of educational language (e.g. Bernstein 1971; Tough 1977; Donaldson 1978). In this chapter we shall explore the nature of the context-dependence of classroom discourse. We suggest that education is best understood as a communicative process that consists largely in the growth of shared mental contexts and terms of reference through which the various discourses of education (the various 'subjects' and their associated academic abilities) come to be intelligible to those who use them.

After a preliminary definition of the terms 'continuity' and 'context', we shall proceed with an examination of the notion of 'context'. This involves us in an essentially Vygotskyan analysis of mental development, and picks up the discussion from chapters 2 and 4 about contextual interpretation, a social-cognitive process that was shown to be essential for 'discourse analysis' and for understanding 'given' and 'new' information. We argue that context is best conceived as mental rather than either linguistic or situational: that is, as a property of the general *understandings* that obtain between people who communicate, rather than a property either of the linguistic system that they use, or of the actual things done and said, or, indeed, of the physical circumstances in which they find themselves. The details of the argument are then worked out in relation to samples of classroom discourse. We examine the ways in which physical contexts are invoked, the use of displaced contexts (out-of-school experiences, past events, etc.), and the relationship between contexts of joint activity and the development of a shared conceptual vocabulary. We look at how classroom discourse depends for its intelligibility upon the gradual accumulation of shared contexts of talk and experience. Finally, we examine some 'discontinuities' and consider some of the problematical aspects of developing shared knowledge.

We shall use the term *context* to refer to everything that the participants in a conversation know and understand, over and above that which is explicit in what they say, that contributes to how they make sense of what is said. *Continuity* is the development of such contexts through time. The notion bears comparison to George Herbert Mead's 'emergent present', which is usefully summarized by Griffin and Mehan (1981) as follows: 'that which is going on in the present inexorably becomes the past, informing and reforming the present, while future events inform the sense of the present' (p. 190). We shall fill out these brief definitions as we proceed.

Context as mental

It is a commonplace observation in studies of language and communication that messages depend for their meanings on the contexts in which they take place. These contexts are of various sorts. A first distinction may be drawn between linguistic and non-linguistic contexts: the linguistic context is the speech or text that precedes and follows any given utterance, while the non-linguistic context includes the time and place, the social occasion, the persons involved, their behaviour and gestures, and so on. Both sorts of context are very relevant to the form or structure of any discourse, and also to its content.

Sequence 5.1 is a fragment of discourse taken from the first of our three video-recorded lessons on the measurement and motions of pendulums. The teacher was discussing with the class how they might measure different angles of swing.

Sequence 5.1   Physical and mental context

T: Right. So Sharon how are you then going to decide on your angle? 'Cause I mean you've got to have a certain/ measurements. Turn it around and let's see if we can give her any ideas. How is she going to decide on her angle?

Sharon has a 3-foot-high wooden pendulum on the table beside her.

Sharon turns pendulum to face T.

ANTONY: On that/ draw angles on there.

Antony points to top plate of pendulum.

JONATHAN: Or hold/ ⌈ set a protractor on the top.

DAVID: ⌊ she could put angles at the top.

All gesturing to top of pendulum.

T: She could/ could/ ⌈ at the top (. . .)
JONATHAN: ⌊ place a protractor up there with sellotape.

SHARON: (. . .) or just draw it.

T: Or just draw it. What else could she do? If she didn't do that what else could she do? To make sure she always had it/ you know at the level she wanted? It doesn't really
⌈ mat(ter . . .)
DAVID: ⌊ put the ruler down here and make/ the height from the ground/ from the table.

David holds pendulum bob out and points to distance between bob and table.

T: So where would/ what would she mark then/ to measure the height from the ground?// What could she mark// on the pendulum?

T pauses, pupils don't respond.

JONATHAN: Oh on on here.

Jonathan points to two places, at different heights on the upright on his pendulum.

T: Right. She could put marks across couldn't she? And it doesn't matter if there's/ er/ it matters if they're even. Right/ so you could start . . .

T indicates upright on Jonathan's pendulum with pencil at three different heights.

We have in sequence 5.1 a piece of discourse which is clearly context-dependent. It is necessary for us to know things about the various physical activities, gestures and props in order to make proper sense of the dialogue, and of course the same is true for the participants. There are the usual textual markers of context-dependent discourse – pronouns (she, it, you), locative expressions (up there, down here), ellipsis (incomplete sentences, etc.), the definite article (the), and so on. But there are two rather less obvious features of this context-dependence that are equally important. These are (1) the fact that *all* of the dialogue can be said to be dependent on context for its meaning, and (2) the fact that the context is not physical but mental. We shall explore these in turn.

The dependence of *all* of the dialogue on a current, or previously established, or implicit context is most clearly seen if we examine particular words. 'Pendulum', for example, has a general, abstracted definition, such as this one from an edition of the *Oxford English Dictionary* – 'suspended body swinging to and fro by force of gravity'. In the dialogue above it also has a much more specific meaning – its situational reference to the particular wooden structure that Sharon has beside her. Similarly, the words 'height', 'ground', 'table', 'mark' (and so on) all have particular situated referents. In addition, these particular meanings are ones that the participants in the dialogue understand jointly. Each person has to understand what the other means. For example, David first uses the word 'ground' and then adjusts this to 'table', this being effectively the ground on which the pendulum stands, rather than, say, the floor of the classroom. His gestures make it clear what he means. The teacher then also uses the word 'ground', relying on the fact that David had already made clear what it refers to. Another example is the teacher's use of the word 'even', near the end of the extract. Here it seems to mean something close to 'equidistant', since she points simultaneously to three points a certain distance apart on the wooden structure, and makes it a major theme of the lesson (we demonstrate this in chapter 6) that scientific measurements have to be accurate and consistent in scale. In order for teacher and pupils to understand each other and develop a shared conception of the work they are doing on pendulums, it is crucially important that they are able to relate discourse to context, and build through time a joint frame of reference.

The notion that the context of a discourse is not physical but mental is an essential part of the link between discourse and knowledge. We normally think of the 'context' of an utterance as something concrete and determinable – the surrounding talk or text, the surrounding actions, gestures and situation. But this is an outsider's view. For the participants, the context of any utterance is more a matter of perception and memory – what they think has been said, what they think was meant, what they perceive to be relevant. For example, as I (one of the authors) write these words, I am seated at a word-processing microcomputer, surrounded by books and papers, a desk, walls painted a particular colour, and so on. It is a university academic's office. You the reader will also be situated in a physical context. The point is that none of this was contextual to what I am writing until the point at which I mentioned it. The physical circumstances of any act of communication, whether spoken or written, could support an infinity of detailed descriptions. What matters is what the participants in the communication understand and see as relevant. Even the surrounding discourse itself is contextual only in so far as it is remembered or understood, whether accurately or not.

All of our data transcripts offer a wealth of material which we could use to illustrate the various points we want to make about context and continuity. Indeed, the reader can check the generality of our interpretations in this chapter against the various fragments of discourse quoted in later ones. For no better reason than that chapters 6 and 7 deal with certain conceptual issues that were realized most obviously in the pendulum experiment lessons, we shall draw for the most part in this chapter on our other main data bases, the series of clay pottery and computer graphics lessons.

The clay pottery and computer graphics lessons were clearly oriented towards the teaching of practical knowledge and skill – how to make a successful piece of clay pottery, and how to instruct the computer to draw desired shapes on its monitor screen. Relevant knowledge was introduced at appropriate points and for practical purposes: the heat from one's hands tends to dry out the clay if it is held for too long; computers are essentially stupid and have to be told precisely what to do or they will get it wrong. Much of the teachers' talk consisted in heavily context-dependent questions, prompts and instructions, of the sort we saw in sequence 5.1. In sequence 5.2 the teacher and Susan are pointing as they speak to various parts of a drawing on a piece of paper.

Sequence 5.2   Planning a LOGO program

T: Now/ which angle did you have to
   measure/ let's have a look at that one.   *T leans forward and Susan gives*
   I notice that you've got all lines drawn   *her the paper.*
   out all over the place haven't ⌈ you?
SUSAN: ⌊ Mm.

T: You've extended your lines/ haven't you?
Did you measure the angles in here?

T showing paper to whole group of 5 pupils.
T points to one of the drawn hexagon's internal angles.

SUSAN: No.

T: No/ which angles/ you've got/ let's see the angles. Right one three seven/ right one twenty.

T and Susan examining diagram, pointing to parts of it as they speak.

SUSAN: One thirty yes.

T: One two eight/ right one three eight/ which angles are those?/ Are those the angles/ inside the hexagon/ or are those the angles outside?

SUSAN: They/ they're the bits where you go forward like that./ Then you've got your arrow pointing that way./ So you straighten it out/ and you go round and measure it/ and go up to that angle.

Susan pointing at monitor.

T: So which turn have you actually measured there? You've measured/ you were pointing that ⌈ way (&)
SUSAN: ⌊ Mm.

T: (&) and you had wanted to go that way/ ⌈ yes?
SUSAN: ⌊ Yes.

T: So you've measured that turn/ is that right/ from there to there?

Let us unpack the contextual knowledge that we need to share with the participants in order to understand what they are talking about. We have given sequence 5.2 a helpful title. As the title and the dialogue imply, the teacher and Susan are discussing Susan's planned set of instructions (in the LOGO computer language) for drawing a regular hexagonal shape (i.e. with six equal sides) on the screen with certain pre-measured angles. (Although they were using LOGO, the teacher had in fact told the class they were using BASIC, a different sort of computer language altogether.) Anyone familiar with LOGO will recognize it from instructions such as 'right 120', which tells the computer to turn the screen cursor (the 'arrow' here: in some other versions it is a 'turtle') to the right (clockwise) through an angle of 120°.

It is clear from the talk in sequence 5.2 that Susan was working with the wrong angles. What she had done was to draw a hexagon, and then use a protractor to measure the drawn internal angles. These were then subject to slight inaccuracies; instead of calculating them as all being 120°, they were measured as 137, 120, 130, 128, etc. As figure 5.1 shows, the correct angles to use should have been the external ones of 60°. The error was never resolved by teacher or pupils and caused some continuing confusion.

We can define for sequence 5.2 two major sorts of mental context that are necessary for joint understanding. First, there is the evocation via words, gestures and direction of gaze of a perceived physical context which includes especially the piece of paper with its drawings and text, and the joint orientation of Susan and teacher to various parts of it. Second, there is the implicit context of relevant shared knowledge that has been established up to this point. This is the second of the three lessons on LOGO graphics, the pupils already having been taught how to instruct the 'arrow' to turn angles and move in certain directions (forwards and backwards). In Lesson 1 they defined a hexagon and discovered how to measure its angles with a protractor. They know that they are about to try out Susan's planned instructions on the computer itself. The measured angles are the hexagon's external ones (see figure 5.1). This is because LOGO draws shapes by travelling on the screen in a forward direction, turning a specified number of degrees, and proceeding forwards again in the new direction. As figure 5.1 shows, this means having to move through the hexagon's external rather than internal angles. That is presumably what Susan was talking about when she said, somewhat

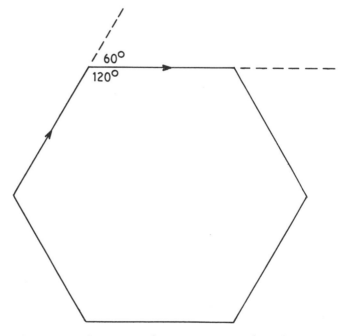

Figure 5.1   Drawing a hexagon: external angles are 60°

cryptically, 'So you straighten it out/ and you go round and measure it'. All of the dialogue proceeds against this sort of cumulative shared mental context. The implications for our understanding of 'education' are profound. We can say that the process of education, in so far as it succeeds, is largely the establishment of these shared mental 'contexts', joint understandings between teacher and children, which enable them to engage together in educational discourse.

Displaced contexts

It is a much-vaunted characteristic of the language of formal schooling that it supposedly transcends the here-and-now context of place and time in which speaker and hearer are situated. Teachers and pupils are assumed to engage, at least to a significant extent, in exchanges of knowledge and thought concerning events remote in time and space, future and past, imagined and hypothetical, invoking abstract generalizations rather than simple descriptions of what is physically real and present to the senses (Bruner 1971; Donaldson 1978; Bernstein 1971). This may to some extent be so, though we would probably have to take it as a goal or end-product of classroom discourse, rather than a description of its typical characteristics. But some important qualifications need to be placed on such notions. One of these qualifications is that the same sorts of claims are also made for *any* kind of human communication that uses language. 'Displacement' of topics of communication from the contextual time and place in which the talking is done is one of the key distinguishing features by which human language itself has been contrasted with the communications of other species (e.g. de Laguna 1927; Hockett and Altmann 1968). Similarly, displacement (as well as other features such as abstraction and rationality) has been held to be a distinguishing feature of middle-class rather than of working-class speech (Bernstein 1971); or else of written text, contrasted this time with ordinary spoken conversation (e.g. Olson 1977; Ong 1967). In fact, there is evidence that many of the characteristics commonly attributed to written text owe themselves either to the influence of formal schooling (Scribner and Cole 1981) or, more generally, to the social and historical circumstances in which literacy is used and acquired (Heath 1983; Street 1984). But let us remain with our prime concern, the exchange of understandings in spoken discourse.

There are two further problems with this characterization of educational language as contextually displaced and abstract. First, displacement is not the same thing as abstraction. We can speak concretely about remote things, and abstractly about present circumstances. Second, there is evidence to suggest that displaced communication is untypical of much of educational talk. Our own researches are in accord with those of others who, on investigating the cognitive content of actual classroom talk (e.g. Cooper 1976; Driver 1983), have found it to be surprisingly and overwhelmingly tied to the concrete activities and situations that occur in classrooms. If pupils are required in school to engage in displaced discourse and to draw abstract generalizations from their experience, then we need to examine what sorts of displaced communications occur, and how they relate to the rest of classroom activity and talk. We shall discuss the nature of generalizations from experience in chapters 6 and 7. Here we shall deal with the more simple question of contextual displacement.

Let us examine some actual references to out-of-school experience. The first thing we have to say about these sorts of displaced communications is that there were not many of them. Most of those occurred in the course of the clay pottery lessons, while the other lessons contained few if any at all. We are able to cite most of the occurrences here as raw dialogue. Sequence 5.3 includes all from pottery lesson 1.

Sequence 5.3   Pottery lesson 1: out-of-school experiences

(a) *Colour expansion*

DAVID: Miss/ Miss.
T: Yes love.
PETER: It says darker colours expand more than lighter colours.
T: Darker colours ⌈ expand
PETER: ⌊ more than lighter.
T: Where did you read that?   *T sounds incredulous.*
PETER: It was on/ erm/ I don't know/ a programme.
T: Oh/ well anyway it's the air inside that expands and . . .

(b) *Pots made at the university*

PATRICIA: Are there any pots left from last time?
T: What/ that the others left?
PATRICIA: Because I didn't get mine.
T: Erm.
PATRICIA: Those pots that we made at the university.
T: I didn't know you'd made any at the university./ Well never mind.
PATRICIA: I made mine/ mine went wrong.

T: Was it/ was it a proper pot or was it
   made out of that funny clay?
PATRICIA: No/ it was made out of clay.
T: Was it/ oh I didn't think you had
   made any.
PATRICIA: I did.
T: Oh.

(c) *Peter's sister*

T: What are you going to use this for/
   what do you think?
PETER: My sister's made one/ she keeps
   it in her room for/
T: Just putting things in.
PETER: Yes.
T: Uh uh.
PETER: That's what I'll use mine for.

(d) *Katie's sister*

T: Going to give this to your little sister/
   or are you going to keep it yourself?
KATIE: Don't know. My sister made
   one.
T: Did she? Oh/   *T moves off to attend to another*
   well pull all these little bits off and   *pupil (Patricia).*
   smooth the inside.

The most notable aspect of the displaced references listed in sequence
5.3, apart, perhaps, from their triviality, is how shortlived they were.
They are not presented here in any prematurely truncated form. Three of
the four were introduced by the pupils, and none of them was taken up by
the teacher and treated as worth pursuing. It was a pervasive feature of all
of our recorded lessons that each of them was heavily concerned with its
own inherent content and activity, this in turn being something controlled and determined by the teacher, through whom each lesson gained
a momentum of talk and activity, planned in advance, from which the talk
was not easily to be distracted. The lessons themselves created contexts of
talk and experience which overwhelmingly predominated over any sorts
of knowledge or experience derived from outside the classroom.
Certainly this falls into a general pattern of control by the teacher over the
creation and validation of shared knowledge, a theme that we shall
consider in some detail in chapter 7. But there is another dimension to the
phenomenon that is more relevant here. It appears that, by relying
heavily on contexts of shared experience and discourse which were

generated within the lessons themselves, the teachers in our sample were able to ensure that all of the talk, instruction and explanation, questions and answers, were founded on a self-contained body of knowledge that was potentially available to everyone. Perhaps this was understood, if only intuitively, to be the soundest contextual basis on which to build joint understandings.

There is some support in the data for such an interpretation, and, ironically, this comes from the exceptions to the general pattern in which external inputs to the lesson were discouraged. Acceptable inputs from out-of-school experience were invariably those to which everyone, or at least several pupils, could relate. Thus the teacher herself described to the pupils the kiln in which the clay pots were to be fired as 'about three times as hot as your mummy's oven at home'. This was typical of appeals by the teacher to out-of-school experience, invoking what could reasonably be assumed to be common knowledge. Other instances included eliciting from the pupils the fact that pigs have ears and tails (so these had to be included on the clay models of pigs), and references to characters from children's television ('That's a Dougal dog. . . . Do you remember Dougal on *The Magic Roundabout*?'; 'The woodmouse has big ears like Mickey Mouse'). When in doubt, as with the dog 'Dougal', the teacher would check that these references were indeed shared ones, as sequence 5.4 shows.

Sequence 5.4   Have you ever seen a pig running?

T: . . . Now/ I don't really like the way they're joined. I think they/ you should do this/ at the front and at the back./ Hold it. Support it/ because it's very very flappy and thin/ and then smooth over what you've been doing/ and his ears can be wavy/ or however you want them to be 'cause pigs' ears look nice/ and they flap about/ don't they/ when they run. Have you ever seen a pig running?

T attending to Ian, working on his model with him.

IAN: Yes.

PUPIL X: No.

(Unidentified pupils speaking off camera.)

PUPIL Y: I've seen them on the farm.

T: Yes/ if you call out pig pig pig they/ often they think it's food time for food and they come running and their ears

flap about. Let's bring them forward a   *Referring to the clay pig's ears.*
bit/

Anecdotal events and stories were the norm for this sort of displaced reference, with television programmes playing a prominent role. In the second of the three pendulum lessons, the teacher recounted what happened in a television programme that she and the pupils had all seen a couple of weeks earlier, in which the Tudor ship *Mary Rose* was seen lifted from the water by a crane. The ship had begun to swing about on the lifting gear rather like the bob of a pendulum, and the teacher helped the pupils to apply what they had learned about pendulums to their understanding of those events. Similarly, in the second pottery lesson (sequence 5.5), the teacher encourages some sharing of anecdotal reminiscences about hedgehogs, which some of the pupils are modelling.

Sequence 5.5 Hedgehog anecdotes

T: Have you got any hedgehogs in your   *T is helping Peter to shape his*
   garden?   *clay hedgehog, addresses*
                                          question to no specific pupil.

IAN: No.
PATRICIA: Yes/ but we don't know
   where it is.
T: No/ has anybody got any hedgehogs
   in their garden?/ You ⌈
PATRICIA: ⌊ Yes/ we/ erm/
   we take erm/ saucers of milk down for
   it and hold it.
T: Ah/ now/ let's have a look.   *T picking up Ian's model.*
KATIE: I've got a photograph of a
   hedgehog.
T: Oh/ I've touched its ears./ You've got
   a photograph of one/ what in your
   garden?
KATIE: Yes he's out. It's daytime and
   he's out in the garden/ and we put a
   saucer of milk out for him.
T: Ah.
JOHN: We found our ⌈ hedgehog
T: ⌊ You write that   *T addressing Ian.*
   on/ can you pull it off/ pull it off love/
   'cause I'm trying to write your initials
   on.
JOHN: on the front lawn.
KATIE: Yes (. . .)

T: You did what?

JOHN: We found our hedgehog on the
front lawn/ so we took it in the back
garden/ so that it wouldn't get run
over.

T: That's the trouble with hedgehogs
isn't it./ Yes/ they go out on to the
road.

PETER: (. . .) they should use the Green   *Pupils laugh.*
Cross code.

T: Perhaps nobody's taught them.

The teacher's observation in sequence 5.4 that 'pigs' ears look nice'
suggests that she is appealing not only to what the pupils may all have
experienced in the world beyond the classroom, but also to some
assumed common aesthetic values. This was indeed the case. Many of her
comments on what the models should look like appealed to a sentimental
cuteness which, in addition to frequent appeals to the chart on the wall
which depicted various animals, was clearly a major criterion of approval
for what the pupils managed to make. Typical comments included: 'Your
ducky's looking quite nice isn't he? Give him a nice tail'; 'How about that.
It looks very cute/ little ducky's tail.' The assumption that the teacher's
aesthetic values were shared by the pupils was probably not fully warranted. As sequence 5.6 demonstrates, the pupils' agreement about such
things was not always automatic.

Sequence 5.6   The aesthetics of clay animals

T: Ian/ what's wrong with him love?   *T examining Ian's model. Other*
                                        pupils laugh.

Now all right/ don't you laugh at Ian
(. . .) come on/ think what's wrong.
Just look at its face.

IAN: Its beak's crooked.

T: Yes/ it's not just crooked/ it's what?//
Something else besides crooked.

IAN: Too thick.

T: Too/ not just thick/

IAN: Big.

T: Too big altogether isn't it.

The aesthetic values by which the teacher judged the pupils' clay animals
were not open for negotiation. To the extent that such values were not
already shared by the pupils, they were imposed upon them, either by the
teacher's implicit usage of them, or else more directly. For example:

Make his ears lie back not stick up like that. I think they look better lying back.

No it doesn't [T denying that a finished model looks like a pony]. It's an Airedale dog. They look like that.

I think it's a bit long don't you? You make it look a bit snakey-looking. It would be better if . . .

The mere assumption of common knowledge and values can be a powerful means of encouraging the pupils to adopt them without question. This is a topic that we shall take up in chapter 7.

The notion that the proper business of the lesson centres around what is 'done' in class, rather than in what the pupils may know and understand from outside the classroom, appeared to be understood by the pupils themselves. They appeared to operate with a ground-rule to the effect that, if the teacher asks a question related to the work done in class, then the answer is to be found in what the lesson has actually covered. It was a local educational variant of the more general principle that one does not ask things of someone of whom we cannot reasonably assume that they may know the answer (see Grice 1975). In sequence 5.7 the teacher was trying to get the pupils to express the principle that large pieces of pottery, if not constructed as hollow from the start (which was the technique taught to the pupils in an earlier lesson), need to have a hollowed-out base to prevent them from exploding in the kiln because of the expansion of air which is trapped inside the clay. The sequence is a long but instructive one, through which we can examine how the pupils sought the required answer.

Sequence 5.7   Making the pot hollow (pottery lesson 3)

T: . . . but the same thing happens with a great lump of clay. You/ you've pushed it around so much that you've probably got air trapped inside. Also when it's a thick lump/ erm it/ it's to do with the way it's heated up in the kiln./ It may burst open. Hey/ steady on girl/ steady on. Now/ erm/ can you think what you might do to make it like Katie's? You've not made it in two pieces so what do you think you might have to do to make it like Katie's?

T to John.

T to John, pointing at Katie. (The taught method of making large hollow figures was to combine two hemispherical 'thumb-pots'.) John looks blank.

KATIE: Put a hole straight through.

T: Not a hole straight through/ exactly.

.

.

.

Any idea Peter?

PETER: No.

T: No?   *T sounds incredulous.*

PETER: No. Can I have the knife please
Ian?

T: What/ listen/ what sort of a shape is
Katie's? Is it solid? What is it?

PETER: Hollow.

T: **Hollow/ hollow/** now think of that
word **hollow/** and what are you going
to do to yours/ hey/ come on think.   *Peter and John both look blank.*

IAN: (. . .)

T: Pardon/, what do you think you're   *John looks blank, and looks down*
going to do to yours then/ make it/   *at the table.*
make it what?

KATIE: Hollow.

T: Why is Katie having to tell you?/
You've got a brain./ You know really
don't you?

JOHN: Yes.

T: Well shout **up** then.

PETER: How **do** you make it hollow?

T: How do you **think** you make it   *T sounds exasperated.*
hollow?

PATRICIA: You done it/ erm/ on
Monday/ when you ⌈ made the pig
and the hedgehog. ⎹

JOHN: ⌊ made two
thumb-pots.

T: Well/ you've not made two
thumb-pots love. You've done it
without making two thumb-pots./ So
how can you hollow something out?
Think about a man that made the first
boats and they chopped down trees.
They've got a lump of tree piece of a
tree trunk. Now/ what did they do/   *Rising intonation on 'they' and*
they/   *pause (for sentence completion*
                                         by pupils).

JOHN: They got something and
   hollowed it out.
T: So what does it mean/ hollowing it
   out? What does that mean?
PETER: Hollow out.
T: Yes/ so what do you have to **do**?
PETER: Dig it out.
T: Pardon?
PETER: Dig it out.   *Peter gestures a digging action.*
T: Dig it out/ yes. So you're going to
   have to dig some out from/ from
   underneath where nobody can see.
   All right?
JOHN: Yes.   *John nods, looking abashed.*

Katie's initial answer to the problem was to suggest what the teacher
had previously demonstrated for *hollow* pots – piercing the pot to allow
the trapped air to escape. After Peter's evidently distracted response, and
non-responses from Peter and Patricia, Katie provides the cued response
'hollow'. In pursuit of how to make a solid pot hollow, Peter asks the
teacher directly, while Patricia and John refer back to what they have been
taught in the previous lessons. The teacher is clearly exasperated,
apparently convinced that she is asking for what is simply common
knowledge. The pupils respond on the basis that what they are required
to do is to find the answer in what the teacher has told them. Only when
the teacher herself provides a new context of shared knowledge for the
question (the construction of prehistoric 'dug-out' canoes) do the pupils
grasp what she is after. The description 'dig it out' probably comes
directly from that newly invoked context; the term 'dug-out', though not
mentioned explicitly here, is conventional. Both concept and word were
derived from the new context of common knowledge invoked by the
teacher. What exasperated the teacher appears to have been the pupils'
insistence on finding the required knowledge within the context of what
they had been explicitly taught in the pottery lessons. Yet it was precisely
within such lesson-bound contexts, as we have seen, that the teacher
herself strove generally (and successfully) to maintain the content of
classroom talk.

Our examination of classroom discourse has emphasized the extent of
its context-embeddedness. Even those references that were made to
contexts beyond the immediate physical circumstances of classroom
activity were not the sorts of displaced generalizations, discussions or
abstractions that one might expect from some of the theoretical perspectives that we listed at the beginning of this chapter. The introduction of
such decontextualized talk was relatively rare, and closely sanctioned by

the teacher. An overriding constraint upon it appeared to be that it should be directly relevant to the business in hand, and should invoke common knowledge rather than idiosyncratic experience. The principle, to put it crudely, that lessons are about what happens in lessons appeared to be a ground-rule that the pupils had themselves acquired.

Action, word and concept

The embeddedness of classroom discourse within a rich context of joint activity and shared experience forces us to re-examine the relationship between actions, words and conceptual understandings. The classical position on the matter, at least in British educational circles, is Piaget's. The important distinguishing feature of Piaget's approach is its insistence that the roots of human intelligence, and particularly its higher, more abstract forms such as our capacity for logical and mathematical reasoning, derive essentially from action rather than from language. As we showed in chapter 2, this is a position which has been criticized in recent years, particularly from perspectives that emphasize the importance of the social context of education and developmental testing, such as those of Donaldson (1978) and Walkerdine (1982). Walkerdine's approach is important from the point of view of this book. Although it is largely concerned with explaining the same sorts of mental achievements as Piaget's own theory – the development of abstract intellectual skills such as logical and mathematical reasoning – we share with Walkerdine an insistence on the importance of socially situated activity and discourse. Our concern, however, is with the content rather than the forms of knowledge and thought.

Let us examine the process through which the teacher's words take on meanings for the pupils. In sequence 5.8, from pottery lesson 2, the teacher is demonstrating to the pupils how to join together, using an additional long piece of clay, the two hemispherical halves of what becomes an enclosed hollow pot, later to become a model animal.

Sequence 5.8   Word and action: joining two pots

T: . . . Now you've got to have it smooth Katie so/ wet your finger/ and get it smooth. Now/ I'm going to/ erm/ join a little bit on to mine/ I think./ Can you pull yours over a bit harder than that love. You've got a big hole to fill up/ big groove there/ so you'll have to really pull it over. Pull it over from one side first/ then turn it round and

T holding and working on her own clay model, with Katie and others watching and manipulating their own.

pull it over from the other side. Now I'm going to give mine a little belt/ to cover up this great groove./ I'm going to make it into/ like a sausage/ first of all./ **Come on** Ian./ Wipe your finger round love/ all wet and sloshy/ just to join it together./ That's it/ come on/ join it up/ very careful with that bit/ 'cause it's very fragile./ Now notice I'm making a nice sausage./ I'm going to flatten it a bit/ and I'm going to put it round/ this bit where it's oh/ groovy/ round there/ not quite big enough./ I'm going to make it a bit bigger./ How am I going to join it on?

T occasionally glancing around to see what the children are doing.

JOHN: With water.

T: With water/ and/ and/ what am I going to make?/ Come on. Think hard./ What are you doing?/ What have you been doing?/ What's Ian doing now?/ And what are you doing?

T staring hard at Ian.

JOHN: Smoothing.

T: No/ you're not/ smoothing.

JOHN: Putting hole in.

IAN: Grooves.

T: Making grooves/ yes./ Make all those little grooves to hold the water.

The teacher's demonstration was not simply the performance of a set of actions which the pupils were obliged to copy. She talked throughout the demonstration about what she was doing, and it is necessary that we understand the importance of that talk. One function it achieved was to direct and hold the pupils' attention to what she was doing, and to orient the *joint attention* of the group to specific aspects of the activity: 'Come on Ian/ wipe your finger round. . . . Come on./ Think hard./ What are you doing?/ . . . What's Ian doing now?/ . . .' Further, the teacher's words served to highlight the *significant aspects* of the activity. They encapsulated what it was about her actions that the pupils ought to be noticing and remembering, what finite meaning should be placed upon them. Indeed, the teacher sometimes expressed this idea explicitly. She remarked during the following lesson:

When you're doing animals/ you/ erm/ the thing to do is to/ think of the most important features on them/ things that you notice most/ and just concentrate on them. Now this tail/ look/ if we look at him that way (*turning the model around*)/ can you tell me what's wrong?

Third, the teacher's words provided for the group a *common vocabulary* for those actions that they all would need in order to communicate these joint understandings to each other (for example, in sequence 5.8, the terms 'grooves', 'smoothing' and 'belt', which was the name given hereafter by pupils and teacher alike to the additional piece of clay used to join two pots together). This notion of acquiring a shared conceptual vocabulary was clearly an important implicit aim of the teacher. She insisted that the pupils learned what to call the various parts of the procedure; 'smoothing' was not 'grooving'. The pupils had to learn the teacher's terms of reference even for actions that they themselves were performing. This is an important educational process that we shall take up again in chapter 7, where it is examined as a feature of the control of knowledge by the teacher.

What began as a physical context of joint activity later came to serve as a shared mental context of experience and understanding. Having gone through the demonstration together, and having established how to talk about it, teacher and pupils could begin to exchange understandings with words alone. The joint activity and discourse of the past became a shared mental context for the present. Sequence 5.9, from pottery lesson 1, shows the process happening overtly. The teacher was explaining how to even out the thickness of the hemispherical pots that the pupils were making, moving from pupil to pupil, monitoring the actions of each in the manner noted by other observers of classroom interaction (Galton, Simon and Croll 1980).

Sequence 5.9   From action to words: getting an even thickness

T: Wait a minute/ now you've got/ can you feel/ put your thumb inside finger outside./ See if you can feel how thick it is.	*T holding Ian's pot.*
	T passes Ian his pot, and he feels inside it as directed.
Yeh? Now/ what do you think you had better do. Peter what do you think?	*T addressing Ian. Peter raises his hand.*
PETER: Thin it up.	
T: Thin it up by doing what?	*To Peter.*
PETER: Pushing.	
T: Or/ squeeze/ squeeze it/ squeeze it so/ it's thinner/ because otherwise you've got a great big thick base to it/ which you don't want. Now thin it out. Let's	*T gestures at the base of Ian's pot.*

have a look at John's. Yes/ yours is
not quite so bad. Give it a good bonk
on the bottom to give it a base to   *T picks John's pot up and bangs*
balance on/ and try and keep the   *it on the table.*
inside nice and smooth as well as the
outside/ OK lovey. Now lets have a   *T turns to Lorraine, and picks*
look at Lorraine's. How are you   *up her pot.*
getting on?

LORRAINE: All right.

T: Now yours is a bit thick around the
bottom isn't it?

LORRAINE: Mm.

T: So give it some more squeezes. Now   *T hands back Lorraine's pot, and*
Patricia.   *turns to Patricia.*

LORRAINE: I can't get my fingers down.

T: You can't get your fingers down. Well
then instead of your thumb going up/
put your fingers down instead   *T gestures to Lorraine how to do*
                                            this.
                                            T turns again to Patricia, and
probably get that better. Now then   *works on her pot as Patricia*
Patricia/ it's a bit thin there can you   *looks on.*
see? You've got a mark where a
thumb's been so/ be very very careful/
feel where it's thick/ and squeeze the
thick bits/ and where it's thin/ like
there/ do you see? You've made a/ big
dent in it. Don't squeeze that part any
more. Just smooth gently round it.

.
.

.

T: Let's see Ian's./ Now Ian you've still   *(Several minutes later.)*
got a lot of thickness in parts.
Couldn't you feel it?

IAN: No.

T: Put your fingers inside/ and squeeze/
and just feel if you can feel where it's
thick in some parts and thin in others/   *Ian does as instructed.*
can you?

IAN: Yes.

T: You can/ right./ Well then where it's
fat give it a squeeze./ Where it's thin/
leave it alone/ until you've got it the
same all the way around.

The teacher in sequence 5.9 began by demonstrating carefully through direct action and a running commentary how to hold the pot, where to place finger and thumb, what to feel for, what to alter and how to do it ('squeezing', not 'pushing' as Peter had suggested). The pupils also performed the action themselves, under close guidance. Returning later to Ian, the teacher's remedial instructions could be much briefer, relying on the words alone to carry what were assumed to be shared meanings. The procedure could now be encapsulated in a simple verbal principle: 'Where it's fat give it a squeeze. Where it's thin leave it alone.' Terms of reference (words) and verbal instructions came during the lessons to carry shared understandings about principles and procedures that teacher and pupils had created through talking in the context of practical activity. Similarly, verbal explanations arose as responses to noticed features of joint activity, as in sequence 5.10:

Sequence 5.10   Activity and explanation

PETER: I haven't got there yet/ and I started before him.

Peter remarking on the fact that John is at a more advanced stage of model forming than he is.

T: His clay was softer than yours. That's why. Condition of the clay makes a great difference.

The importance of co-ordinated joint activity as a context for the creation of shared understandings of word meanings, verbal instructions and explanations was evident in all of our recorded lessons. We shall examine some problematical aspects of that dependence in the next chapter, through an examination of the pendulum lessons. But now we must pursue the growth of contexts of shared understanding through time – the notion of 'continuity'. It was not only the meanings of words and verbal expressions that mattered, but the whole context of shared experience and activity. This was a feature of common knowledge to which the teachers themselves made explicit reference, but which mostly happened implicitly, becoming the unspoken backcloth against which all new talk would have to make sense.

Explicit continuity: recaps and summaries

Our purpose in recording lessons in sequences of three was precisely in order to gain some information about how curriculum knowledge was built from lesson to lesson, as well as within lessons. The time when the continuity of common knowledge was made most explicit was at the beginnings of lessons. Sequence 5.11 is the opening talk from the first two lessons on computer graphics.

Sequence 5.11   Introducing the lesson

T: Right/ this is our new computer/ the
four eighty zed. You haven't seen this
one before. Erm when you've used
computer programs before/ what's
happened is that the words have
come up on the screen/ or the
instructions/ for you/ have come up
on the screen/ and you've just
answered the questions/ and/ typed
in/ what the/ computer wanted you to
do. This program is different. In this
program the computer doesn't know
what to do. You've got to tell it what
to do/ so you have got to instruct the
computer.

(An RM 480Z microcomputer.)

*Teacher gestures with arm
towards screen.*

Lesson 2

T: Now you've got your programs from
last week have you/ to show me what
⌈ you're (&)
PUPILS: ⌊ Yes.
T: (&) going to do/ with angles not
ninety degrees./ We had to try
something else didn't we. What did
you find most difficult Susan? What's
yours?

*T reminds pupils of instructions
she gave last week.*

The teacher began lesson 1 by introducing the pupils to their new
computer, and immediately established a context for it in terms of their
previous experience with computers in the classroom. Lesson 2, recorded
a week later, began with a back reference to where the previous computer
lesson had left off, the pupils having been required in the meantime to
work out how to instruct the computer to draw non-rectangular shapes.
The lessons typically began in this manner, with introductions to the
work to be done, and continuity links established with what had been
done previously. Similarly, the third of the lessons on pendulums began
with the teacher directly asking the pupils to recall the discourse of the
previous lessons:

Right. Now then./ Do you remember the work we've been doing/ on
pendulums?/ You remember we talked about the parts of a pendulum.
What do we call/ the weight on the end . . .

Besides these opening links, explicit references were also made during the lessons to what had been done and said earlier. Sequence 5.12 lists the teacher's back references from pottery lesson 3.

Sequence 5.12 Back references to shared experience and talk

What did I tell you about thin bits? What happens when they dry?

What did I tell you about eyes?

Can you remember what you forgot to do Patricia/ when you put that little belt thing round?

Look when you put its eyes in./ I did tell you this before Lorraine.

John/ you seem to have forgotten everything you've learned don't you?

Don't forget/ if it's too wide chop it off.

As the teacher's remarks to John and to Lorraine imply, the continuity of common knowledge was not something that developed unproblematically. Indeed, all of the cases listed in sequence 5.12 occurred in the context of some difficulty arising with regard to the understanding that teacher and pupils had established up to that point in the lesson. Explicit back references to common knowledge were generally made by the teacher at moments when the very status of the commonality of that knowledge was in doubt. The teacher made these sorts of metacognitive and metadiscursive comments (i.e. comments on mental processes like knowing or remembering, and on the discourse itself) at moments when the pupils seemed not to have grasped some significant principle, procedure or instruction that had been dealt with previously.

This appears to be a general feature, one that we have found in other contexts such as adult conversation (Edwards and Middleton 1986) and parent–child conversation during early language learning (Edwards and Goodwin 1986). People who are engaged in working out a common understanding of events, or a common language for describing their experience, tend to resort to direct talk about the mental processes involved, and about the conversation itself, at precisely those points where there appear to be disagreements, mismatches or incongruities in the different participants' understandings. In the asymmetry of teacher–pupil and parent–child conversations, these mismatches are an important part of the learning process. As transactions between child and adult, they occur in Vygotsky's 'zone of proximal development' (see chapter 2), at precisely the points at which common knowledge is being created. And it is the adult who takes the leading role in drawing attention to them, talking about them, establishing knowledge which is both common and communicable. We can see the process clearly in sequence 5.13.

Sequence 5.13   Continuity: what have you been doing all along?

T: Now/ how are you fixing them on
Katie?

KATIE: Putting them/ well it's (. . .)   *Katie mutters hesitantly.*

T: Now/ what do you think you should
do what have you been doing all
along every time you've joined
anything?

KATIE: Putting grooves in it.

T: Putting grooves in it/ haven't you and
water/ grooves and water/ the water
to fill up the grooves/ on both bits of
clay./ You must do it/ otherwise it will
dry/ and when it's dry like those are
dry/ those ears will just be lying on
the floor/ or on the table. Take them   *Katie refits the ears.*
off/ otherwise you'll be very sad./
You've got to do things the right way
round with clay or they just don't
work.

Sequence 5.13 is taken from pottery lesson 2. The teacher, having
noticed that Katie was having difficulty with her model, intervened and
appealed explicitly to a continuity of shared contextual experience: 'what
have you been doing all along?' The IRF exchange succeeded in focusing
Katie's awareness on to what the teacher perceived to be the salient part of
her actions, and this then became the necessary shared mental context for
the teacher's explanation of why those actions were important – 'You
must do it/ otherwise it will dry'. Explanation was built, therefore, upon a
shared understanding, communicated in the discourse, of the nature and
significance of selected aspects of joint experience and activity.

So the function of these explicit recaps was to ensure that the pupils had
developed a joint understanding with the teacher of the significant
aspects of what had already been said and done, and how to conceptualize and describe them. The establishment of these shared understandings
could then become the basis of further teaching, serving as shared mental
contexts for what was to follow. Sequence 5.14, from computer graphics
lesson 2, is a clear example of this.

Sequence 5.14   Recaps as contexts for new understandings

T: Just to recap on that/ whatever you
draw/ and that's why we use the
square paper/ whatever you draw/

you've got to measure exactly/ the
lengths and the turns/ in order to
convert it to the language of the   *T points to computer.*
computer.// OK/ so/ and the main
difficulty there's the angles/ the actual   *T demonstrates by turning top*
angle we want to turn. You've seen   *half of her body to one side.*
that all for yourselves haven't you?
Now/ everything we've done so far/
has been with the arrow on the screen   *T points to screen, then mimes*
all the time/ like the pen being on the   *drawing on paper with pen.*
paper all the time. Now/ we know
that we don't write and draw with the
pen on the paper all the time/ so this
machine has got a command/ that lets
you put your pen on and lift your pen   *T gestures lifting pen off paper.*
off . . .

The teacher's explicit recap in sequence 5.14 has a very clear Janus-like quality. It faces both ways: backwards in encapsulating a conceptualization of significant joint experience and activity in a common language; forwards in creating the shared mental context that served as a joint conceptual framework for understanding the new activity and teaching which was to follow – that is, how to tell the computer to move the cursor with or without drawing a line on the screen as it moved. Sequence 5.14 is a particularly overt expression of the nature of context and continuity.

Contexts, scaffolds and discontinuities

The notions of 'scaffolding' and of the 'zone of proximal development' (discussed in chapter 2) have two important properties that are important to our analysis of context and continuity. First, they embody the important principle that much of the acquisition of culture, including both formal and informal education, takes place in the context of guidance by some person, whether parent, teacher or more competent peer. It is a process of guided discovery, in which an individual's competence begins as his or her part in a social transaction. Joint activity and shared conceptions carried by language are the major constituents. Second, there is the notion of internalization, in which the natural end-product of the learning process is a competent individual who has become able to perform alone, or in new contexts, activities and conceptualizations which could earlier be achieved only with the teacher's help. In his account of early language learning, Bruner (1983a) calls this a 'handover' process: the knowledge and competence of the adult is eventually possessed by the child. It is this second aspect of scaffolded learning that is especially problematical when we look at formal education. While more or less all of us successfully learn to talk, for most of us the experience of formal education is marked by compromise and failure.

We shall be examining some failures of 'handover' in chapters 6 and 7. First, we must practise our own preaching and establish a context for that discussion. We noted earlier (see discussion of sequence 5.7) that not only the teacher but also the pupils tended to see the talk and activity that took place in the lessons themselves as creating the context for what should be done and said next. This was realized most explicitly at those points in lessons where the pupils were expected to put into effect what they had earlier been taught. At the start of pottery lesson 3, the pupils were set the task of making some clay models without close supervision by the teacher. Sequence 5.15 shows Katie's response to the task.

Sequence 5.15   Pupil-initiated continuity

KATIE: Do we have to make the animals
   the same way as we did the piggies?
T: Do we have to do what dear?
KATIE: Make the animals the same way
   as we did the piggies?
T: Well/ you know how to make them
   that way don't you?/ Now/ I'll show
   you a little bird./ Erm/ a little bird is   *T fetches and places on the table*
   made in exactly the same way . . .   *a ready-made clay model of a*
                                                  bird.

In sequence 5.15 Katie and the teacher established explicitly what the teacher had implicitly intended that the pupils should do – use the specific knowledge and skills acquired in the previous two lessons to create their own clay models. Both speakers were able to refer to that past learning as common knowledge that needed no explication – 'the same way as we did the piggies' (Katie), 'you know how to make them that way don't you?' (teacher). The teacher here was clearly putting into practice the Vygotsky–Bruner principle of scaffolded learning. The pupils were required to do by themselves what had in previous lessons needed close tuitional support, including explicit instruction and direct assistance from the teacher. What we have called 'context and continuity' are important characteristics of that process. However, all of our transcripts of classroom talk force us to take account of the *context-specific* nature of what is taught and learned. Both Katie and the teacher were clearly referring to particular knowledge and techniques. The pupils' learning was embedded in a specific context of talk and activity. However independent of adult supervision the pupils may become, their knowledge and understanding remain socially constructed and conceptualized, and contextualized by particular talk and activity.

All the teachers in our sample appeared to operate with something like the scaffolding and handover principle as an implicit part of their teaching method, though none of them talked of it in interview, where their conceptions of the nature of education appeared to be dominated by the twin principles of Piagetian experiential learning and of innate intellectual ability. Sequence 5.16 shows the clay pottery teacher in lesson 1 informing the pupils of her plans for succeeding lessons.

Sequence 5.16   Planning for handover

IAN: Can I do a pattern?

Ian referring to the patterns that could be engraved into the soft clay using the special tools provided.

T: Yes love/ do you want one of these? You'll find/ choose one that you want. You'll have to think about making something yourselves/ without my help/ for next week something you can do (. . .) that's based on what what you have been doing today. Don't forget when you're going right round the pattern's got to meet just/ at the last few bits./ Judge it because you may have to make your pattern a little bit smaller/ or larger/ so that it meets round the other side/ . . .

T placing the jar of tools to within Ian's reach.

T working on her own pot.

Note how the teacher, by telling the pupils in advance that they will later be expected to make clay pottery by themselves, uses this as a context for focusing the pupils' attention on an important technique that they ought therefore to commit to memory; she immediately goes on to point out the general necessity of making sure that engraved patterns take account of the different dimensions of clay pots, and are accurately aligned so that when joined together their edges meet nicely. The handover process is explicated as part of a continuity of shared understanding. It begins when the teacher takes up Ian's request to use one of the engraving tools, and is invoked as a rationale for paying attention to the teacher's words and actions, offered now as generalized principles that may be applicable to new circumstances, rather than merely one-off routines relevant only to the activity of the present.

The teachers in our other sets of three lessons were also overt in their use of the handover principle. The third pendulum lesson was designed as an opportunity for the pupils to transfer what they had learned about pendulums to the new context of swinging on ropes in the gymnasium. Similarly, in the computer graphics lessons, the pupils were required to carry out by themselves the procedure taught to them earlier: 'What we're going to do for next week is/ you're going to go away and you're going to try and do it on your own' (computer graphics lesson 1). Indeed, the pupils were informed at the end of lesson 2 that they would be 'showing others how to do it next week. I'm having nothing to do with it next week'; the teacher clearly intended the handover process to go all the way, and include being able to take the role of teacher! However, in none of the lessons was the handover process anything like a complete success. In the third pendulum lesson, the new context of the gymnasium proved to be no simple context for discussing pendulums. Experimental controls present in the original lessons were lacking, and even the teachers (two were present) appeared to confuse the swinging of pendulums with the notion of leverage. However, in talking later with the teachers concerned it transpired that the third lesson was essentially an afterthought performed to fulfil the investigators' initial request for a sequence of three lessons. So let us set that lesson apart.

Despite her insistence that the pupils should later make pottery 'based on what you have been doing today' (sequence 5.16), several of the pottery pupils in fact proceeded in lesson 3 to construct solid models rather than joined-up hollow pots. They performed what probably was for them a technically simpler *sculpturing* task, rather than the more difficult taught procedure of forming and joining together two hemispherical *pots*. As sequence 5.7 showed, they had encountered difficulty in establishing the context in their earlier lessons for applying the principle of hollowing out ('digging out') the base of their solid sculptures. Since the major planned task of the lessons was the matter of learning how to make pottery models from joined-up 'thumb-pots', something quite basic appears to have gone wrong. The teacher at one point, as we have seen, became exasperated and declared, 'John/ you seem to have forgotten everything you've learned don't you?' (sequence 5.12).

Again, in the computer graphics lessons, the pupils ran into trouble when required by the teacher to construct by themselves a LOGO program to draw a hexagon. The sources of difficulty this time were easier to identify, but only, we should stress, for observers who, unlike the teacher, had the luxury of a reviewable video recording of the proceedings! In this case, the problem arose because the prerequisite context from which the pupils had to work had not been properly established in the first place. It turned out to be a false assumption on the teacher's part that the pupils possessed a full understanding of what a hexagon is, and, moreover, it became clear that even the teacher did not fully grasp how to write the appropriate program, needing to resort to the manual to find what commands were available. She attempted to teach the ready-made LOGO command BUILD, as in BUILD HEXAGON, but appeared not to realize that HEXAGON would have to be defined first before it could be used in the program. So Susan's program, using BUILD, failed to work, and was postponed for another week: 'That's what we're going to have to do for next week/ think of a way to iron out Susan's bug' (lesson 2).

The following week, in lesson 3, Susan was asked to take the role of teacher, and show some pupils who had not been present in the previous lessons how to move the screen cursor (the 'arrow') around using the simple commands that had been learned (FORWARD, RIGHT, etc.). Sequence 5.17 is Susan's attempt.

Sequence 5.17   Susan as teacher

SUSAN: This is a program called Arrow/ and another is/ a completely new program because it hasn't got a brain like us and you have to tell it what to do/ and it goes off in degrees/ and you have to press Forward and Right/ and instead of just writing the whole word Forward you can press/ Forward/ or Right/ or Left or Repeat/ or Fresh/ and it/ it goes up on degrees/ and things like that/ erm//

Susan pauses, apparently at a loss.

T: Perhaps you'd like to tell them what this thing here is Susan.

T pointing at screen cursor.

SUSAN: Oh yes/ that's the Arrow/ and erm/ and you have to press in Fresh and every time you've finished a command./ You don't put in Forward/ so many/ and then/ Left/ so many. You have to put/ Return/ Forward so many/ and then Return/ and then Left so many/ Return. Otherwise it will say something like/ sorry I don't understand Forward twenty/ Right ninety/ something like that. So you have to remember to press/ Return erm/ that's about it.

T: Can you show them what to do when you press code Enter and Return/ what happens. Is the screen clear?

Susan was one of the most responsive and involved pupils in the earlier two lessons, and was chosen by the teacher because of her competence. Nevertheless, she was clearly very inept as a teacher. Her speech echoed the *content* of what the teacher had talked about – the contrast between the computer's ignorance and the knowledgeable brains of the pupils themselves was a favourite theme – but she failed to communicate instructions in any comprehensible way. It was all decontextualized talk, with no demonstration, and no IRFs with her 'pupils'. The (real) teacher was obliged to offer her some helpful prompts. Susan was still very much dependent on the teacher for help in explicating her understanding of things. When the scaffolding was removed, she fell over.

Now it is not the purpose of teaching to make pupils into teachers. At least, not in the space of a week. But Susan's efforts at teaching do raise issues for the notion of a handover of competence from teacher to child. If she was not learning how to act like the teacher, then what *was* she supposed to be learning? What the pupils were apparently being prepared for was more and more education in the same vein. Indeed, the pendulums teacher went so far as to anticipate at one point that 'when you get up to A-level physics that's the sort of thing you'll be doing'. In their role as pupils, they remained dependent on the teacher to set the agenda, define the tasks and the criteria for success, furnish the significant concepts, and generally control the learning process. It is, indeed, in this asymmetry of power and knowledge, a characteristic of all of our recorded lessons, that we shall locate many of the problems that formal education faces in accomplishing the handover of competence from teacher to child. This will be the major theme of chapter 7.

6
Ritual and principle

In this chapter and the next we shall examine extracts of classroom discourse in order to explore some ways in which joint understandings are established, or may fail to be established. This chapter examines the *curriculum content* of the lessons, looking in turn at how the various major concepts or principles at stake in the lessons were dealt with. These 'principles' are basically what the lessons were 'about', what the teacher hoped the pupils would come to understand. The following chapter will concentrate more explicitly on the various *communicative processes* identifiable in the discourse, through which understandings and misunderstandings appear to arise.

In chapter 5 teachers and pupils were seen to build their common understandings on the basis of a continuity of experience and discourse which becomes, as it proceeds, the implicit context for the meaningfulness of further activity and talk. The teacher's role as expert, in control of the development of knowledge through careful guidance and 'scaffolding', was seen as part of a more general process of human development in which children acquire such basic cultural knowledge and skills as their first language (Bruner 1983a), and indeed all of their language-based mental processes in what Vygotsky (1978) termed the 'zone of proximal development'. But the process of formal education is fraught with problems. It is a process often strongly contrasted with that of everyday life and learning (e.g. Donaldson 1978), a seemingly unnatural process quite different from that of learning one's first language. Bruner draws the distinction strongly:

> The fact that we learn the culture as readily and effectively as we do must give us pause – considering how poorly we do at certain artificial, 'madeup' subjects that we teach in . . . schools that set out to teach a subject without the advice or consent of the pupils involved and without the task having any contextualization in the children's lives. (Bruner 1985, p. 29)

The differences between everyday learning at home and learning in school are obviously not restricted to the artificiality and disembeddedness of the curriculum. Even ignoring the probability of innate predispositions in the learning of a first language, contrasts between everyday learning and school learning include the fact that teachers in schools are generally faced with much larger numbers of pupils, children they do not know outside that context, children who are required to attend by law or some other irresistible authority, in whose name the teacher may need to act to coerce attendance and compliance. Often an externally imposed curriculum has to be taught, and, of course, teachers themselves receive explicit training in the psychology of child development, and in educational principles and practice, which most parents do not. We shall turn our attention in this and the following chapter to the problematics of common knowledge, and it is in precisely these contrasts between formal and informal education that we shall try to identify what goes wrong.

The particular issue we shall be dealing with is that of the relationship between practical experience and principled understanding. Although we are concerned primarily with classroom activity and discourse, the pedagogic nature of this derives from the ways in which the practice of classroom education is an embodiment of the sorts of educational assumptions and ideology that we looked at in chapter 3. Educational practice is founded on assumptions about the nature of the educational process, which may be conceived in terms of transmission and teaching, or of discovery and learning: of covering syllabuses or of developing skills and abilities, and so on. Teachers acquire through their training and experience ideas about how teaching and learning are best conducted (at least, best conducted under such constraints and circumstances as class size, resources, etc.), and these ideas are shaped within a particular historical and cultural milieu. As we noted earlier, many of our primary schools have been strongly influenced by the educational principles of experiential and practical learning, in which the teacher's role is to facilitate discovery and involvement on the part of pupils who, given the right sorts of learning opportunities, will be able to generate deeper understandings than could be the case if they were simply talked at or directly instructed.

In the last chapter we established that the physical contexts of classroom discourse, the physical props and materials and the activities of teacher and pupils, are essential constituents of each lesson. Much of the classroom discourse that we have collected is highly context-dependent, closely related to physical actions and circumstances in the classroom. Moreover, in an ethos of learning by doing, of discovering and inventing conceptual understandings through practical action and experience, these physical activities are not merely 'contexts' that conveniently assist participants and observers alike to make sense of the dialogue. They are, to a large extent, as far as the participants are concerned, the lesson itself.

Occasionally, in the clay pottery lessons, matters of scientific principle were raised, such as the effects of heat on the expansion of air inside the clay, and the consequent dangers of cracks appearing. But the predominant aim of the lessons, and indeed of discussing such principles, was to teach the pupils or help them learn how to do clay pottery: 'I wanted them to learn the skills/ to be able to make their own pots and know how to do it correctly.' The major issue that we wish to address in this chapter concerns this relationship between practical activity and principled understanding. It is not always the case that a scientific principle such as that of the expansion of gases is subservient to the more practical business of learning a physical skill. Sometimes the essential business of a lesson is one that is oriented to principles, getting the children to understand some principles of scientific method or theory, for example, in which the practical activities constitute the experiential base on which such concepts may be understood, or from which they will, it is hoped, arise.

The lessons on pendulums are the clearest ones we have in which the essential aim was to teach scientific concepts and principles. We shall be concentrating here on those lessons. But first let us raise an issue. Let us say that it is the teacher's aim in a lesson to get the pupils to understand the importance of careful observation, scientific testing and measurement, and the use of experimental controls in testing hypotheses, and to learn that only one of several possible variables (in our case, the length of the pendulum's string) actually has a measurable effect on the pendulum's motion (its 'period of swing' – the time taken by each complete swing). As we shall see, these were indeed some of the principles at stake in our lessons. The question is, why go to all the trouble of constructing physical pendulums, of testing out hypotheses, of getting the pupils to do it all themselves and work it all out for themselves through practical discovery, across a series of four lessons (including a preliminary one in which they constructed three wooden pendulums), when the teacher could simply present these ideas in a few words, explain their importance and how they work, even demonstrate them to the children so that they can see for themselves, all in less than, say, half an hour?

The answer is simple – or, at least, it appears to be so. Apart from the problem of sustaining the pupils' attention and motivation, we would have no guarantee that the children had 'really understood' the concepts. Children cannot learn things simply by being told; they need to be able to relate such principles to their own actions, experiences and conceptions, otherwise they will simply be acquiring empty words, verbal formulae taught and learned, with no real understanding. As we saw in chapter 3, these are the educational assumptions that have led to the undoubted changes in British primary education, and to some extent secondary education, since the Plowden Report and the popularization of the theories and findings of Jean Piaget.

However, learning by doing has problems of its own. In the case of clay pottery, it is easy to see how practical experience and activity are essential in acquiring the skills involved, and even how such practice would lend itself to an understanding of the principles that underlie the process. But it surely remains true that a great deal of what we know as educated adults is not derived from direct experience. Indeed, as we remarked in chapter 1, this is often held to be the great distinction between ourselves and the rest of the animal kingdom, that we have the power, largely due to language, of transcending the limitations of our own individual experience and participating in knowledge and ideas generated by other people and communicated to us. The philosophy of learning by doing, of experiential and inductive learning, must ultimately confront this issue: how do we come to know and understand things from beyond our own experience, and, indeed, how do we know what interpretation to put on that experience, and how to share and compare such experiences and interpretations with those of other people? Just as the older pedagogy of chalk and talk encountered the problem of ensuring that pupils actually understood the concepts purveyed, so the newer pedagogy of learning from practical experience must deal with the problem of culture, of how people come to understand things in the same ways and in the same terms as each other – that is, the problem of common knowledge.

One of the real dangers of an emphasis on children's capacities to learn from their own activity and experience is that their understanding of things will remain at the level of specific experiences and practical procedures, while the hoped-for principled understandings are never grasped or articulated. A rather extreme example of such procedural or 'ritual' knowledge comes from some research by Taba and Elzey (1964), who cite the instance of a girl who regularly achieved good marks in mathematics, and who described her procedures as follows:

I know what to do by looking at the examples. If there are only two numbers I subtract. If there are lots of numbers I add. If there are just two numbers and one is smaller than the other it is a hard problem. I divide to see if it comes out even and if it doesn't I multiply.

The pupil in Taba and Elzey's example had worked out for herself a ritual procedure which was capable in most cases of generating an acceptable result for the teacher. But it seems that she had a serious misunderstanding of the proper rules of arithmetic. The fact is that there are such rules, and the teacher knows what they are, and the curriculum defines them and requires that they are taught. Pupils are seldom free to reinvent the curriculum. Taba and Elzey's is an extreme example, but it is not difficult to identify many other instances of essentially ritual rather than principled knowledge. It is possible to learn how to do many algebraic operations without understanding why or how they work, just as pupils and even university students are quite capable of using the various practices of experimental design, statistical analysis and formal laboratory reports without understanding the underlying principles by which all of those procedures are justified and interrelated. Similarly, in preparation for a 1964 O-level English examination, one of us was taught how to write an essay, complete with formulaic phrases rather like those of a modern mail-merging word processor ('on the other hand . . .', 'from the above points we can see that . . .', etc.). The plan to follow was:

Introduction
Paragraph for (the proposition in the title)
Paragraph against
Paragraph for
Paragraph against
Conclusion

We do not wish to imply that formulaic procedures even such as the essay plan are necessarily or inherently poor sorts of pedagogy. What matters is how they are presented and used, how they are taken up by teacher and pupils and developed. The essay plan is in some respects laudable. If we imagine that the teacher's task is to move pupils from a competence that they probably already possess, for engaging in rhetorical debate and argument, towards the ability to write essays, then the format has some merit as a first step in that process. An essay can be understood as a dialogue expressed as a monologue. Written by a single hand, it must nevertheless include argument, counter-argument and refutation. In conversational argument, each speaker provides the other with the disagreements, comments, additional information and alternative interpretations which prompt the other's thoughts, and which give structure and sequence to the debate. In an essay, the flow and continuity of argument have to be achieved by the writer alone. The ritual essay plan can be seen as a dialogic 'scaffold' within which an argument can be constructed by a single speaker/writer. Its most favourable interpretation is as a transitional step in a Vygotskyan development from social discourse to verbal self-expression. Of course, the essay plan was not presented by the teacher in those terms. In fact, it was all the tuition we received. It was given (and taken) as a blueprint, the correct procedure for writing essays, and may well have remained for many pupils an inhibiting constraint on their ability to write.

What we are calling *ritual* knowledge is a particular sort of procedural knowledge, knowing how to do something. In many contexts, of course, procedural knowledge is entirely appropriate and exactly what is required. This was the case with learning to do clay pottery, and was also an important part of the lessons on pendulums; the pupils had to know how to operate their apparatus, their stop watches and calculators, and much of their ability to get through the lessons required knowledge which was essentially procedural. Procedural knowledge becomes 'ritual' where it substitutes for an understanding of underlying principles. Ritual knowledge is the sort exhibited rather crudely by the pupil in Taba and Elzey's example, and in the less spectacular cases cited above. *Principled* knowledge is defined as essentially explanatory, oriented towards an understanding of how procedures and processes work, of why certain conclusions are necessary or valid, rather than being arbitrary things to say because they seem to please the teacher.

The ritual–principle distinction, like any such distinction, is not absolute, and succeeds only in so far as it is useful. Similar sorts of distinctions can be found in work as diverse as that of Kuhn (1962), in describing the procedural, routine work of ordinary science; of Piaget (1970), in accounting for the development of higher forms of thought and understanding out of the earlier co-ordinations of practical actions; and even that of Bernstein (1971), where a distinction is drawn between an active, autonomous orientation to 'principles' that he attributes to middle-class pupils, and a more passive orientation to 'operations' or 'how things work', attributed to working-class pupils. The relationship between practical action and principled understanding is clearly of fundamental importance in educational and developmental theories. We shall make no assumptions here of social-class differences, or even of individual differences between pupils. Rather, our concern is with establishing the ways in which ritual and principled knowledge arise out of the situated discourse of school lessons, as matters of joint understanding. Our emphasis on the importance of joint understanding arising out of joint activity and discourse is, as we have stressed, more akin to the Vygotskyan perspective than to any other.

In many contexts, procedural knowledge is a great advantage. It would be grossly inefficient if we were constantly to return to first principles in solving problems. Rote learning produces fast answers. And the ritualization of discourse and action is a great aid to memory. Knowing one's 'times tables', or how to use a pocket calculator, is preferable for many everyday purposes to having to resort to a principled understanding of multiplication. Knowing a good recipe may be a quicker and surer route to preparing a good meal than having first to seek an understanding of ingredients, flavours and the principles of *haute cuisine*. The recipe is fast but finite, particular rather than general, brittle when inappropriate – lacking the proper ingredients, one would require a more principled knowledge to adapt successfully. Procedural knowledge is fast and efficient, provided that all of its conditions for appropriateness are met. Where those conditions fail, and there is no principled understanding to resort to, performance becomes ritual.

We do not wish the notion of 'principled' knowledge to be confused with any notion of epistemological universals, of rationality, operational intelligence or scientific truth. Indeed, we are wary of providing a hard and universal definition of principled knowledge, for reasons which are not difficult to appreciate. All of human knowledge is ultimately questionable; all of our scientific and literary practices and products are open to critical scrutiny, as are the epistemological and aesthetic assumptions on which such ideas are based. We are in no position to offer a universal rule by which we can identify absolute principled truths. Even the most universally accepted principles are no more than that – subject to social *acceptance*, agreement, validation, and embodied in a context of accepted knowledge and procedure. Both ritual and principled understandings, in school and in the outside world, belong to frameworks of communicated understandings, of common knowledge sustained through discourse. Our distinction between ritual and principled knowledge is a pragmatic one, designed to help us examine some ways in which educational knowledge develops through classroom talk and action as a shared system of thought and practice. It enables us to address problems concerning the relatedness of ideologies, practices and outcomes of education. The fact that curriculum content, as far as the pupils are concerned, is virtually all predetermined, leads naturally to an examination of the nature of education as socialization into a pre-existing epistemological world. Our conception of 'principles' is therefore a local one, dependent on the particular context of the lessons we have observed. We shall take as our focus those principles of understanding, however well or ill founded these may ultimately turn out to be, which were at stake in the lessons we observed. The way in which these principles were identified is discussed below.

The major issue that we shall be dealing with here is the relationship between principles and procedures – between the conceptual understandings at stake in the lessons, and the practical activities and discourse which constituted the lessons themselves. Our strategy will be to identify what appeared to be the main conceptual principles that the lesson was designed to teach (if we may use the word 'teach' loosely for now), and to examine how these were handled during the lesson in terms of what was actually done and said.

It is important that we distinguish between the principles at stake in the lessons, and the notion of principled understandings on the part of teacher and pupils. At one level we have the lesson as something planned and done, the set of concepts and issues that the lesson is 'about' (scientific method, the concepts of democracy and division of labour, or whatever), and the actual activities through which these concepts were meant to be learned or developed (doing experiments with pendulums, creative role-playing, etc.). At another level, we have the participants' knowledge and competence, what they understand of these things, and this can be dichotomized for our purposes as either principled (understanding the issues and concepts, and their relationship to the activities) or ritual (embedded in the paraphernalia of the activities themselves, without any grasp of what it was all really about). We hope to demonstrate the usefulness of this dichotomy in examining the point at which we believe many of the problems of classroom teaching and learning arise – the relationship between what is done and what is understood, as these are embodied in teacher–pupil discourse.

We shall take as our main focus the set of lessons on pendulums. The major principles at stake here were these:

the generation of hypotheses (making testable predictions);
empiricism (learning by direct experience, doing and testing);
controlling variables (e.g. allowing only one at a time to vary);
accuracy of measurement (quantification, etc.).

We derive these principles mainly from what the teacher said in interview, but also from the lesson transcripts themselves. For example, the importance of controlling extraneous variables was derived not from interview but from the video transcripts of the lessons, where it was a pervasive feature of what the pupils were required to do, and necessary to their results' making any sense at all. Additionally, we had at our disposal the materials used by the teacher to plan the lessons at the outset. The day before lesson 1 was recorded, the teacher had got a group of six pupils to construct, in pairs, three wooden pendulums about a metre high (see figure 6.1).

The teacher explained when interviewed in advance that she had planned that the lessons would involve the testing of three hypotheses concerning the effects of different variables on the 'period' of swing (the average time taken by each swing). Her basic source was the maths book

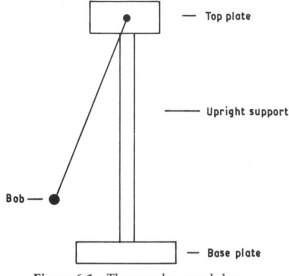

Figure 6.1 The wooden pendulum

that the pupils were using, which included a brief piece about pendulums, and the effects of varying the length of string from which the bob was suspended. Only one of the six pupils (Antony) had reached this part of the book in their reading. The teacher had decided to get the children to test for themselves the effects of varying length of string, as well as two other variables not mentioned in the book, which ought to have no effect on the period of swing: the weight of the bob, and the angle or height from which the swing is started. These additional variables were introduced, the teacher told us, 'to help the children to actually learn the concept'. It was the aim of the lessons that 'the children should learn about scientific methods/ to test out hypotheses and use the experimental method', and also that they should 'find out for themselves how pendulums work'.

Before looking at each principle in turn, we can gain some idea of the sorts of issues we shall be dealing with by examining how the pupils expressed their understandings of things in interviews (conducted after the three lessons had been completed, after the researchers had made a preliminary examination of the video recordings), and also their various spontaneous suggestions made during the lessons.

Pupils' conceptions

After the set of three lessons was completed, we interviewed each of the pupils individually, primarily to discover the extent to which they appeared to have grasped certain key concepts, including the four principles defined above, which we had previously identified by examining the video transcripts of the lessons. These interviews generally supported our impression that the lessons had been successful. The pupils had been actively engaged in work which appeared both interesting and challenging to them, and they appeared to have grasped most of the essential information and ideas. They had a good conception of what pendulums were and how they worked, and of how to do experiments. But our major interest was in the processes through which such understandings were achieved, and through which they may sometimes have failed; as many researchers have noted before, it is often the failures which are most revealing. So, against the background of a well-organized piece of teaching and learning, rich in joint activity and conversation, we shall be looking for clues as to how joint understandings and misunderstandings arise, and relating these directly to what was done and said in the lessons.

Our purpose in conducting the interviews with the children was to gain additional data relevant to particular questions raised by our preliminary examinations of the video transcripts of the lessons. We asked the pupils questions concerning the extent to which they had dealt with similar concepts and procedures in other lessons, or outside school, and we asked them questions directed at discovering how far they appeared to have understood the various concepts and procedures covered in the lessons. The interviews were themselves, of course, discourses with the pupils which have to be taken as additional information, and not simply as true indications of what the pupils had learned.

As well as their answers to questions in interview, other useful bases for assessing the pupils' understandings of things were their spontaneous comments and ideas expressed during the lessons. These were suggestions or ideas expressed by the pupils other than those that reflected what the teacher had told them, or had prompted them to say. These are particularly important in the context of one of the major issues that we shall be dealing with: how, in an essentially discovery-oriented sort of classroom education, do pupils manage to discover what they are meant to?

It is important that we establish here that it is not our intention to be critical of the teacher. That would be grossly unjust. It is impossible for any teacher to keep track of all that is said and done, and all that is implied, in any lesson. There are many distractions, and other priorities apart from strictly pedagogic ones. We are merely using our privileged position as observers who have unique access to a permanent record of events, to try to identify what actually happened, in the belief that it is essentially in the discourse between teacher and pupils that education is done, or fails to be done.

In sequence 6.1, the teacher is at the stage of establishing what the hypotheses to be tested will be. Mass, length of string and angle have been suggested as appropriate variables (see sequences 6.3–6.5 below), and the teacher is asking for hypotheses about the effects of altering the angle of swing.

Sequence 6.1   The compensatory principle (David)

T: What sort of a difference/ Jonathan/ do you think? If I held it up here?

T holding pendulum bob out away from the upright support.

JONATHAN: ⎡ Well it might make a difference.

DAVID: ⎣ I don't think it'll make a difference. I know it's got further to go but/

JONATHAN: It's got faster.

DAVID: But it's ⎡ going faster/ and so it won't (&)

T: ⎣ go faster.

DAVID: (&) make any difference because it's equal.

ANTONY: Well I think it'll go slower because it's got further to go.

T: So if it goes up here/ right/ and we let it go/ you reckon it'll go much slower.

T holds bob out.
T looks at Antony.

DAVID: Miss it's got more power than if you did it from about there.

David holds his bob out low, then high.

T: So you think it'll go//

DAVID: Faster.

T: Faster. What do you think Karen?

KAREN: I think it'll go faster as well.

T: Why?

KAREN: 'Cause if you can bring it up there it's bound to go faster because it's going to drop down faster.

T holds bob high, as Karen talks.

In sequence 6.1, David suggests that altering the angle will make no difference to the pendulum's period of swing, and indeed this is later proved to be correct. He also offers a rationale based on some sort of compensatory relationship between angle (the distance the pendulum has to travel) and speed of swing. The teacher ignores David's rather sophisticated suggestion in favour of Antony's simple hypothesis that a greater angle will produce a slower swing. David again attempts to suggest that increased angle is countered by increased 'power' which will make the pendulum go faster. But, in answering the teacher's sentence-completion question 'So you think it'll go . . . (pause)', David falls into the pattern of providing a simple hypothesis, 'faster'.

It is not difficult to discern what is happening here. The teacher is engaged in fulfilling her plan for the lesson, eliciting a predetermined set of variables for the pupils to test on their three pendulums, and eliciting simple hypotheses about the effects of each single variable. She is not prepared (literally) for a discussion of the influence of one variable on another, and in fact never discusses this in any of the lessons. Antony and Karen provided the simple single-variable hypotheses that she was after. For David, and perhaps for the others too, it was a missed opportunity. The fact that angle of swing, and also the mass of the bob, turn out to have no effect on the pendulum's period of swing is presumably due to some such compensatory principle as David tried to express. The pursuit of his suggestion might well have led to a principled understanding of two very important concepts at stake in the lesson – that is, how and why pendulums work as they do, and also the principle of experimental control, based on the ways in which different variables influence each other: why it is necessary to control variations in angle, say, while measuring the effects of length and mass. Immediately after sequence 6.1, Jonathan also tried to express some sort of compensatory principle, this time through an analogy.

Sequence 6.2   The compensatory principle (Jonathan)

JONATHAN: If you had two quarters of
  a circle and erm you've got two
  snooker balls at each point/ one at the
  halfway point and one at the top and
  you let them both go at the same time
  they'll both get to the bottom at the
  same time so it might be the same as   *Jonathan moves finger in an arc.*
  this won't it?
T: Good boy. That's very good
  observation Jonathan. Well now   *T turning to rest of group.*
  what's the only way we're going to
  find out for sure?
DAVID: Do it.
ANTONY: Try it.
T: Well I think we should. We've got to
  remember then that we've got to be
  very accurate and know how to use
  our stop watch . . .

Jonathan's observation was accepted by the teacher, but not pursued. Instead, she turned her attention away from the issue of mechanisms and explanations and towards the need for empirical testing and accuracy of measurement. It appears that the teacher was not easily to be deflected from her notion of where the lesson was going, and what had to be done next. The business of getting the group through the organized activity of the lesson appeared to be a pedagogic aim that was more important than pursuing spontaneous understandings on the part of the pupils of the principles underlying what they were doing. David's eventual understanding of how and why the various variables and hypotheses were chosen was correspondingly arbitrary, reflecting the teacher's lesson plan rather than any principles of science. As he said in interview, 'there was three of us and there was really three things to change on the pendulum so we done one each.'

The issue raised here is a serious one. In the pursuit of practical activities on which experiential learning is assumed to be based, it is quite possible for the teacher to fail to deal with the pupils' understandings of the essential principles underlying the work they are doing, even when these understandings, or at least a substantial basis for them, are offered by the pupils themselves. Sequence 6.3 occurred near the end of lesson 1, when the pupils had tested and measured the effects of angle, length and mass (weight), but Antony and David had proceeded spontaneously to try altering a variable which the teacher had earlier discouraged, that is, the substance from which the string was made. It had already been accepted that angle and mass had no effect, that the measured effects were insignificant, and the teacher clearly expected string substance to have no effect either. Here she is suggesting that the measured times for the two string substances (1.78 and 1.70 seconds) are essentially equivalent.

Sequence 6.3   Wool versus string

T: So it **is**/ **prac**tically the **same** isn't it?   *T raising her voice above others.*
DAVID: No that/ goes ⌈ **fas**ter.
ANTONY: ⌊ It's point/
T: Point/ **why**?
DAVID: This taut/ this is tauter.   *David pulling at woollen string*
                                           on pendulum.

ANTONY: The other string/ the other is   *T picks up a piece of string from*
   you know it's up a bit. It wasn't   *the table and holds it against*
   exactly the same.   *pendulum.*
T: That goes faster/ than ⌈ this one?
DAVID: ⌊ Yeh.
T: I wonder if the string **does** make all
   that much difference/ and **why** it
   does.

DAVID: I reckon it's because/ that/ you need a real/ a really big weight to keep that right down.

David reaches and takes second string from T.

T: So it wasn't down/ mm// Beautiful pair of scissors you've got there isn't it// (. . .)

Pause, 5 seconds, with T and David looking at Antony cutting the pendulum's woollen string.

We shall deal later with the issue of how various measurements came to be treated as equivalent, but at this point in the lesson it was understood by everyone that, despite small differences in measured timings, the variables angle and mass had been shown to have no effect on period of swing. David and Antony resisted the teacher's attempt to impose the same interpretation on the timings for altering string substance, and eventually the teacher abandoned the issue and left it unresolved, switching her attention rather clumsily to the 'beautiful pair of scissors', and subsequently to the other pupils who were ready to draw graphs. It appears that the string and the wool may not have been the same length, so that perhaps the measured difference was indeed a real one, but attributable to an uncontrolled difference in length rather than to the use of wool. Further, David was offering a different interpretation, also reducible to the effects of length, that the tension on wool and string may have stretched one of them more than the other. So, again, we have pupils pursuing their own investigations and explanations which are close to yielding insights about the importance of experimental controls and the workings of pendulums, but the teacher does not take advantage of the opportunity. The pupils appear to be interpreting things differently from how the teacher did, but, rather than this being an opportunity for some genuine negotiation of understandings, the moment is allowed to pass. Altering string substance had not been part of the planned activity, and in any case it ought to have had no effect.

This brief examination of some of the pupils' spontaneous conceptions suggests that a close examination of the discourse and activity of classroom lessons is necessary if we are to understand how particular conceptions are created, fostered or ignored, how particular understandings and procedures become jointly understood while others are neglected, and how pupils' own insights and conceptions of things may be taken up and developed, or else ignored or discounted. We shall now examine how the four principles identified above were handled in the pendulums lessons.

Generation of hypotheses

The teacher in these lessons was a firm believer in the educational principle that children do not learn simply by being told. As she said in interview, 'they learn by discovering things for themselves.' It was important that the pupils should 'learn the concept through testing out a number of different hypotheses', and she was sure before the lessons began that the pupils would generate the hypotheses for themselves; for instance, 'they should be able to hypothesize that if the mass is varied this might make a difference because they are used to investigative science.' Again, in interview before the lessons began, the teacher explained that her lesson plan included coverage of the generation of hypotheses, 'and then the children will do the experiment and record their results on changing the mass, amplitude [angle] of swing and length, over twenty swings.' But the question is, given that the children are to discover things for themselves, how does the teacher then ensure that they come up with sensible hypotheses, testable ones, the ones planned in advance? Let us examine how the three variables (length, angle and weight) and their associated hypotheses were generated.

Sequence 6.4   The length hypothesis

The teacher has spent the first part of lesson 1 introducing the concept of pendulums and making sure that the pupils are able to operate their stop watches and calculate an average period of swing from a set of timed swings.

T: Look at David's./ Now suppose David and his partner were to change something on that pendulum. Can you suggest something that he might change to test whether it's still the same?

ANTONY: The length of the string.

T: He could change the length of the string. Right now/ suppose that he did. Suppose say/ he took the string say up to here and shortened it. What do you think might happen then? *T indicates halfway up pendulum post. David raises hand.*

Do you think the **time**/ *Rising intonation on 'time'. T looking at David.*

DAVID: Yes because it won't come out as far.

JONATHAN: It would go like that. *Jonathan holds pendulum string halfway down the upright support, swings bob which very clearly moves with a much faster period than before.*

SHARON: It would be slower.

T: ⌈ What do you
                        reckon/   ⌈Sharon?
JONATHAN: ⊢Much faster.
SHARON: ⌊Slower./   ⌊Faster.
    I think it would be faster.

T: You think it would be faster if we
    shortened the string. What do you
                    ⌈think yourself David?
JONATHAN: ⌊Much faster.

DAVID: I reckon it'll go faster as well
    'cause say when I done there   *David holds string halfway*
                                                                    down support.

T: Yes/ you think it goes faster?   *David lets bob swing.*

DAVID: I think it goes much faster.

SHARON: Yeh but you haven't held it   *(Sharon off screen.)*
    out right to here.

T: Like you were doing before.

Sequence 6.4 begins with a recognizable IRF exchange in which Antony (David's partner) provides the teacher with the variable 'length of the string'. We know from our interview with the teacher that Antony was the only pupil to have reached the section on pendulums in his maths book, where it is stated that the pendulum's period of swing depends on the length of the string. Despite their being apparently new to these concepts, David and Jonathan appear on the face of it to have an understanding of some of the ideas to be dealt with in the lesson that is to follow. David eventually articulates the hypothesis that shortening the string will produce a faster swing, together with a quick demonstration (as Jonathan had done previously and also earlier in the lesson) by holding the string halfway up against the upright and letting it swing. He further offers the suggestion that a compensatory principle is at work – 'because it won't come out as far' (see the discussion of sequences 6.1 and 6.2 above). Despite having by now seen three such demonstrations, Sharon suggests that the shortened swing might be slower, but then changes her mind, and says something which suggests that she also has some understanding of the compensatory principle – 'Yeh but you haven't held it out right to here.'

The teacher has succeeded in obtaining from the pupils the first variable and hypothesis. But three more interesting things have happened as well:

1 The pupils have tried to articulate a rationale for their hypothesis based on some principle of compensation, but the teacher has not taken this up and incorporated it into the lesson (here or elsewhere, despite several similar opportunities to do so).

2 Sharon has apparently contradicted the evidence of her senses and offered a false hypothesis.
3 Sharon changes her mind.

Item 1 falls into a general pattern that we shall examine in the next chapter; the teacher is able to control the extent to which pupils' contributions are given significance, the extent to which they are incorporated into shared understanding. Items 2 and 3 call into question how much pupils learn from direct experience and activity. As we saw in chapter 2, classroom discourse has a structure and momentum of its own, irrespective of the content of what is being discussed. Teacher and pupils are frequently locked into a routine pattern of question-and-answer dialogue (the IRF structure) in which the teacher elicits and evaluates, assigns turns at speaking, and so on. In items 2 and 3, Sharon appears to be carried along by the flow of the discourse, ignoring the evidence of her senses in favour of providing what seemed to be the appropriate responses to the teacher's prompts. We shall return to this important matter of discourse overriding experience when we examine the principles of empiricism and accuracy of measurement later in this chapter.

In sequence 6.5 Jonathan suggests the next variable, 'weight'. Note the teacher's use of the term 'mass', offered as a preferential alternative to 'weight':

Sequence 6.5   The weight hypothesis

T: What about you Jonathan? What
   could we change on yours perhaps
   which might produce a different
   result?
JONATHAN: Weight?   *Jonathan holds up bob.*
T: We could/ we could change the mass.
   What could we do there then?
JONATHAN: Er we could put more than   *Jonathan holds and looks at bob.*
   one washer on it.
T: We could.   *Rising intonation (inviting
                                     further suggestions).*

JONATHAN: Or/
T: And what would we be looking at?
   What would we be wanting to find
   out?
JONATHAN: If the time is different.
T: If/ if the time is different when we
   ⎡change the number of
   washers (&) ⎢
JONATHAN: ⎣Mm yeh.

T: (&) if we change the mass of the bob
in other words. Right/ That would be
an interesting thing. What about
yours Sharon? David's changing the
length of the string to see if that
makes any difference. What's
Jonathan going to do Karen?

*'That . . . thing' said quickly
and quietly.*

KAREN: Change the weight.
T: Change the mass. Now what could
Sharon do?

Having elicited the variable 'weight', and suggested the term 'mass', the
teacher takes stock of where the group has reached, checking via an IRF
exchange with Karen that the group has a joint understanding of what has
been established up to this point in the discourse; the length and weight
variables are established, and it is now the turn of the third pair to choose
a variable to measure. The group this time overlooks the business of
making a hypothesis, of predicting how altering the mass would affect the
period of swing.

The pupils did not immediately or spontaneously suggest the remaining variable planned by the teacher – angle – and so she had to devise
some way of eliciting it from them without resorting to the apparently
taboo strategy of telling them directly what it should be.

Sequence 6.6   Eliciting the angle variable

T: Watch me/ operate this pendulum
here. Watch what I'm doing. I'm
touching the string. I'm touching the
bob. What other thing can I change?
I'm changing/ **now**.

*T reaches for the bob on
Jonathan's pendulum.*

*T holds bob out and lets it go,
then (on 'now') holds it out
much higher (further), lets it go
and catches it.*

ANTONY: You could hold it right up.
T: So you could change the/
ANTONY: The distance [of the swing.
T: [What do we
call this?

*T pointing at gap between post
and outheld string, moves finger
around the triangular gap.*

JONATHAN: The erm.
PUPILS: Angle.
JONATHAN: Angle.

T: The angle that we start our swing
   from. I wonder if that would make a
   difference.
JONATHAN: Yeh.

The discourse following that of sequence 6.6 is the section examined earlier in sequences 6.1 and 6.2, where David and Jonathan offer hypotheses and rationales based on the principle of compensation, but eventually settle for the simple (and false) hypotheses that the teacher had planned that they should formulate and test. In sequence 6.6 itself, the teacher gets the pupils to suggest the variable 'angle of swing' by resorting to an elaborate mime and physical demonstration. This is clearly a strategy forced by her adherence both to the pedagogic principle of *e-ducare*, and also to the not altogether compatible procedure of planning the activities and ideas of the lesson in advance, so that the ideas that the pupils must arrive at from their own thought and experience are actually preordained. The teacher's solution is to ask a question while simultaneously providing heavy clues to the answer via bodily gestures and demonstrations. We shall call this sort of situated discourse 'cued elicitation', and examine it and its consequences more closely in the next chapter.

We have examined how the three variables, and a set of hypotheses about their effects, were elicited from the pupils. There were in fact other suggestions made by the pupils which were not encouraged by the teacher, and which were not taken up as variables to be measured and tested. One of these ideas was that they might alter the substance or thickness of the pendulum's string. (As we saw in sequence 6.3, Antony and David eventually managed to test for this at the end of the lesson.) Sequence 6.7 is the dialogue which connects sequences 6.5 and 6.6; the group has agreed on weight as a variable, and are now in pursuit of the third variable, which, as we have seen, is angle.

Sequence 6.7   The string substance variable

SHARON: Would it make any difference
   if I changed/ maybe the wood/ I mean
   not/ not the/ but the length of the
   wood?
ANTONY: No but that's what David is
   changing.
T: Yes.
DAVID: You could change the string.
T: ⌈ How could she change/
ANTONY: ⌊ You could make the weight
   lighter.

T: Well that would roughly be what
   Jonathan is doing.
LUCY: ⌈Perhaps she could do
   both.
JONATHAN: ⌊Change/ change the
   thicknesses of the string.
T: Well that would be a good thing to
   do. Why would that make any
   difference? You see David's string is
   thick and heavy and Sharon's is
   lighter. What would you expect to
   happen in the case of David's string   *T points in turn to each*
   and Sharon's string? What would you   *pendulum.*
   expect to happen?//
   What ⌈would/
DAVID: ⌊Perhaps her weight wouldn't
   pull the string down so much.   *David holds his own string.*
T: And so/ what would happen to the
   bob in that case?
ANTONY: ⌈It would go slower.
DAVID: ⊦Well it would   *Jonathan and David are waving*
JONATHAN: ⌊It would/ bob about a   *their bobs about.*
   bit.
T: Yes it probably would. Right now we
   still haven't decided how Sharon's
   going to change her pendulum./

The teacher's first reaction is one of encouragement: 'Well that would be a good thing to do.' It is an important part of her educational philosophy, as we have seen, as well as an overt part of her plan for the lesson, that the children should come up with their own ideas and test them out. But, again, we have a conflict with the fact that the variables to be measured, their number and nature, have actually been determined in advance. The pupils' task is not really that of generating ideas of their own, so much as discovering what the teacher has in mind. So, before resorting to cued elicitation of the variable 'angle' (sequence 6.6), the teacher uses the familiar 'Right now' format to mark the string substance discussion as closed, and to mark the start of a fresh attempt to find the third variable: 'we still haven't decided how Sharon's going to change her pendulum.' The teacher is very much in control of the establishment of joint understandings – in this case, of which variables are selected for examination, of what to call them, of which to ignore and which to incorporate into the lesson. This control that the teacher exercises over the content and definition of joint knowledge and activity is an important and pervasive phenomenon, which we shall return to in chapter 7.

Our examination of how the various variables and hypotheses were generated and defined has raised several points which we shall take up in the following sections and chapters:

1 The teacher is pursuing an overt policy by which the children themselves are required to generate ideas, and to learn by direct experience.

2 The ideas to be generated are in fact largely preordained, though the pupils are not explicitly made aware of this in the lessons.

3 The pupils' real task is, to a significant degree at least, one of inferring and discovering what the teacher wants them to say and do.

4 Point 3 is definable as a general pedagogic ground-rule which under-lies the discourse of the lesson, and which at least some of the pupils may be aware of.

5 It appears that pupils' interpretations of their own experiences are strongly determined by the way those experiences are conceptual-ized and communicated. The fate of any *a priori* assumptions and interpretations made by pupils will depend on whether or not these are articulated in classroom discourse. If they are articulated, they may then be legitimized, modified or overridden without ever having been explicitly confronted and discussed.

6 The teacher seems able, despite what appears to be a relatively open, pupil-oriented and conversational style of teaching, to maintain a close control over the selection, expression and direction of ideas and activities.

Empiricism and the control of variables

The principle of empiricism arises in these lessons in two distinct but related senses. First, there is the scientific principle that knowledge is acquired through observation, trial and test, rather than through simply thinking things through or believing what we are told. Second, there is the pedagogic principle (discussed in chapter 3) that pupils learn most and best through their own practical experiences, rather than, say, by being spoon-fed words and concepts by the teacher. We shall treat these two notions together here because it is not always clear in our data which particular version of empiricism is being invoked. In fact, it may well be the case here that the two senses are generally conflated – which itself has consequences for what teacher and pupils think they are doing and learning.

Our reason for discussing the principle of controlling variables together here with the principle of empiricism is that they were not clearly distinguished in the lessons; indeed, there appeared to be some confusion about their relationship. It is important that we recognize that the principle of controlling variables, realized here mainly as the need to alter one variable at a time, is not the same as the principle of empiricism. Its scientific justification is not simply one of trying things out and observing what happens, but, rather, one of restricting possible explanations to particular causal factors. Its importance lies in the process of deciding what exactly is causing the observed effects.

Apart from the fact that both pedagogic and scientific empiricism pervaded the lessons as background assumptions to all that occurred, there were occasions on which the principle was made explicit by both teacher and pupils, as in sequence 6.8.

Sequence 6.8   The principle of empiricism

T: Good boy. That's very good
   observation Jonathan. Well now   *T turning to rest of group.*
   what's the only way we're going to
   find out for sure?
DAVID: Do it.
ANTONY: Try it.
T: Well I think we should.
.
.
.
T: Well I think it might be worth trying
   just to be sure.
.
.
.
T: You want to try it using wool? Why
   not. Yes.

The responses by Antony and David were immediate and confident; the general principle of empirical testing and observation was one readily grasped by all of the pupils, and appeared to be a well-established assumption in everyone's understanding of what they were doing and why. Indeed, it seemed to be the teacher's favourite principle, since she invoked it many times to justify particular conceptions and procedures (as later, 'Are you going to try it any shorter just for kicks?'). It was evidently the importance to the teacher of the principles of empiricism, both scientific and pedagogic, that led her eventually to allow David and Antony to do their additional experiment with the wool ('Why not').

Not only was it important to conduct empirical investigations and to subject hypotheses to empirical test; it was also the principle invoked, beyond its usual range of meaning, to justify other principles, such as why the group needed to control variables, holding others constant while one was being varied and measured. In sequence 6.9 we find the principle of scientific empiricism invoked in the context of altering variables. Jonathan and Lucy had been assigned the variable 'weight' (or 'mass'), and were in the process of varying the number of metal washers that constituted their pendulum's bob, and measuring the period of swing for each different weight. However, what they actually did was to vary two things, weight and angle, with the possible problem of not then knowing which of these variables was responsible for any measured effects. Since neither of these variables affects a pendulum's period of swing, their results were fortunately not as messy as they could have been; all of their measurements were judged to be roughly equivalent. However, the important issue for us here is the conceptual one: how does the activity and discourse embody and create shared understandings of the scientific principles involved?

Sequence 6.9   Empiricism and experimental control

T: How are **you** doing? Are you all right?
JONATHAN: We've done three of them/
that one that one that one with one   *Jonathan points in turn to three*
washer/ with two washers and it's   *marks at top of pendulum, and*
exactly the same at that point there   *again at first two marks*
and that point there.   *('points').*
T: Exactly the same at those two points?
JONATHAN: Yeh.
T: What about this one is it slower?   *T pointing to third mark.*
JONATHAN: (. . .)   *(Inaudible: his back to camera.)*
T: You can always recheck them./ Do
you think it might be wrong because
it's that time?
JONATHAN: I think this one might be   *Jonathan points to one of the*
wrong.   *numbers they have recorded.*
T: Do you?
JONATHAN: I think it might not be
⌜ quite/
T: ⌊ What's the only way to find out   *T to Jonathan.*
⌜ whether that/
LUCY: ⌊ Do it again.   *Lucy smiling.*
T: Do it again. However keep going and   *T smiling at Lucy and Jonathan.*
I'll see how you get on after the next   *T touches Jonathan lightly on*
one. Right?   *the arm.*

T makes a move to leave
Jonathan and Lucy, but stays
and looks up at top of their
pendulum.

.
.

.

T: What/ 'cause the answer to this one is   *T pointing at matrix scores.*
two isn't it? So how is it working out
do you think? Do you think it's
making a difference the fact that you
are ⌈ holding it up higher?
LUCY: ⌊ Not really.   *Quietly, shaking head.*
JONATHAN: No/ it isn't.   *Jonathan looking at Lucy.*
T: It's not is it?
JONATHAN: And nor is the weight.
T: No. ⌈ The weight isn't making   *T to Jonathan.*
any | *T turns to Lucy who is talking*
| *simultaneously.*
LUCY: ⌊ Perhaps we'd better do that
again because/ perhaps we'd
better ⌈
T: | No you're ⌈ not really.
JONATHAN: ⌊ I think it's
round about two seconds.   *Jonathan and T looking at*
matrix (presumably at time for
each swing: 10 ÷ 5 = 2 secs).

T: Point two of a second/ two seconds
each time.   *Jonathan scratches his head.*
Do you think if you put **three** on it's   *(Three washers.)*
going to make a difference?
JONATHAN: No.   *Jonathan shakes his head.*
T: Is it worth making sure?

The 'points' indicated by Jonathan at the top of the pendulum were marks that indicated the different angles from which the pendulum was allowed to swing. The two pupils seemed to be aware that something was wrong, but it is not clear exactly what; apart from the problem of attributing measured effects to the two different variables, they may simply have made false measurements. The teacher's response was to assume such an empirical error and to invoke the principle of empiricism: 'You can always recheck them. . . . What's the only way to find out? . . . Do it again. . . . Is it worth making sure? . . . Try it with the three . . .' Later the teacher explicitly addressed the issue of altering variables one at a time, and suggested to Jonathan and Lucy that they might do so. But, again, no rationale was offered that appealed to the difficulty of explaining effects when several possible causes are at work. The teacher instead invoked again the principle of empiricism:

Sequence 6.10   Altering one variable at a time

T: Mm.// Erm perhaps if you only change **one** thing each time.// It **might** be different. It would be worth investigating wouldn't it.// What would you change/ do you reckon?

T examining Jonathan's and Lucy's recorded measurements.

JONATHAN: The washer.

T: You just change that and start at the same angle. It **might** make a difference.//

It would be a good idea to try though. Anyway we won't do it today. We'll do it some other day. I reckon it would be worth doing.

Jonathan silent during pause.

In sequence 6.10, and again at other points in the lessons, the teacher's only rationales for altering variables one at a time were 'accuracy' (which we shall examine below) and general empiricism: 'It might make a difference. It would be a good idea to try.' Controlling variables was treated as if it were itself another variable to try, and one unimportant enough to be postponed for 'some other day', rather than a principle governing the sense that can be made of empirical findings.

We should not be surprised, therefore, if the pupils' understanding of why their experiments were designed around the control and measurement of variables is essentially ritual or procedure-oriented; it was offered to them as something simply worth trying, something they were required to do to see what happened. An essentially procedural rather than principled understanding of this aspect of scientific experimentation would be a natural outcome of the discourse of the lesson. Any conception of the principle that the pupils possess must therefore be either procedural and reducible to simple empiricism, or else based on understandings that they had already achieved. There is some evidence of such prior conceptions; when setting up their experiment to vary length of string, Antony and David spontaneously controlled for angle of swing. However, when we talked to the pupils individually after the lessons were completed, their conceptions of why variables were altered one at a time were disappointing. Four of them offered explanations, of which only Lucy's comes close to expressing the principle involved:

SHARON: If we did too many things at a time it would get too/ the graph would get cluttered up and be much more difficult/ it's easier.

LUCY: Because if you did two things then you wouldn't really be able to work it out properly but if you only changed one thing it's easier to work out.

JONATHAN: We did the weight and the angle but we didn't do them at the same time because it's much easier to do the weight first and then the angle, and then we did them together afterwards.

DAVID: You couldn't have us all doing the same thing, so we/ there was three of us and there was really three things to change on the pendulum so we done one each.

Apart from Lucy's formulation, which is not explicit but may be referring to the principle of being able to choose between alternative possible causes, the pupils' suggestions are all couched in terms of practical and procedural difficulty.

It is worth reminding ourselves of how the notion of controlling variables was introduced into the lessons. We have seen that the teacher handled the notion as essentially a *procedure* justified by the principle of empiricism. The selection of individual variables (length, angle and weight), to be systematically varied one at a time, was never introduced or discussed as an explicit principle but, rather, was from the beginning the planned activity of the lesson – the pupils divided into three pairs, each with its own pendulum and variable to measure. As we saw earlier, in the section on the selection of hypotheses, the teacher chose early in lesson 1 to elicit three single-variable hypotheses from successive pairs of pupils. The isolation of single variables for examination was introduced, therefore, not as an explicit scientific principle, but implicitly and arbitrarily through the discursive device of turn-taking dialogue, itself oriented to the organization of the lesson in terms of its physical props and behavioural activity. It was during this selection of hypotheses, when the thickness of the string was being discussed (following sequence 6.7 above), that the teacher came closest to providing a principled justification. Lucy suggested that Sharon might try altering both the weight of the bob and also the thickness of the string. The teacher replied: 'She could try doing both but perhaps she might get a more accurate result if she just changes one thing', and then immediately moved on to the elicitation of the variable 'angle' (sequence 6.6). The explanations offered by the four pupils are therefore consistent with the ways in which the principle of the control of variables was dealt with during the lesson – a matter of practical convenience, ease of execution, accuracy of measurement, and even, as we noted earlier with David's response, a practical consequence of how the lesson happened to be organized. Their understanding of the rationale for altering variables singly was therefore, as far as we can ascertain, procedural, ritual rather than principled, and was made so in the lesson itself.

Measurement and accuracy

One of the scientific principles which the teacher particularly wanted the pupils to come to appreciate was the importance of making accurate measurements. This was linked in the lessons directly to the principle of scientific empiricism. Part of the dialogue omitted from sequence 6.8 above, where the teacher and pupils overtly expressed the principle of empiricism, was the teacher's instruction, 'We've got to remember then that we've got to be very accurate and know how to use our stop watch'. The principle had been implicitly invoked earlier when the pupils were learning how to use the stop watches. Lucy read off the answer 'nearly ten', which proved unacceptably vague; the teacher replied: 'Nearly ten? Right shall we do that one again 'cause it doesn't sound as if we were doing it very scientific that time.'

One feature of this value placed on the importance of precise measurement was the insistence on doing properly controlled tests and measurements even when differences were very obvious to casual observation. We saw this principle at work in sequence 6.4, when, early in lesson 1, David and Jonathan made quick preliminary demonstrations of how shortened strings would produce faster swings. Sequence 6.11 is taken from the second of the three lessons, when the teacher was recapping the findings of lesson 1, and demonstrated with Jonathan's help how an obviously shortened string produced an obviously faster swing.

Sequence 6.11　Making accurate measurements

T: . . . Shall I start from here and you start from there. Let's see if that is in fact true that/ the shorter pendulum goes faster than my longer one. We ought to be able to see it oughtn't we?

T and Jonathan hold their respective pendulum bobs out ready.

T and Jonathan release bobs. Jonathan's one has a shorter string and swings obviously faster.

PUPILS: Yes.

JONATHAN: Yes it is yes.

T: You reckon it is. The way to find out for sure is to time it again/ and that's something we could do. Right.

The principles emphasized by the teacher, of empiricism and accuracy of measurement, were readily appreciated and adopted by the pupils. The principle of controlling variables and its importance in explaining results was, as we have seen, never explained, but rather invoked as a sub-principle which could itself be justified by reference to the primary notions of empricism and accuracy of measurement. What the two emphasized principles have in common that the other does not is that they are essentially oriented towards procedures rather than conceptual understanding or explanation. Empiricism and accuracy are principles which closely govern the practical activities of the lesson. It is possible, therefore, to discern in these lessons an overriding concern on the part of the teacher with the practicalities of joint action, with getting things done properly, making sure that the pupils know what to do and how to do it, rather than with the pupils' conceptual understanding of how science explains things and how pendulums work. However, even empiricism and accuracy were not absolutes. They were subject to a higher constraint, and were sometimes suspended or overridden. This higher constraint was not a scientific principle but a pedagogic one – that the teacher was in control of the proceedings, knew in advance what the findings ought to be, and, without having to explain the basis for doing so, was able to introduce rules of thumb whereby empiricism and strict accuracy could be suspended. We shall examine some instances.

Much time was spent ensuring that procedures and measurements were done properly and accurately. The teacher spent at least as much time on these matters as on the business of performing the experiments themselves. She took pains to ensure that the pupils learned or demonstrated how to operate their stop watches and knew how to measure the swing of a pendulum accurately, that they could calibrate the pendulums to measure angles, that they took accurate timings and entered them clearly as numbers in prepared matrices. But despite the general insistence on precision and accuracy, communicated explicitly to the pupils, there were notable occasions when strict accuracy was not required. These were the occasions on which different measurements were to be read as equivalent, while on other occasions differences in measurements were taken to be significant. Sequence 6.12 lists some cases where different measurements were treated as equivalent.

Sequence 6.12   Treating differences as unimportant

Teacher and pupils are in the preliminary stages of establishing how to measure pendulum swings. A first reading has previously been recorded as 9.73 seconds.

T: What did you get?   *To Karen.*

KAREN: I got ten seconds.

T: Well that's near enough isn't it? Nine seventy three is near enough to ten. Now/ what will we do? Will we round it off to ten?

T writes '10 seconds'.

PUPILS: Mm/ yeh.

T: OK? So that makes ten seconds.

.

.

.

Further swings and timings are obtained, from Antony 10.12 seconds, and 8.5 from both Karen and Lucy.

T: Yes it is. Eight point five the same. Right. So it looks as if/ if we round off the two eight point fives and take into account the ten point twelve/ ten point one two./

T writes '8.5'.
Voice louder and slower.

ANTONY: ⌈ Nine.

SHARON: ⌊ Nine.

T: We're going to call it nine./ Right/

T nods at Antony and Sharon.
T is now checking that the group can calculate the average of five swings.

.

.

.

T's speech slow and loud.

T: One point six five/ So it's not very far away from two which was David's/ and from Jonathan's. What/ what conclusion do you come to? How far away from two is one point six five?

DAVID: Four ⌈ four

T: ⌊ Point what of a second?

T ignores David (presumably requires different answer).

DAVID: Four.

ANTONY: Three five.

T: Point three five of a second. Do you think it's worth worrying about point three five of a second?

T starts to shake head.
All shaking heads.

PUPILS: No ⌈ no.

T: ⌊ It's not really is it? So what conclusion have you come to?

ANTONY: They're all the ⌈ same.

T: ⌊ They're all the same.
That whatever way/ er/ whatever you do/ that they still come to the same.

In any sort of scientific measurement, it is common, and generally necessary, to recognize that small measured differences sometimes have to be ignored, being within the range of error of the measurement procedures, or matters of random fluctuation, or whatever. What concerns us here is not that different measures were taken as equivalent, but the manner in which this was done, and the grounds on which the pupils came to accept and understand it. Sequence 6.12 contains the first three occasions on which the teacher suggested that differences be discounted. Notably absent was any explanation or rationale for the procedure. The teacher established the understanding that the scores were to be rounded off, that they were 'near enough' and 'not worth worrying about', and the pupils appeared to adopt the idea, being prompted and cued (by some well-timed head shaking, for instance) to describe the different measures as equivalent. But what had they learned? Did they understand the rational basis for such manœuvres? Our interviews with the pupils suggested that some of them at least understood that small differences were to be expected as inevitable errors of measurement – 'It's difficult to get it exact/ exactly on with a stop watch', as Jonathan explained – but none of them was able to explain why some small differences should be discounted while others should not. However, the interviews were part of our research, not part of the pupils' education. What really matters is the extent to which such understandings were created or fostered in the lessons.

Arguably, despite the absence of explanation by the teacher, the pupils might have been able to infer the principles from the numbers themselves. For example, it could be the case that those differences which were taken as unimportant were obviously much smaller than those which were taken as important, and that the pupils may have been able to work this out for themselves. We can examine that possibility in terms of the classroom discourse.

It makes no sense to deal with absolute scores, since a difference of, say, 2.5 is clearly more significant for the numbers 3.2 and 5.7 than for the numbers 83.2 and 85.7. We shall therefore consider the differences as proportions of the numbers concerned. If we take the difference between scores from sequence 6.12 as proportions of the larger of the actual scores measured, we obtain these figures:

$$10.0 - 9.73 = 0.27 \text{ as a proportion of } 10$$
$$10.12 - 8.5 = 1.62 \text{ as a proportion of } 10.12$$
$$2.0 - 1.65 = 0.35 \text{ as a proportion of } 2$$

The first of these proportions is one thirty-seventh. The second and third are roughly one-sixth. Are these differences inherently small enough to be ignored? The question is not yet sensible – we would need to take account of the likely margins of error in our apparatus and procedures.

The inferential task required of our pupils is clearly considerable. But what of the scores that were not treated as equivalent – were those of an obviously different order? The clearest case occurred when Antony and David measured the effects of variations in the pendulum's length of string. This was, of course, as the teacher knew in advance, the one variable that should, according to textbook physics, produce significant differences in the pendulum's period of swing. Their first two measures were 1.41 and 1.78, with a difference of 0.37, which is about one-fifth of 1.78. This was accepted without question by pupils and teacher as a significant difference. It would, of course, have been larger or smaller given a greater or lesser alteration of the string's length. Nobody suggested or raised the issue of rounding off or taking the scores as equivalent. Although a proportional difference of one-fifth is a bit larger than one of one-sixth, these are hardly, we would argue, the sort of figures on which the pupils could be expected to understand why some scores should be treated as equivalent while others were taken as absolute.

Given that certain measured differences were taken to be insignificant, and that the grounds for so doing were not made clear, we may ask how the pupils came to accept such judgements as proper, and how far they appeared to understand the reasons for what they were agreeing to. The variables altered by the other two pairs of pupils, angle (Karen and Sharon) and weight (Lucy and Jonathan), were the ones which the teacher expected to have no effect on the pendulums' period of swing. Sequence 6.13 is the part of the lesson where teacher and pupils looked at the results of the experiment that varied weight.

Sequence 6.13   Equivalence of different measures: weight

LUCY: Ten point/ ten point two.

Lucy reading time from stop watch.

T: Ten point two seconds. How does that compare with the others?

Jonathan writes '10.2' into the matrix.

JONATHAN: Different.

LUCY: Different.

//Pause. No response from T.

JONATHAN: A little bit different/ it's about average.

Jonathan waves his hand from side to side, gesturing balance.

T: Is it just points of a second?

T gets up and looks at Jonathan's and Lucy's data matrix.

JONATHAN: It could be that we're not quite accurate.

Jonathan nodding.

T: What/ 'cause the answer to this one is two isn't it? So how is it working out do you think? Do you think it's

T pointing at matrix scores.

making a difference the fact that you
are ⎡ holding it up higher?
LUCY: ⎣ Not really.

Quietly, shaking head.
Jonathan looking at Lucy.

JONATHAN: No/ it isn't.
T: It's not is it?

The immediate reaction of both Jonathan and Lucy was to declare their new score 'different' from the others obtained previously with different weights. The teacher made no response. As we noted in chapter 4, silences which occur as the feedback part of IRF sequences may be read as equivalent to repeated questions, signalling that the previous answer was incorrect, that the teacher's question remains 'on the table'. Jonathan modified his reply to 'a little bit different'. The teacher then took up the notion that the measured differences were very small, and both pupils eventually declared that they had found no real differences at all. They had, of course, already been made familiar (see sequence 6.12 above) with the notion that measured differences should sometimes be treated as equivalent. But, again, we have little evidence here that the pupils were doing anything other than going along with what the teacher apparently wanted them to say. Certainly the general principle that weight has no effect on period of swing was not yet clear to them; asked subsequently by the teacher, 'What do you think you should do now?', Jonathan's reply was 'Try a much heavier weight'.

In sequence 6.14, Sharon and Karen have been measuring variations in the angle of swing.

Sequence 6.14   Equivalence of different measures: angle

T: What are you finding? Any results at
  all Sharon?
SHARON: One point seven two three/
  one point seven two two/ one point
  seven five six.
KAREN: We had to/ we had to do three
  digits after the point because
  otherwise ⎡ it would have been the
  same.   ⎢
T: ⎣ Otherwise it wasn't/ you
  weren't getting a result.
KAREN: That one would be ⎡ the same.
T: ⎣ But if you
  took it just to the first digit/ to the
  tenths.

KAREN: All be the same.

(The actual scores were 1.723, 1.722, 1.756.)

T: They would all be the same. If you took it to the second/ hundredths?

KAREN: Those two would be the same.

Karen pointing to written scores.

T: Those two would be the same. So what are you concluding so far what do you think is happening?

SHARON: They're all really the same.

T: They're all/ so you're getting the same results roughly aren't you? Only/ points/ only thousandths of a second out. Did you think that was going to happen?

SHARON: ⌈ No.
KAREN: ⌊ No.

Sharon and Karen both laugh.

T: I wonder if it will happen when you get to the top?

T points to highest angle mark on top of pendulum; Karen and Sharon have not done the fourth and last trial yet.

SHARON: I should think it probably will but on the top it's going to be much more different.

Sharon holding head in both hands.

KAREN: I think the top one will be the same as that one because those two are roughly the same.

Karen looking at matrix scores.

Again, the pupils appear at first to be disposed to treat their results as significant. Karen points out that they took their calculation of average timings to three decimal places precisely in order to show that the scores were different. Soon, however, they realize that what they have found is a set of figures of the sort that the teacher has been defining as 'really the same'. But, as with Lucy and Jonathan, Sharon at least has not yet grasped the general principle that angle does not affect period of swing. It appears that these pupils have acquiesced with some judgements made by the teacher, on no basis that is ever explained to them, and according to no criterion evident in our data. The pupils therefore were offered no rational basis on which to judge measured differences as real or insignificant, and lacked also what may well have been the teacher's grounds for making such judgements – she knew in advance which scores *ought* to be different, and which should be 'the same'.

Learning from experience, and the power of discourse

Our analysis of the issue of how different findings came to be agreed as equivalent has been detailed and painstaking. This is because an important issue is at stake. The analysis calls into question the notion that the pupils were engaged in any simple process of learning by experience, finding things out for themselves, forming their own concepts through practical activity and observation. In fact, their conceptions of the nature and meaning of their discoveries were strongly governed by interpretations offered them by the teacher through a variety of communicative devices ranging from gestures and silences to the uses of implication and verbal descriptions which imposed particular interpretations upon their experience. The pupils were quite capable of contradicting the experiential evidence of simple demonstrations, as we saw in sequence 6.4, when apparently driven along by a dialogue with the teacher in which her requirement that a succession of alternative hypotheses be offered seemed to override what the pupils themselves could see and think.

In her excellent study *The Pupil as Scientist?* Rosalind Driver (1983, p. 67) notes that 'One of the difficulties with younger adolescent pupils is to help them to distinguish between these two aspects: the empirical data and the explanation.' Our examination of how the concepts of scientific empiricism, and of accurate observation and measurement, were handled in our lessons with younger children suggests that this is a difficulty which is, in part at least, attributable to the ways in which common knowledge is created through teacher–pupil discourse, rather than to any inherent cognitive confusion in the heads of the pupils. Driver suggests that the problem arises from teachers' adherence to a false view of science as empiricist and inductive, the view that underlies the heuristic, learning-through-experience approach that is popular in secondary science teaching. The solution that she offers is to replace that model of science with one based on a constructivist, hypothetico-deductivist view, which emphasizes the importance of hypothesis testing, focused observation, the testing of prior expectations, and so on. But although these matters – hypothesis testing, and so on – were overt in the aims and practices of the pendulum lessons that we have examined here, we are still faced with the same problems of the relationship between experience and interpretation, and especially between those of the pupils and those of the teacher, that Driver encountered.

While Driver cites examples of classroom discourse as evidence of how pupils think – the ways in which they entertain idiosyncratic hypotheses, expectations and inferences, for example – our own emphasis has been on the importance of teacher–pupil dialogue for the development of joint understandings. As Walkerdine (1982, p. 153) notes: 'Children do not have raw experiences of concrete objects: meaning is created at the intersection of the material and the discursive . . . located in, and under-stood in terms of, actual social practices, represented in speech as discourse.' The importance of teacher–pupil discourse is recognized by Driver, though mainly negatively in terms of its omissions:

> It is common to see science lessons which end with the clearing up after the practical work is finished. The time for the important discussion of how the important experiences gained relate to the new ideas is missed. Activity by itself is not enough. It is the sense that is made of it that matters. (Driver 1983, p. 49)

Our observations agree with those of Driver, though we would stress that it is largely within the teacher–pupil discourse through which the lesson is conducted that whatever understandings are eventually created are in the first place shaped, interpreted, made salient or peripheral, reinter-preted, and so on. And it is a process that remains essentially dominated by the teacher's own aims and expectations – a view that we shall substantiate in chapter 7.

Driver is well aware of the teacher's dilemma, the problem of reconcil-ing experiential, pupil-centred learning with the requirement that pupils rediscover what they are supposed to:

> Secondary school pupils are quick to recognize the rules of the game when they ask 'Is this what was supposed to happen?' or 'Have I got the right answer?' The intellectual dishonesty of the approach derives from expecting two outcomes from pupils' laboratory activities which are possibly incompatible. On the one hand pupils are expected to explore a phenomenon for themselves, collect data and make inferences based on it; on the other hand this process is intended to lead to the currently accepted law or principle. (Driver 1983, p. 3).

The teacher's solution to this dilemma is to resort to less overt means of maintaining discursive control over the establishment of common under-standings. Again, we shall be examining these in the next chapter. What concern us here are the consequences of this dilemma, and its various solutions, for the pupils' understandings of the principles that the lesson, or the curriculum in general, was designed to teach. The teacher's dilemma is to have to inculcate knowledge while apparently eliciting it. This gives rise to a general ground-rule of classroom discourse, in which the pupils' task is to come up with the correct solutions to problems seemingly spontaneously, while all the time trying to discern in the teacher's clues, cues, questions and presuppositions what that required solution actually is. Ritual knowledge is a measure of both the success and the failure of this ground-rule; pupils succeed in the sense that they can say or do the right things, but fail in the manner so insightfully analysed by John Holt (1969), in having acquired a procedural, 'right-answer'-

oriented competence instead of a principled, explanation-oriented one. In the next chapter we shall examine the various discursive devices through which such understandings were established in our recorded lessons.

7
Communication and control

In the last chapter we looked at some ways in which ritual or procedure-oriented understandings, rather than principled ones, may be fostered by certain sorts of classroom communications. Our examination of those communications was organized in terms of the principles of scientific experimentation that were at stake in the lessons, rather than in terms of the communicative processes that could be identified. We shall now examine the same sorts of phenomena, but this time concentrating on the sorts of communications that are involved. We shall be looking at how certain sorts of communication may foster or hinder the development of common knowledge in the classroom.

Although our focus of attention is switching from the content of knowledge to the processes of communication, we remain concerned with knowledge rather than with thought processes – with what people say and talk about rather than with their capacity for rational argument, for example. Similarly, we are not concerned with patterns of communication or structures of discourse for their own sake – with the range and types of non-verbal signals, for example, or the patterning of IRF-structures in classroom talk (discussed in chapter 2). Our central issue is how teachers and pupils establish shared understandings of curriculum content, so that our examination of various sorts of classroom communication is oriented to the ways in which information, arguments, ideas or analyses are expressed. So, when we discussed in the last chapter some spontaneous contributions offered by the pupils, these were occasions on which pupils offered their own ideas or explanations, rather than simply occasions when pupils took a turn at speaking without being invited. The same concern with the content of shared knowledge will constrain what we investigate here.

Our account in chapter 4 of the ground-rules of joint understanding pointed to the importance of the form and content of spoken and written discourse in signalling the proper occasions on which particular sorts of understandings should operate. The ground-rules of educational practice and mutual understanding generally rely on the ability of participants to recognize that some sorts of communication – the use of particular words or types of questions in recognized contexts – mark the appropriateness of particular related cognitive strategies. Recognizing disembedded questions, pseudo-narrative mathematical problems, test questions in IRF sequences, and so on, depends primarily on familiarity with the ways in which educational discourse functions to embody, question and test educational knowledge. Since our data are principally transcripts of classroom dialogue, we shall inevitably be looking for these processes in spoken classroom communications. It is our purpose in this chapter to examine how particular sorts of classroom discourse carry classroom knowledge. Our first impression of the lessons was that they were relatively informal, progressive, child-centred sorts of pedagogy of the type advocated by the Plowden Report (see chapter 3). It is an unforeseen consequence of examining the data more closely that we are in fact largely concerned here with control processes, that is, with ways in which the teacher maintained a tight definition of what became joint versions of events, and joint understandings of curriculum content.

The process of creating joint understandings in the classroom is a problematical one, as we have seen. There appear to be a set of properties and constraints under which the educational process works, which are not always harmonious, and which make the process problematical. These include:

1 the assumption on the part of teachers that educational failure in individual pupils can be attributed to individual factors, and principally to innate ability;
2 a philosophy of education which assumes a self-actualizing process of inductive and experiental learning through practical activity;
3 the socializing function of education, in which the teacher exercises a large degree of control over what is done, said and understood;
4 the separation of formal education from the contexts of everyday, out-of-school experience and learning;
5 the largely implicit basis of much classroom activity and discourse.

The notions of 'scaffolding' (Bruner) and of the 'zone of proximal development' (Vygotsky) appear to be appropriate to the description of classroom education, but are often compromised by the somewhat inconsistent nature of these listed properties. While teachers engage in a great deal of skilled tuition, prompting and helping children to develop their understanding of curriculum topics, their own conceptions of what they are doing may be at odds with such a process. Success and failure are conceived largely in terms of inherent properties of pupils rather than as outcomes of the communicative process of education itself, and understandings on the part of pupils are seen as essentially inductive insights that the pupils themselves must achieve on the basis of their own experiences. The fact that a particular syllabus has to be taught, or, at least, that a planned set of concepts and activities has to be covered, leads to the sort of 'teacher's dilemma' that we discussed at the end of the last chapter: how to get the pupils to learn for themselves what has been planned for them in advance.

We shall argue that these dilemmas and compromises can have a destructive effect on the effectiveness of education, by spoiling the essential purpose of the Vygotskyan process: that is, the process often remains incomplete, with no final *handover* of knowledge and control to the pupils. The pupils frequently remain embedded in rituals and procedures, having failed to grasp the overall purpose of what they have done, including the general concepts and principles that a particular lesson's activities was designed to inculcate.

In looking for some way of organizing our treatment of these communicative processes, we have chosen what appears to be a central theme of classroom talk, the extent of teacher control over both the discourse and, through that, the content of knowledge. The following list of classroom communications is presented as a scale of teacher control of the nature, content and coding of knowledge, with the extent of control increasing as we descend the list. It is not an exhaustive list, and the qualitative nature of its contents precludes any precise notion of hierarchy or order. Nevertheless, it is useful in that it helps us to define the sorts of phenomena that we shall be dealing with, and their role in the establishment of shared understandings. We shall argue that it is essentially through the pervasive phenomena of teacher control over the expression of knowledge that pupils' understandings of things are frequently created as procedural rather than principled – saying and doing what seems to be required, rather than working out a principled understanding of how and why certain actions, expressions and procedures are appropriate or correct.

The following list of features of classroom discourse is cast in terms of the teacher's role in them.

Elicitation of pupils' contributions
Significance markers, e.g. special enunciation
                                          formulaic phrases
                                          ignoring pupils' contributions
Joint-knowledge markers, e.g. simultaneous speech
                                          'royal' plurals
                                          repeated discourse formats
    Cued elicitation of pupils' contributions
    Paraphrastic interpretations of pupils' contributions
    Reconstructive recaps
    Implicit and presupposed knowledge

The following sections of this chapter will deal with each of these phenomena in turn, roughly in the order listed. Omitted from the list, at the top and bottom, are non-elicited contributions by pupils (which we shall discuss below in the context of elicited ones), and direct lecturing-style tuition by teachers, in which little or no contribution was asked of or offered by pupils. In the pendulums lessons this sort of direct teaching was minimal. The discourse was mostly interactive, based more on IRF sorts of dialogue, with direct teaching limited to occasional explanations or definitions of words ('this is called the bob', holding it up for the pupils to see), or the recounting of stories of relevance to the lesson (of Galileo's observations of the swinging of incense burners in church, and of the raising of the *Mary Rose*). While these sorts of teaching are interesting in their own right, and indeed make important 'common knowledge' assumptions about shared experience and the sorts of things that will interest and inform the pupils, we shall concentrate here on the more overtly interactive sorts of classroom discourse.

Spontaneous and elicited contributions

The *spontaneous contributions* offered by the pupils were by definition those communications least influenced by teacher control. But they were not devoid of it. It was the teacher who had set the agenda, defined the topic of discussion, and established in advance the criteria of relevance and appropriateness of any contributions that the pupils might offer. And the teacher generally remained in control of the ultimate fate of any such contributions – of whether they were acted on, taken up and incorporated into the development of ideas in further classroom discourse, or whether they were discouraged, disapproved or ignored. Apart from those considerations, it may well also have been from some other lesson (as we emphasized in our discussion of 'continuity' in chapter 5) that the thoughts expressed had ultimately derived. We examined some spontaneous contributions in the last chapter, where it was clear that the teacher remained in control of their fate; she was able to ignore and discourage any development of the idea of compensatory mechanisms at work in the motion of pendulums, to define the variation of string substance as peripheral and inconclusive, and generally provided the detailed framework of activity and discourse within which any such pupil contributions were made.

Let us begin, then, with a definition of pupils' spontaneous contributions. These were occasions when pupils offered, without explicit invitation from the teacher, information, suggestions or analyses of the curriculum subject matter which had not, according to our observations and interviews, been taught or demonstrated by the teacher. So we would include here Jonathan's observation about the action of snooker balls, and David's suggestion of a compensatory relationship between velocity and distance (sequences 6.1 and 6.2). However, most contributions to classroom discourse offered by the pupils were, as other research has abundantly demonstrated (e.g. Galton, Simon and Croll 1980; see chapter 2), made by invitation from the teacher. *Elicited contributions* were those that fell into the familiar and pervasive IRF structure, where pupils' contributions were directly constrained by teachers' questions, and by the normal requirements on any answer to a question – that it should be relevant, appropriate, informative, and so on (Grice 1975).

The importance of IRFs in the establishment of joint understanding lies in the way in which they express the complementarity of teacher's and pupil's knowledge. As we saw in chapter 4, teachers' questions are of a special sort, in that they do not carry the usual presupposition that the speaker does not know the answer to the question asked. In chapter 5 we showed how they function as discursive devices through which the teacher is able to keep a continual check on the pupils' understandings, to ensure that various concepts, information or terms of reference are jointly understood, so that subsequent discourse may be predicated on a developing continuity and context of intersubjectivity. IRF structures also function in defining and controlling what that knowledge and understanding will be. They are part of a set of communicative devices whereby the teacher acts as a kind of filter or gateway through which all knowledge must pass in order to be included in the lesson as a valid or useful contribution. This is particularly noticeable in instances of what may be called 'retrospective elicitation', where the teacher invites a pupil's response after it has already been made (sequence 7.1).

Sequence 7.1   Retrospective elicitations

T: . . . Right any problems so far any
   questions you want to ask any ideas./   *Sharon shaking her head.*

SHARON: I think me [and Karen are   *Sharon points to top of*
   going to (&)   *pendulum.*
T: [What do you
   think Sharon?
SHARON: (&) do across the top.
T: You're going to measure across the
   top for your angle. Karen/ you reckon   *T turns to Karen.*
   that? All right . . .

Pendulum session 2:
T: . . . What is it/ that **makes** the
   pendulum **swing** in a downward
   direction/ for instance until it gets to   *Taps with pencil to mark 'there'*
   there?/   *at bottom of plinth.*
JONATHAN: [Gravity.   *Jonathan puts hand up as he*
                              speaks.
T: [Just watch it./ What is it
   Jonathan?
JONATHAN: Gravity.
T: Yes./ Now we mentioned gravity
   when we were actually doing the
   experiments but we didn't discuss it
   too much. OK so it's gravity then that
   pulls it down. What causes it to go up
   again at the other side?   *T lets bob swing.*
ANTONY: The string/ it forces up the
   string/ going down   *Level intonation: Antony not*
                              finished speaking yet.
T: It gets up speed going down./ Does   *Rising intonation on 'down': T*
   anyone know the word for it when   *prompting for more information.*
   you get up speed/ as in a car when
   you press the pedal? Does anyone
   know the word for it when you/
JONATHAN: Accelerate.
ANTONY: Momentum.
T: You get momentum/   *T points to Antony.*
   Jonathan?   *T points to Jonathan.*
JONATHAN: Accelerates.
T: It accelerates going down doesn't it?

The responses of Sharon and Jonathan in sequence 7.1 were invited or
reinvited by the teacher, to be repeated and made salient, marked out as
the required responses for everyone to hear. A particularly interesting
example of retrospective elicitation occurred as part of sequence 6.4,

where the teacher was eliciting hypotheses about the effect on period of swing of shortening the pendulum's string:

SHARON: It would be slower.
T: ⎡What do you reckon/ ⎡Sharon?
JONATHAN: ⎨Much faster.
SHARON: ⎣Slower./   ⎣Faster.
     I think it would be faster.

Sharon first offered the hypothesis 'It would be slower.' The teacher then retrospectively defined Sharon's contribution as welcome and proper, by explicitly inviting it. Sharon then vacillated and changed her mind. Two things may have influenced her. First, Jonathan was simultaneously suggesting that the pendulum bob would swing faster. Second, and at least as important, there may have been another ground-rule at work. Rather than making a retrospective invitation, the teacher may have been interpreted by Sharon as repeating the question, as asking the same question after having received an answer. As we noted in chapter 4, this is generally a signal that the first answer is wrong, and that an alternative answer is expected. What we have here is probably a conflict between two alternative discursive ground-rules. While the teacher sought to make a retrospective elicitation of Sharon's answer, Sharon herself read this as a repeated question and changed her mind.

     We saw also in chapter 6 the fate of less welcome responses. The teacher ignored, or simply failed to encourage or develop, several attempts to introduce ideas that were not part of the planned course of the lesson, such as the notion of reciprocal compensatory effects of velocity and angle of swing, and the suggestion that string substance might be a good variable to alter (sequences 6.1, 6.2 and 6.7); similarly, she showed a lack of interest in David and Antony's eventual insistence that they had measured a significant effect due to altering string substance (sequence 6.3). The teacher not only checked and predicated her remarks on joint understandings then, but also managed to keep a tight rein on the introduction and establishment of what was to count as significant shared knowledge. She controlled both prospectively and retrospectively the content of what was introduced, included, validated and made prominent. She was able to ignore or discourage pupils' contributions, to prompt or welcome them, to highlight some, and generally to control their order, nature and significance.

Marking knowledge as significant and joint

Apart from the pervasive phenomenon of inviting pupils' contributions, and of occasionally ignoring them, expressed knowledge was sometimes given special prominence by discursive devices such as special enunciation and the use of formulaic phrases. Shifts of intonation served pedagogic functions by highlighting important information, and marking other comments as 'asides', or as having different functions. Apart from the conventional use of devices such as pauses and rising intonation to mark the asking of questions, or of falling intonation to mark the confirmation of answers, shifts particularly in the rate and loudness of speech generally occurred at the boundaries of shifts of pedagogic significance, rather than merely of conversational function.

Sequence 7.2   Intonation and knowledge

(Note: relevant speech segments italicized.)

Pendulum lesson 1: T is establishing that the pupils know how to measure pendulum swings, and can calculate an average period of swing.

T: OK? So that makes ten seconds. So how much then is each swing roughly?	*T looks at Antony.*
ANTONY: Two seconds.	
T: Two seconds. Good. OK We'll write that down.	*T writes '2 seconds'.*
Everybody understood that bit?	*Spoken quickly.*
Now then. I wonder if this pendulum would also take the same time.	*T reaches for Jonathan's pendulum. T's intonation now slow, deliberate, in marked contrast to preceding speech.*

.
.
.

T: What did you get darling?	*T looks beyond Lucy to Karen.*
KAREN: Mine says eight and a half.	
T: Eight point five and a half. What did you get Lucy?	*T writes down '8.5'.*
LUCY: Er I think/ I think mine's eight and a half.	*Lucy showing T the watch.*
T: No. Yours is/ yes/ *yes it is actually I haven't got my glasses on. I can't see. Yes it is. Eight point five the same.*	*T speaking quickly and quietly. T writes '8.5'.*
Right. So it looks as if/ if we round off the two eight point fives and take into account the ten point twelve/ ten point one two/	*Voice louder and slower.*

.
.
.

JONATHAN: Five into eight goes one/
   and/

*Jonathan pauses, pen over
paper, frowning.*

T: Anybody help him?

JONATHAN: I think it's three isn't it?

In fact the sum is: $\dfrac{1.65}{5\overline{)8.250}}$

T: Three/ yeh/
JONATHAN: Fives into three/ is that it?
   Fives into three go
PUPIL: Fives into thirty goes six/
JONATHAN: Fives into thirty goes six.
   Fives into two goes/
   one point six five

Jonathan mumbles from here.

T: *One point six five/*
   So it's not very far away from two
   which was David's

T's speech slow and loud.

.

.

.

*T elicits suggestions for the total
number of swings from which an
average swing will be calculated;
see sequence 7.7.*

T: An even number/ makes it/ you
   reckon you can divide by six better
   than you can divide by five.//
   Will it make any difference to the
   accuracy/ *of what she's doing if she did a*
   larger/ *number of swings?*
   For instance if she decided that if it
   was/ erm/ five swings she was going
   to do/ right/ and then she divided by
   five/ but suppose she decided as
   you've just said on ten.
   Which one of those readings would
   be the more accurate?

T looking at Antony.

T laughs, then Sharon does.
*T speaking slowly and clearly,
with small pauses as indicated.*

*T writes '5' on sheet of paper on
table.*

T writes '10' next to '5'.
*T prods her pen back and forth
from '5' to '10'.*

.

.

.

Pendulum lesson 2: T is displaying results of pupils' experiments on an
   overhead projector.

T: . . . There/ bit hard to see but there
   you can see quite clearly/ that there is
   a definite difference and in **fact**/ *the
   only pendulum that changed was in fact
   the one where the string/ was/*

*T placing a transparency on to
overhead projector screen.*

Speaking slowly, with emphasis.

$$\left[\begin{array}{l}\text{shortened. That was/ and}\\ (\&)\end{array}\right.$$

ANTONY: shorter.

T: (&) you didn't expect that I don't   *T looks around group.*
suppose did you?

The italicized speech in sequence 7.2 is that to which the contextual comments about intonation apply. It is speech marked by intonation as having a special significance in relation to the rest of what is said. The choice of slow, deliberate enunciation, or of faster and quieter speech, was clearly determined by the content of what was said, and its pedagogic function. The important curriculum-oriented content was given prominence with careful, clear enunciation, while 'asides' about the teacher's vision, and the check on continuity of understanding, were marked by a drop in volume, and a sudden increase in rate of speech.

Another way in which the discourse reflected the pedagogic status of what was said was in the use of repeated *formulaic phrases*. These acted as memorable formulae through which certain observations and conclusions were given prominence, were repeated, and became established as expressions of shared understanding. They arose during the lessons out of teacher–pupil dialogue, sometimes initiated by the pupils, but were taken up and encouraged by the teacher as correct and appropriate things to say. Sequence 7.3 shows the development of a rhyming couplet, 'the shorter the string, the faster the swing', which came to serve as a mnemonic encapsulation of the lesson's main empirical finding.

Sequence 7.3   The string length formula

T: (. . .) point seven three. So the   *T looking with Antony at his*
shorter the string/ what? What   *matrix of recorded timings.*
happens when you shorten the
string?

ANTONY: The faster it gets.

T: The shorter the string the faster the   *T raising head and voice in slow,*
swing. Right. That's good isn't it?   *formal enunciation of the*
                                              principle.

Ask Jonathan how he went/ with his.   *T pointing towards Jonathan*
                                              (off camera).

.
.
.

SHARON: God I don't understand
really. They're all/
different ⌈

T: ⌊ They're all different. So
theirs is the only pendulum that's/
makes a ⌈ difference.
DAVID: ⌊ It's just the string really.

T: So you don't think that it's the
pendulum.

DAVID: It's just the string.

T: It's the length of the ⌈ string mm (&)
DAVID: ⌊ length of the
string.

T: (&) so that's **very** ⌈ interesting isn't it?
LUCY: ⌊ Say if the string's/
erm/ shorter it'll go faster.

T: Yes.

DAVID: Yeh.

T: We made up a little rhyme didn't we.
What did we say?// The shorter

DAVID: The
shorter ⌈ the string the faster
the swing.

ANTONY AND T: ⌊ the string the faster
the swing.

Sharon looking at David and
Antony's matrix, speaking
quietly.

David gestures a swing.
T nodding. (Did David mean
length?)

T, Antony and David recite it
together.

The string length formula was essentially invented by the teacher, as an encapsulation of the principle established in the first instance in two parts – that is, the teacher's question and Antony's answer. Later the rhyme was recalled and recited jointly, as something that 'we made up'. The reading that the teacher was putting on these events was one of joint inductive learning; 'we' had made our observations, had drawn the proper conclusions, and had jointly invented a verbal formula in terms of which it could be expressed and remembered. In a similar fashion, Sharon and Karen came repeatedly to describe their results, the effects of varying angle of swing, as 'just the same', or 'it all comes out the same'. Again, as in sequence 7.3, the phrases came to be recited in unison, as jointly recognized formulae:

Sequence 7.4   The equivalence formula

T: And what about the times?

T moves finger along middle row
of matrix.

Matrix:

Time for 20	34.47	34.44	35.13	35.47
Time	1.723	1.722	1.756	1.733
Angle	40°	55°	70°	85°

KAREN: The times are all **roughly** the
  same.

T: Roughly the same aren't they?
  So

SHARON: And **these** are all roughly   *Sharon points to top row.*
  the same as well.

T: Yeh./ So what conclusion
  have you come to?

SHARON: It doesn't make

KAREN: It doesn't matter

T: doesn't make any   *T tries to talk simultaneously*
  difference whatever it still comes out   *with Sharon and Karen (to*
  the same.   *signal joint understanding?).*

Pendulum lesson 2: T is recapping on the findings of lesson 1.

T: **So** we can see then that your graph
  ended up almost as a/ what would
  you say Sharon?

SHARON: // It's just the same.   *T smiles at Sharon as Sharon*
        pauses looking at graph.

In the last segment of sequence 7.4, taken from lesson 2, the teacher
was trying to get the pupils to describe their graphs, and in this instance
very probably wanted Sharon to describe it as being almost a straight line
(which were indeed the words eventually adopted). However, Sharon
remembered from lesson 1 how to describe her results: they were 'all the
same'. It was not only the teacher who provided such phrases for all to
rehearse and recite, though, in the event of their being introduced by a
pupil, it was nevertheless the teacher who drew attention to them, cued
their repetition, and generally defined them as significant. In sequence
7.5, Lucy's suggestion that, in varying the weight of the pendulum's
bob, 'even a ton' would make no difference was taken up by the teacher,
repeated and encouraged, and later recalled as a memorable formulaic
phrase which encapsulated the essential empirical finding of the
experiments on varying weight.

Sequence 7.5   The 'even a ton' formula

JONATHAN: Eleven/ twelve/ thirteen/   *T with Jonathan and Lucy.*
  fourteen/ fifteen/ sixteen/ seventeen/   *Jonathan counting pendulum*
  eighteen/   *swings with increased weight on*

LUCY: ⌈ nineteen/ twenty.
⌊ I don't believe it. ⌈ Nine point
                          six again.
T: ⌊ You can't
believe it Lucy?

bob (large blob of plasticine).
Lucy stopping watch.

Lucy and T eye contact and both
laughing.

LUCY: I think even if we stuck a whole
ton on there it wouldn't make any
difference.

T: You think even if you stuck a ton on
    ⌈ it wouldn't make any difference
    | a ton? (&)
LUCY: ⌊ No/ no/ not even a ton.

T shaking head; everyone
smiling.

Lucy shaking head.

T: (&) it would still be about ten seconds
apart from it collapsing? (. . .) Is that
what you expected?
JONATHAN: Yeh.

T looks at Jonathan.

.
.
.

About fifteen minutes later;
Antony and Jonathan are
examining Jonathan's written
results.

JONATHAN: Two seconds for each
swing. Whatever we put on it even
that it ended up two seconds for each
swing.
ANTONY: With all of that?

Jonathan picks up and puts
down the blob of plasticine.

Antony picking up the
plasticine.

JONATHAN: Yeh still ended
    ⌈ up two seconds
LUCY: | Still ended up two
seconds. So even if you stuck a ton on
it it would still be two seconds.
JONATHAN: Any angle ⌈ you put on
(. . .) |

(Jonathan apparently varied
angle as well as weight; see
chapter 6 and below.)

T: ⌊ The angle
didn't make any difference either
Jonathan.// No.// Lucy reckoned that
if you/ What did you reckon Lucy?
JONATHAN: That even if you put a ton
on it wouldn't make any difference.

Jonathan silent, through two
pauses of 2 and 4 seconds.

Do these formulaic phrases have a pedagogic function, and, if so, what is it? They appear to operate as jointly understood encapsulations of the significant empirical findings that the pupils have been guided to dis- cover in the course of the activity and discourse of the lessons. Lucy's 'even a ton' phrase constitutes a powerful generalization, though not quite an expression of a general principle, concerning the effects on period of swing of varying the mass of the bob. The 'just the same' phrase similarly embodies the essential equivalence of the results derived from varying angle of swing. The rhyme 'the shorter the string, the faster the swing' is an explicit principle, capturing the one positive finding. As they are carefully guided in how to interpret and place significance on their experiences, the pupils are in the same process offered a common language through which these common understandings may be expressed.

The status of certain understandings, achieved in the lessons, as 'common knowledge' was often marked overtly in the discourse by the development and repetitive use of such formulaic phrases, together with other devices such as simultaneous speech (which we saw particularly in sequences 7.3 and 7.4), and in the teacher's use of 'we' when making claims for what had been done, said and understood, as when reminding Antony and David of the 'faster the swing' formula (sequence 7.3). These were not isolated cases. In sequence 6.12, when the teacher was en- couraging the pupils to see small differences as unimportant, the use of 'we' implied a joint understanding in which there was no difference between the teacher's intentions and interpretations, and those of the pupils: 'Well that's near enough isn't it? Nine seventy three is near enough to ten. Now/ what will we do? Will we round it off to ten?' And, in another instance, 'Well I only think we need it to hundredths don't we? Seven two three five what are we going to call it?' The shift from 'I' to the 'royal plural' (if we may borrow that term) was an overt expression of the teacher's communicative purpose to establish certain observations and interpretations as joint.

Speech in unison was similarly an overt marker of common knowledge, in which teacher and pupils rehearsed their common understanding through the simultaneous enunciation of common language. It is import- ant that we make a clear distinction between, on the one hand, simul- taneous speech in which people happen to be talking at the same time, perhaps interrupting or avoiding 'giving the floor' to an interrupter, and, on the other hand, speaking in unison, where people are jointly giving voice to the same words or meanings. It is remarkable in the sequences of dialogue that we have presented in chapters 6 and 7 (see, for example, sequences 6.12, 6.14, 7.2, 7.3, 7.4) how this second sort of simultaneous speech occurred at precisely those points where important issues of joint understanding were at stake; where the teacher was at pains to ensure, for example, that her own interpretations of 'equivalent measurements' should prevail (sequences 6.12, 6.14, 7.4), and that the major empirical finding, the 'shorter string, shorter swing' law, was understood (7.2, 7.3). Common knowledge is thus founded upon the establishment of the teacher's understandings as joint understandings, embodied in a common discourse – in this case, in a very simple and direct manner.

Cued elicitation

The process of cued elicitation was a pervasive one in our data transcripts. We encountered examples of it in our earlier discussion of the physical and gestural context of classroom discourse (chapter 5), and in our discussion of how the teacher elicited from the pupils the various hypotheses for testing in the pendulum experiments (chapter 6, e.g. sequence 6.6). Cued elicitations are IRF types of discourse in which the teacher asks questions while simultaneously providing heavy clues to the information required. This simultaneous provision of information may be achieved merely by the wording of the question, but is often accomplished via some other communicative channel such as intonation, pausing, gestures or physical demonstrations. It may also be done implicitly, by an unspoken appeal to shared knowledge. Sequence 7.6 is a clear example.

Sequence 7.6   Cued elicitation: Galileo's pulse

T: Now he didn't have a watch/ but he
had on **him** something that was a
very good timekeeper that he could
use to hand straight away/

> *T snaps fingers on 'straight away', and looks invitingly at pupils as if posing a question or inviting a response.*

You've got it. **I**'ve got it. What is it?//
What could we use to count beats?
What have **you** got? //

> *T points on 'You've' and 'I've'. T beats hand on table slowly, looks around group of pupils, who smile and shrug.*

You can feel it **here**.

> *T puts fingers on T's wrist pulse.*

PUPILS: Pulse.

> *(In near unison.)*

T: A pulse. Everybody see if you can find it.

> *All copy T, feeling for wrist pulses.*

Cued elicitation is an important process for at least two reasons:

1 It demonstrates a general point of method and theory – that, if we are going to make proper sense of the process of classroom education, then

we need careful records of gesture and activity as well as detailed transcripts of classroom discourse, that these need to be closely integrated, and that we do not make the error of trying to account for educational processes solely in terms of classroom talk and discourse structures.

2 It is a communicative process of substantial intrinsic interest. Classroom questions and answers have peculiar characteristics, as we noted in chapter 4; the teacher, who knows the answers, asks most of the questions, asks questions to which she already knows the answers, and, additionally, it appears, may ask questions while simultaneously doing her best to provide the answers via an alternative channel. We have to seek an understanding of the pedagogic function of this sort of thing.

The best interpretation that we can make of the pedagogic function of cued elicitation is that it embodies an educational process in which the pupils are neither being drawn out of themselves, in the *e-ducare* sense, nor simply being taught directly, in the 'transmission' sense. Rather, they are being inculcated into what becomes for them a shared discourse with the teacher (discourse in the broadest sense, including concepts and terminology as well as dialogue). As such, it falls neatly into the sort of educational process defined by Vygotsky's 'zone of proximal development', in which pupils' knowledge is aided and 'scaffolded' by the teacher's questions, clues and prompts to achieve insights that the pupils by themselves seemed incapable of. It is a device which requires that the pupils actively participate in the creation of shared knowledge, rather than merely sit and listen to the teacher talking. Cued elicitation is also a process which constitutes a solution to what we have called the *teacher's dilemma* – a necessary compromise between two conflicting requirements that the lesson had to achieve. These requirements were that the pupils should (apparently, at least) generate their own understandings of things through their own thought and experience, and that they should come to do and to understand specific activities and concepts planned at the outset – to test three specified hypotheses, to find that only one of the variables was effective, to calculate average times over twenty swings, and to make matrices and draw graphs of the results. This is, of course, the conflict noted by Rosalind Driver (1983) in her discussion of the limitations of inductive science teaching, which we discussed in chapter 6. Sequence 7.7 shows how the teacher managed to get the pupils to agree to perform the pre-planned twenty swings.

Sequence 7.7   Eliciting twenty swings

T: Right/ now how many swings will she   *T referring to Sharon.*
   have to do do you think// before she

can work out for instance suppose
she starts from here and she counts
the swings and divides OK. Now
we did five. Do you think that's a
good number to do and divide
by?

T holding Jonathan's pendulum
bob out at an angle.

LUCY AND KAREN: Yes.

Both nodding.

JONATHAN: Yeh.

DAVID: Yeh.

(Pause of 3 seconds.)

T: I don't know. ⌈ Why

DAVID: ⌊ Ten Miss./ Ten.

David shouts to interrupt T.

ANTONY: Six/ an even number six.

T: An even number/ makes it/ you
reckon you can divide by six better
than you can divide by five.//
Will it make any difference to the
accuracy/ of what she's doing if she
did a **larger**/ number of swings?
For instance if she decided that if it
was/ erm/ five swings she was going
to do/ right/ and then she divided by
five/ but suppose she decided as
you've just said on ten. Which one of
those readings would be the more
accurate?

T looking at Antony.

T laughs, then Sharon does.
T speaking slowly and clearly,
with small pauses as indicated.

T writes '5' on sheet of paper on
table.

T writes '10' next to '5'.
T prods her pen back and forth from
'5' to '10'. Pupils watch the pen.

ANTONY: Five.

Antony points to the '5'.
(Pause of 3 seconds.)

ANTONY: ⌈Ten.

DAVID: ⌊Ten.

T: Why?

ANTONY: Because it cuts it down more.

Antony gestures with two hands
held out, horizontal, flat,
pointing towards T.

T: Good boy. It cuts down/ what we call
the margin of error doesn't it. It
makes the error that much smaller. I
think we could cut it down even
smaller than ten.

ANTONY: Twenty.

T: Make the error

T continuing.

ANTONY: Hundred.

DAVID: ⌈Sixteen.

T: ⌊Counting a hundred swings

Antony we'd be here till the
Christmas [holidays.   *Antony smiles.*
DAVID: [Sixteen.
SHARON: [Fifteen.
T: [Let's make it an easier
    number to [work with
ANTONY: [Twenty. Twenty.
T: What do you reckon on twenty?
SHARON: [Yeh.
OTHERS: [Yeh.
T: That would be all right wouldn't it?
    So if we **all** use twenty/ so we'll do   *T writes down '20'.*
    twenty swings/ get the time/ divide by
    twenty and we can use the calculator/   *T picks up and shows calculator*
    then we should get the time pretty   *to pupils.*
    accurately/ possibly in hundredths of
    seconds. OK?   *T looking round, pupils' faces*
                                                   turned down, eyes downcast
                                                   (confused?).

Lucy, Karen, Jonathan and David appeared in the first instance to be
ready and willing to accept five swings as a good number to use. Through
a series of pauses and prompts, they eventually hit upon the required
number – 'twenty' – justified by the teacher in terms of some undefined
concept called 'the margin of error'. It is here that we can see plainly the
problematical nature of cued elicitation. It is difficult to avoid the impression that the pupils were essentially trying to read all the signals available
in a guessing game in which they had to work out, more by communicative skill than by the application of any known principle of measurement,
what it was that the teacher was trying to get them to say. There was no
indication that any of the pupils understood what was meant by the term
'margin of error', though Antony's suggestion 'because it cuts it down
more' looked a promising insight. In the end, the pupils had been guided
to accept twenty swings as a good number to use, but seemed (from their
averted gaze) unsure of the grounds for doing so. We asked them in the
interviews what they thought was the reason for doing twenty swings.
Only Jonathan seemed to grasp the importance of accuracy and error
reduction, though he made no use of the notion 'margin of error'. Sharon
replied:

Well/ because it's sort of not too fast/ not too slow and [the teacher] said
well/ we weren't sure what she wanted us to do. Well she said it would
probably be best to do what the others were doing/ twenty swings/ and
so we all done the same.

Sharon's answer was entirely procedural, and couched in terms of doing what the teacher wanted them to do. David's reply was equally procedural and lacking in principled understanding:

> Because that was one of the best to divide with. . . . I think it was five the first time we done it when we were over there and then we thought well if we done ten it's just not that far away from five so we did twenty. We were going to do fifteen at first but then we changed to twenty times.

David's reconstruction of the process by which they arrived at the number twenty is all in terms of what 'we' decided to do, in the form of a narrative reconstruction of the course taken by the dialogue at the time. The teacher's prompting role is not represented in his account, and neither is there any mention of the principle of reducing the margin of error. Lucy did invoke the term 'margin of error', though it is unclear whether she understood its meaning:

> 'cause you have less margin of error/ I think that was it and it's going to be more accurate really than if you just do five . . . 'cause you kind of get more chance to compare it/ kind of.

Again, the expression 'I think that was it' suggests an effort to remember the teacher's words, while again it is not clear what Lucy understood of the principle.

The important point is not which pupils understood the principle and which did not, but that the discourse and activity of the lesson did not promote such understanding. The danger of cued elicitation is that, until it is examined closely, it can give a false impression (presumably to the participants as well as to the observers) of the extent to which pupils understand, and are ultimately responsible for, what they are saying and doing. It can easily mask rather than bridge the gap between teacher and child that is the basis of Vygotsky's developmental process, and can lead therefore to the sorts of procedural, 'ritual' understandings that we identified in chapter 6.

Reconstructions, presuppositions and paraphrases

Moving down our scaled list of communicative processes, we come next to a set of discursive devices through which the teacher was able to maintain a strict control over the content of common knowledge. Through paraphrasing what the pupils said, and through reconstructing what occurred in the lesson when recapping later, she was able to redefine these things as altogether neater, nicer and closer to the intended lesson plan. Similarly, by presupposing certain things as known or understood, she was able to forestall disagreement, and shape the direction of the discourse and the interpretations put upon experience. Paraphrases were often seemingly small and accidental, as when, in pendulum lesson 2, Lucy appeared to misremember one of the timed scores obtained in lesson 1 when she and Jonathan had varied the weight of the pendulum bob:

Sequence 7.8   Paraphrasing Lucy

T: Now what about when you had **one**   *T points to the '1 washer'*
   washer. Can you remember what the   *position on graph.*
   time was there Lucy?
LUCY: Erm/ one point one four.
T: One point nine four?
LUCY: ⌈ Yes.
T: ⌊ That's right there it is.   *T pointing to where the number*
                                                 is plotted on the graph.

The teacher also used paraphrasing more directly as a teaching method, as in sequence 7.9, when she tried to elicit as much as possible of the explanation from the pupils, and then recast the explanation offered by Antony into a preferred (and, indeed, more precise) form:

Sequence 7.9   Paraphrasing Antony

Pendulum lesson 2: The teacher is discussing what makes the pendulum continue its swing past the mid-point, against gravity; see sequence 7.1.

T: Ok so it's gravity that pulls it down.
   What causes it to go up again at the   *T swings one of the pendulums.*
   other side?
ANTONY: The string/ it forces up the
   string/ going down.
T: It gets up speed going down.
.
.
.
   And it's the/ energy the force that it
   builds up that takes it up the other
   side.

These reconstructive paraphrases demonstrate another function of the 'feedback' stage of IRF sequences; they provide an opportunity for the teacher not only to confirm what the pupils say, but to recast it in a more acceptable form, more explicit perhaps, or simply couched in a preferred terminology. The most extensive reconstructions occurred during the second of the pendulum lessons, when the teacher was recapping (via the familiar sorts of IRF elicitations) on the material covered in lesson 1. Both teacher and pupils took advantage of the opportunity to reconstruct a more acceptable version of events. Contextual to sequence 7.10 below, each pair of pupils was in the process of recalling in turn their main empirical findings. Here we have Jonathan's version.

Sequence 7.10   Recapping the main empirical findings

T: Jonathan/ you and Lucy.
JONATHAN: Well we tried different
   weights/ on the end of the/   *Pauses, points to pendulum.*
   on the end of the pen thing whatever
   you call it.
T: And how did you change the weight?
   What did you use?
JONATHAN: Erm/ washers.   *Points with pencil at pendulum*
                                                  off screen right.

T: That's right yes.
JONATHAN: And did them at the same
   height each time/ and then/ they all
   came out/ the same.
T: Which surprised you didn't it?
JONATHAN: Yeh.   *Jonathan nods.*

The most notable reconstruction in sequence 7.10 is Jonathan's declaration that he and his partner had varied weight alone, that they changed the number of washers 'and did them at the same height [i.e. angle] each time'. As we noted in chapter 6, Jonathan and Lucy actually altered angle as well as weight, a fact that the teacher chose consistently to ignore, and it was never established whether or not they had used the proper controls when altering the two variables. By the time we came to lesson 2, the importance of altering variables one at a time had been grasped, and pupils and teacher were prepared to collude in a blatant revision of what had actually occurred. Similarly, Jonathan's confirmatory response to the suggestion that the results surprised him was a direct contradiction of his declaration in lesson 1 (see sequence 7.5) that the results were just as he had predicted. Indeed, he goes on in lesson 2, shortly after sequence 7.10, to articulate the reconstructed hypothesis: 'I thought it might go faster because it has a different weight.' Whatever the truth of the matter, the experimental findings have now become jointly understood as results that disconfirmed a hypothesis. Perhaps Jonathan was originally unwilling to admit to what may have seemed at the time an error of judgement, that he had made a false prediction. In any event, by lesson 2 he has chosen to confirm the teacher's prompted question ('Which surprised you didn't it?') that the results were unexpected. Certainly, it is far more acceptable to have one's hypothesis scientifically disconfirmed than simply to have made an error of judgement.

Another notable piece of reconstructive recapping occurred in lesson 2, when teacher and pupils were recalling the experiment that varied angle of swing:

Sequence 7.11   Reconstructing a principle of equal intervals

T: Right we started off at/ what was this one?

T indicates leftmost position on x-axis of graph displayed on OHP.

SHARON: Forty degrees.

T: Forty?

T pointing to next position (55°).

SHARON: Fifty-five degrees.

T: Yes.

T pointing to 70°, then to 85° marks on x-axis of graph.

SHARON: Seventy degrees and eighty-five degrees.

T: Yes/ erm/ did you follow any particular pattern? Is there any reason why you chose those angles or did you just sort of chalk/

SHARON: Fifteen degrees' difference.

T: Good girl fifteen degrees' difference between the two. That's valuable when you're doing an experiment/ to try and establish some sort of a pattern/ in the numbers/ or the erm timing or/ whatever it is that you're using. Try and keep the pattern the same/ the **interval** the same/ for example between the degrees.

T looking around group, using upturned hand with finger tips joined (precision gesture).
T holds palms of hand a fixed interval apart and moves them sideways through the air.

It would appear from sequence 7.11 that Sharon and Karen chose angles that were equal distances apart, 15°, as a matter of proper scientific procedure. In fact, as sequence 7.12 (from lesson 1) demonstrates quite clearly, the four angles were first marked without measurement on the top of the pendulum, and then, only after the experiment was completed, were they estimated, under the teacher's guidance, to be equidistant at intervals of 15°. Sharon and Karen had in fact determined their various angles of swing earlier in the lesson by uncalibrated trial and error, constrained by the angles at which the string was found to snag on the pendulum upright.

Sequence 7.12   How the equal intervals were measured

SHARON: We're stuck.

T: You're stuck Sharon?

T gets up and moves round table to Sharon and Karen.

SHARON: We're going to find ⌈ (. . .)
T: ⌊ What
 love?

T moving into position in front of Sharon and Karen's pendulum.

SHARON: I'm going to find the angles/ and/

T: The angles that you've ⌈ used
KAREN: ⌊ We can't get
 the protractor on there.

Karen pointing to top plate of pendulum where lines are marked at different angles.

T: Well what I always do in cases like that I usually guess.

Sharon turns away laughing.

KAREN: I know that that one's roughly ninety degrees.

Karen pointing to the uppermost line.

T: What one would that one be Karen?

KAREN: That's roughly ninety degrees.

Karen still pointing.

T: Roughly/ is it **quite** ninety or would it be   more/ less?

KAREN: Not quite/ just less I think.

T: So what then?

KAREN: Just/

SHARON: Eighty-five?

Sharon to Karen.

KAREN: Yeh.

T: Come on then/ eighty-five/ Now what

Sharon, T and Karen bend forward, watching as Sharon writes on her notepad.

about this one at the bottom then? That's ninety.

T points in turn to bottom line and then to top (90°) line.

KAREN: That one's ninety. That one's roughly forty-five.

Karen points appropriately, to top and bottom lines in turn.

T: More or less than forty-five?

KAREN: Less.

T: Less than forty-five so/

KAREN: Forty.

T: Forty.//

> *Rising intonation; all bend forward and watch again as Sharon writes on pad.*

And what about the ones in between?

> *T and Karen look up at top plate.*

KAREN: Well/ that's going to be/

> *Karen points to third line down.*

SHARON: That one will be seventy then//

> *Sharon points up towards second line down, then writes on pad.*

KAREN: So that one must be about/

> *T walks over to Antony and David as Karen and Sharon work out the remaining angle, between 70° and 40°.*

SHARON: Thirty.

KAREN: Thirty-five?

> *(Note that 30° and 35° are both less than 40°; these impossible estimates were later replaced by the figure '55°'.)*

The notion that four equidistant intervals were used to measure angles of swing was constructed during the first lesson out of a mixture of the casual positioning of marks on the pendulum and prompting by the teacher, and it was later reconstructed in the discourse of lesson 2 as a scientific principle constraining the proper conduct of experiments. The way in which the intervals were actually arrived at was never articulated. It would clearly be false to place too much emphasis on the importance of what pupils learn simply from their own activity and experience, even when working in pairs or groups. What really matters is the interpretation put upon that experience, the words that define and communicate it, the principles encapsulated in the words. And it is largely the teacher who provides those words while eliminating others from the common vocabulary, governing the discursive process in which particular descriptions and versions of events are established as the basis of joint understanding.

One of the teacher's most powerful means of imposing her definition of how things should be interpreted was through the use of implication and presupposition. Simply by assuming that a particular interpretation was correct, by not raising it as an open issue, she was able to keep a close constraint on the direction of the pupils' thinking. For example, Antony and David were the pupils who altered the one effective variable, length of string. Contrast her questions to Sharon and Karen ('What are you finding? Any results at all Sharon?') with the question to Antony and David: 'Now is it the shorter string which is going faster or the longer string?' While Sharon was offered the possibility of denying that she was finding any results at all, with Antony and David the presupposition was that strings of different length go faster or slower, the question being which length produced a faster speed. David's answer duly obliged: 'No the shorter one is going faster.'

We stressed in chapter 5 that it is an essential feature of educational discourse, indeed of discourse in general, that it is always predicated on contextual assumptions of some sort. In school classrooms, these contextual assumptions constitute the body of common knowledge and thought which is in the process of creation as lessons proceed. But contextual assumptions do not have to involve information or ideas that have previously been explicitly communicated. Information can be *introduced* into a conversation through its role as an implicit context for what is explicitly stated. The implicit part of a message can be recovered from the situational context and from what is explicitly said, and this again is a normal feature of everyday discourse. If someone asks us in the street for directions to the nearest post office, we would have reasonable grounds for assuming that they want to go there, do not know the way, and so on. The use of presuppositional implication in educational contexts has a pedagogic function over and above its uses in many other contexts (though much persuasive rhetoric, propaganda, advertising, and so on, clearly works in a similar fashion); it serves to introduce certain items of knowledge and assumption as things to be accepted without question, as understood but not on the agenda for discussion or disagreement, and, in a more general sense, is therefore available to the teacher as an instrument of control over what is known and understood.

A particular instance of implicit teaching occurred when the teacher introduced preferred terminology, scientific jargon such as 'mass' and 'momentum'. Sometimes these terms would be introduced through what we may call 'direct teaching', where the teacher explicitly introduced the words, defined them and encouraged the pupils to use them. At other times new terms of reference were introduced by elicitation, or cued elicitation, as was the case with the terms 'momentum' and 'acceleration' in lesson 2 ('Does anyone know the word for it when you get up speed/ as in a car when you press the pedal?'). Sequence 7.13 shows how various terms were introduced simply by the teacher's using them in an understood context, as an alternative, implicitly preferred vocabulary.

Sequence 7.13   Acquiring a shared vocabulary: teacher's usage

(Video camera concentrating on T's actions; pupils sometimes unidentified.)

T: Yes. Let's have a closer look at this one. Right. Now then. What does the   *T takes off the pendant she is wearing and puts it on the table.*

pendulum have to have to be a
pendulum?
BOY: String.
T: A string/ yes. In this case it's a/   *T holds pendant chain up.*
PUPILS: Chain.
T: Chain/
So it has to be suspended doesn't it?   *T raises and suspends pendant*
                                                by its chain.

BOY: A weight.
T: It has to have a weight doesn't it/ a
mass at the end which this one has.
OK?/ Right/ let's have a closer look at
mine. Is it a pendulum// now?   *T lays pendant flat on table,*
                                                looks at Lucy.
LUCY: No.   *Rising intonation (signalling 'is*
                                                this the answer you want?').
T: You agreed Jon?   *Jonathan nods.*
LUCY: Mm.
T: Not./ What does it have to do then to
be a pendulum?
BOY: Be straight.
T: It has to be straight.   *T straightens the pendant's*
                                                chain, still flat on table.
Is it a pendulum now?   *Pupils shake heads.*
PUPILS: No.
GIRL: Hanging.
T: It's got to hang.   *T lifts pendant and holds chain*
                                                stretched out between her two
                                                hands.

GIRL: Hang straight.
BOY: Hang straight down ⌈ from one
finger.
T: ⌊ Why isn't it
a pendulum now?
SAME BOY: ⌈ 'Cause it won't swing.   *Boy quiet, almost mumbles.*
T: ⌊ You've said it's got to have
a weight on the end/ You've said that
it has to have a string to be suspended
and it **has**.// Why isn't it a pendulum
then?
KAREN: It has to hang straight down.
T: It has to hang straight down Karen/
there it is/ so that's right isn't it? So it   *T holds pendant string in the*
has to/   *finger and thumb of one hand,*

*suspended now in a straight
vertical line with the pendant at
the bottom.*

hang from a fixed point./

*T points to fingers holding chain
with free hand.*

It has to be suspended/
from a string or a chain or whatever/
and it has to have a mass at the end.
Right/

Runs hand down chain.

While the pupils have used everyday terms such as 'weight' and 'hang straight down from one finger', the teacher herself not only has used these terms, but has also introduced the more technical jargon 'mass', 'suspended' and 'from a fixed point' (see sequence 7.1, where the teacher elicits the term 'accelerate' to replace Antony's expression 'it forces up the string/ going down'). Having established the various component attributes of a pendulum, the teacher then recaps these with the pupils:

Sequence 7.14   Acquiring a shared vocabulary: pupils' usage

T: Now what did we say that they had to
have Jonathan? A pendulum?

*Jonathan is next to his
pendulum.*

JONATHAN: A weight at the bottom.
T: Yes and yours **has**/ OK? And yours is
a washer.
JONATHAN: Mm.
T: Right. David what else does a
pendulum have to have?
DAVID: A mass.
T: Jonathan's mentioned that.
DAVID: A string.
T: A string or a chain or some means of
suspending the mass/ of hanging it
down.
Whoops/

*Pendulum topples and is caught
by Sharon and Antony; all
laugh.*

Right/ and Antony what was the third
thing it had to have?
ANTONY: Suspended.
T: Right./ From?
ANTONY: A fixed point.

The pupils have quickly grasped the new terminology introduced by the teacher, and have begun to use it themselves. It is not clear that they immediately understood what it all meant. David's suggestion 'a mass' is ambiguous between his not understanding that 'mass' means something equivalent here to 'weight', and his sense that the teacher simply prefers the term 'mass', which makes it worth mentioning. Despite the absence of direct teaching – the teacher has not explicitly taught these terms, nor required or overtly encouraged the pupils to adopt them – they have become common terms of reference to signal common understanding. Simply by using the terms in a context in which they could be understood, in this case as alternatives for everyday words used by the pupils, the teacher has managed to induct the pupils into a shared scientific discourse, a shared frame of reference and conception. Indeed, this is probably the best description we could offer of the nature of the sort of teaching and learning that we have examined in the last three chapters: it is all about the induction of children into the academic world of knowledge and discourse inhabited by the teacher. It is a process of cognitive socialization through discourse, a process akin at least as much to general behavioural and ideological socialization as to the cognitive psychological notions of mental growth or development.

Classroom discourse and classroom knowledge

In the 'traditional' classroom in Britain, the pupils passively received the teacher's communicated wisdom. They were required to remain largely silent until invited to speak, to speak only to the teacher, and to learn by rote a large number of pieces of factual knowledge – from the dates of succession of the kings and queens of England to the correct spellings of words, the number of hundredweights in a ton and the multiplication tables. Under the influence of psychological theory and research (mainly Piaget's), together with changes of educational ideology, primary education in Britain has been largely transformed along more 'progressive' lines. It is understood that learning by rote is not the same as achieving understanding, and that children learn best when they are actively involved with the subject matter, rather than passively immersed in teacher talk. Although these are, we think, undoubted improvements on the traditional methods of teaching, they still give rise to problems of their own, some of which we have tried to describe in the last two chapters.

One general finding that surprised us was the extent of control exercised by the teacher, even in lessons that were characterized by the more progressive sorts of teaching. In the pendulum lessons, for example, the pupils worked in small groups, subdivided into pairs of pupils working jointly on each pendulum, discovering through their own activities the principles that govern the motion of pendulums. At first sight, the teacher's role appeared to be essentially facilitative, shaping the general direction of the lesson, but largely relying on the pupils themselves to invent hypotheses, procedures and criteria for testing, performing the experiments themselves and making their own observations and measurements. On closer examination, the extent of teacher control became clearer. As we have demonstrated in this chapter, the freedom of pupils to introduce their own ideas was largely illusory; the teacher retained a strict control over what was said and done, what decisions were reached, and what interpretations were put upon experience.

We are, of course, wary of generalizing from a small sample of classroom discourse to an analysis of the general state of British primary education. That is not our purpose, and this is the reason why we have not coded and counted the various types of phenomena we have identified. Such a procedure would lend itself to the sorts of statistical comparisons between different classrooms and schools that our research was not designed to achieve. Rather, we have chosen to subject small samples of classroom discourse and activity to close quantitative analysis, in the hope of discovering in that discourse clues to how knowledge is actually built and shared between teacher and pupils.

Nevertheless, the discovery of an overwhelming sense of control by the teacher, in setting the agenda, determining in advance of the lesson what the knowledge outcomes should be, and, in general, expressing the authoritative social role of teacher in terms of epistemic as well as behavioural control, is a discovery that others too have made. Some, such as Edwards and Furlong (1978), base their analysis on classroom discourse as we have done. Others use more specific and quantified linguistic indices. Feldman and Wertsch (1976), for example, measured the frequency with which American teachers used a set of auxiliary verbs that express degrees of uncertainty (may, might, could, etc.). They found a greater use of them in the staffroom than in the classroom; classroom talk was judged to be authoritative, certain of its facts, and 'closed' in comparison to the more open, hypothetical and uncertain talk between teachers.

Our findings suggest these main conclusions about the educational processes we have observed:

1 *Experiential learning and teacher control.* Despite the fact that the lessons were organized in terms of practical actions and small-group joint activity between the pupils, the sort of learning that took place was not essentially a matter of experiential learning and communication between pupils. The role of the teacher was crucial throughout, both in shaping the general pattern and content of the lesson, and in producing the fine-grained definition of what was done, said and understood. The pupils were in no sense left to create their own understandings and interpretations.

2 *Ritual and principle.* While maintaining a tight control over activity

and discourse, the teacher nevertheless overtly espoused and attempted to act upon the educational principle of pupil-centred experiential learning, and the importance of pupils' engagement in practical activity and discovery. This led to the pupils' grasp of certain important concepts being essentially 'ritual', a matter of what to do or say, rather than 'principled', i.e. based on conceptual understanding. Particular sorts of classroom discourse that appeared to underlie the creation of such procedural knowledge included a heavy reliance on 'cued elicitation', together with an overriding concern to conduct the lessons in terms of getting through the set of planned activities, rather than, say, making sure that a planned set of concepts were understood by everyone. The sheer extent of teacher control over activity, discourse and interpretation was also likely to have contributed to the fact that the pupils' understanding of the lessons often became a matter of knowing what was done (or, at least, the official reconstructed version of this), and what one was required to say.

3 *Language and the socialization of cognition.* We have concentrated on the 'content' of knowledge and discourse, on what was said and done, the words used, the concepts at issue, the actions performed. Others have looked largely at the 'form' of classroom discourse, either its sociolinguistic structures (e.g. Sinclair and Coulthard 1975; Mehan 1979), or its relations to formal properties of thought, such as logical reasoning abilities (Walkerdine 1984). The overriding impression from our studies is that classroom discourse functions to establish joint understandings between teacher and pupils, shared frames of reference and conception, in which the basic process (including the problematical features of that process) is one of introducing pupils into the conceptual world of the teacher and, through her, of the educational community. To the extent that the process of education can be observed taking place in the situated discourse of classrooms, it is on our evidence essentially a process of cognitive socialization through language.

The relation of power and control to the creation of joint understandings is both problematical and of great importance. According to Habermas (1970, p. 143), 'pure intersubjectivity' is achieved only under conditions of 'complete symmetry in the distribution of assertion and disputation, revelation and hiding, prescription and following, among the partners of communication'. But education is inherently concerned with introducing children and adults into a pre-existing culture of thought and language. However active a part pupils are allowed to play in their learning, we cannot assume that they can simply reinvent that culture through their own activity and experience. It is necessarily a social and communicative process, and one which has as an inherent part of it an asymmetry of roles between teacher and learner. Pre-school cultural learning, and especially the learning of a first language, has been described by Lock (1979) as a process of 'guided reinvention'. In schools the power asymmetry is more marked; schooling is compulsory, separated from life at home, more formal, and with a more arbitrary syllabus. Many children go unwilling to school. Teachers are often perceived primarily as sources of punishment (Hood, McDermott and Cole 1980). If the educational process is not to be completely compromised by the asymmetry of teacher and learner, then we need to develop an understanding of the process which recognizes and encourages that asymmetry in a manner that fosters rather than hinders learning.

Part of the problem for pupils is that much of the process remains mysterious to them. In however friendly and informal a manner, they are frequently asked to do things, learn things, understand things, for no apparent reason other than that it is what the teacher wants them to do. The goals and purposes of the lesson are not revealed. Indeed, neither often are the concepts that the lesson may have been designed to 'cover'. In the ethos of pupil-centred inductive learning, it is not acceptable to tell the pupils what they were supposed to discover for themselves, even after they have completed the various activities involved. Recall from chapter 4 (p. 53) the interviews with the children who had done the 'desert island' simulation exercise, in which we asked them what they thought the lesson had been about, and what they thought they were supposed to learn from it. Their answers showed that most of them made sense of it as survival training, something which might be of practical use to them should they ever find themselves marooned. A lesson that had been devised to help the pupils conceptualize aspects of the society in which they lived served only to teach them what a peculiar sort of existence one would have living on a desert island or in Africa.

The major components of the teacher–pupil learning process as we have presented it are present in Vygotsky's conception of it. The asymmetry of teacher and learner is essential to the 'zone of proximal development', and so also is the notion of control. Children do not simply acquire knowledge and vocabulary. They acquire at the same time the capacity for self-regulation. Just as verbal thought originates as social discourse, so self-regulated behaviour begins with the regulation of one's behaviour by other people. The successful process involves a gradual handover of control from teacher to learner, as the learner becomes able to do alone what could previously be done only with help. In formal education, this part of the process is seldom realized. For most pupils, education remains a mystery beyond their control, rather than a resource of knowledge and skill with which they can freely operate. The contrast between formal schooling and first-language learning is stark, as Bruner (1985) and others have pointed out. Here, for example, formal education is contrasted with learning to play peekaboo:

the mother initially enacts the entire script herself and then the child takes an increasingly active role, eventually speaking all the parts initially spoken by the mother. The contrast between such learning environments and the classroom is striking. In school lessons, teachers give directions and children nonverbally carry them out; teachers ask questions and children answer them, frequently with only a word or a phrase. Most importantly, these roles are not reversed. . . . Children never give directions to teachers, and questions addressed to teachers are rare except for asking permission. (Forman and Cazden 1985, p. 344)

A successful educational process is one which transfers competence to the learner. It is almost as if formal education, for most pupils, is designed to prevent that from happening.

8
Conclusions and implications

We shall begin this final chapter by summarizing the main points we have made in the book so far.

1 We have adopted a perspective on human thought and understanding which emphasizes their basis in social relations and communication. Knowledge and thought are not just to do with how individuals think, but are intrinsically social and cultural. We have therefore focused on what we call 'common knowledge', looking at how this is constructed through joint activity and discourse.

2 Through discourse and joint action, two or more people build a body of common knowledge which becomes the contextual basis for further communication. Overt messages, things actually said, are only a small part of the total communication. They are only the tips of icebergs, in which the great hidden mass beneath is essential to the nature of what is openly visible above the waterline. This is why *context* and *continuity* are essential considerations in the analysis of discourse.

3 'Context' is essentially a mental phenomenon. Things 'out there' become contextual only when they are invoked – that is, referred to, assumed or implied in what is communicated. The very act of naming things, or of assuming shared understandings of them, makes their reality for communicators a social and conceptual one, rather than one of

simple physical existence in the surrounding world. Context *is* the common knowledge of the speakers invoked by the discourse. It is problematical both for the participants and for any observing investigator. Participants' conceptions of each other's mental contexts may be wrong or, more likely, only partially right. The investigators similarly have the problem of determining what is contextual. Any physical set of circumstances could lend itself to an infinity of possible shared conceptions and relevances, and, in any case, the mental contexts of conversational communication are by no means restricted to the physical circumstances of acts of speech. 'Continuity' is likewise problematical because it too is mental (or, more accurately, inter-mental). Continuity is a characteristic of context, being context as it develops through time in the process of joint talk and action. It exists as shared memory and intention, the conceptions and assumptions that participants hold, of what they have done and said, of its significance, of what the interaction is all about and of where it is going.

4 One important function of education may be described as *cognitive socialization*. The particular research that we have discussed in this book has examined some features of this process within one particular cultural setting, that of some English primary classrooms. Within a society the education system has its own epistemological culture. This culture, and the institutional framework within which children are educated, are what distinguish education from other kinds of cultural learning. Teachers have the task of 'scaffolding' children's first steps towards and into this culture, of supervising their entry into the universe of educational discourse. This is done by creating, through joint action and talk with the child, a contextual framework for educational activities. One of the main purposes of education is thus to develop a common knowledge. This is a problematical process, not only because the creation of successful discourse is in itself problematical (involving as it does the development of adequate context and continuity), but also because education is necessarily ideological and predicated upon social relations in which power and control figure largely. The extent to which educational knowledge is made 'common' through classroom discourse is one measure of the effectiveness of the educational process. The importance of a teacher–child asymmetry of power also makes problematical one of the major goals of education – the eventual 'handover' of control over knowledge and learning from the teacher to the child, whereby the pupil achieves autonomy.

5 Educated discourse is not talk which is 'disembedded' from context and which differs from less elevated forms of discourse by being more explicit. On the contrary, it is talk which relies for its intelligibility on speakers' access to particular, implicit contextual frameworks. The discourse of educated people conversing about their specialism –

mathematics, philosophy, literary criticism or whatever – is explicit only to the initiated.

6 An important part of the contextual basis of classroom discourse is a body of rules which define educational activities and which are required for successful participation in educational discourse. These *educational ground-rules* have both social and cognitive functions. They represent both a set of social conventions for presenting knowledge in school, and also a set (or sets) of cognitive procedures for defining and solving problems. These rules are problematical for both teachers and pupils, for reasons which stem from the fact that they normally remain implicit. They form part of the 'hidden agenda' of school work which is rarely, if ever, available for scrutiny and discussion by teachers and children together. This means that they are tacitly contextual, and participants in education rarely check the adequacy of their assumed shared understanding of the requirements or purpose of their mutual pursuit. It is also difficult for teachers, or pupils, to judge the educational value of these rules in any general sense, or to assess the appropriateness of applying any particular rule or subset of rules to a particular activity or problem. Furthermore, we have argued that the maintenance of the tacit/implicit status of these rules is itself a tenet of the dominant pedagogy or educational ideology.

7 We have drawn a rather simple, but useful distinction between different kinds of educational knowledge. There is knowledge which is essentially procedural, routinized, expedient; we have called this *ritual knowledge*. There is also knowledge which is explanatory and reflective, which is not tied to specific courses of action; we have called this *principled knowledge*. A problematical aspect of education is that even well-intentioned joint action and discourse will not necessarily ensure that teachers and pupils establish a common understanding of both procedures and principles. The ritual–principle distinction is also one that we have tried to relate to matters of educational ideology and the practices that derive from it.

Two of the theoretical perspectives that have most influenced our analysis have been those of Lev Vygotsky and of Jerome Bruner. Bruner's recent writings serve as an excellent starting point for a discussion of some points that we have raised in our own study.

A dialogue with Jerome Bruner

Jerome Bruner (1983b, 1986) has recently been taking stock of a remarkably fruitful life's work on the nature of the human mind and its development in children, and on the process of education. In *Actual Minds, Possible Worlds* (1986) he remarks on a development in his own thinking: 'I have come increasingly to recognize that most learning in most settings is a communal activity, a sharing of the culture' (p. 127). Bruner's words, as usual, carry a great deal of wisdom. His depiction of the nature of education is intended to be both descriptive and prescriptive. He is interested not only in what education is, but also in what it could be. He is particularly clear on what it should not be – the notion of education as the transmission of a body of unchanging facts, from teacher to passive pupil, is clearly inappropriate. Bruner prefers the notion of culture (and therefore of education) as a 'forum', in which teacher and learners engage in a negotiation of shared meaning, the teacher interacting with her pupils in an essentially Vygotskyan manner, guiding them through successive zones of proximal development:

> It follows from this view of culture as a forum that induction into the culture through education, if it is to prepare the young for life as lived, should also partake of the spirit of a forum, of negotiation, of the recreating of meaning. But this conclusion runs counter to traditions of pedagogy that derive from another time, another interpretation of culture, another conception of authority – one that looked at the process of education as a *transmission* of knowledge and values. (1986, p. 123)

Much of our discussion of classroom talk has been an investigation of the problematics of this process. But the lessons we have examined were by no means the old-style didactic sort; they were the modern sort, characterized by exploration and discovery, joint activity and talk, scaffolded learning, and an educational ideology – notwithstanding Piaget's influence – not far removed from Bruner's own. A similar notion of education as a negotiation of meanings between teacher and pupils is characteristic of Hugh Mehan's work (Mehan 1979; Griffin and Mehan 1981), on which Bruner draws. It is an excellent depiction but, as we have stressed, an idealized one. Our own depiction has been of a more compromised process, where the negotiation is a rather one-sided affair in which the teacher's role as authoritative bearer of the ready-made knowledge simply finds alternative, more subtle means of realizing itself than the crudities of brute 'transmission'. Perhaps it is itself a cultural difference between Britain and the United States, whether of the classrooms studied or of the investigators themselves; in either case, our analysis of the compromises of the newer pedagogy clearly echoes that of another British study (Edwards and Furlong 1978). The process that Bruner describes is indeed the one that we have investigated. We have simply been at least as interested in its problems and difficulties as in its actual or possible achievements.

It appears to be a major issue for research and theorizing about Vygotsky's 'zone of proximal development' that there occurs within pedagogic activities a tension between the demands of, on the one hand, inducting children into an established, ready-made culture and, on the other hand, developing creative and autonomous participants in a culture which is not ready-made but continually in the making. An emphasis on one aspect or the other is what characterizes the familiar dichotomies of educational ideology, between transmissional teaching and the child-centred approach, 'traditional' and 'progressive' education, and so on. The value of Vygotsky's and Bruner's approach is to see the dichotomy as false, to stress the participatory, future-orientated process of culture and education. This is what Bruner's notion of a 'forum' implies. Peg Griffin and Michael Cole similarly merge description with idealization:

> Social organization and leading activities provide a gap within which the child can develop novel creative analysis . . . a zoped [zone of proximal development] is a dialogue between the child and his future; it is not a dialogue between the child and an adult's past. (Griffin and Cole 1984, p. 62)

We agree with Bruner's emphasis on the communal basis of knowledge and thought, a view that he uses to judge different pedagogies in terms of the sorts of thought and understanding they may be expected to foster. Bruner depicts knowledge and the educational process as essentially rhetorical:

> the language of education, if it is to be an invitation to reflection and culture creating, cannot be the so-called uncontaminated language of fact and 'objectivity'. It must express stance and counter-stance and in the process leave place for reflection, for metacognition. It is this that permits one to reach higher ground, this process of objectifying in language or image what one has thought and then turning around on it and reconsidering it. (1986, p. 129)

The expression of stance and counter-stance is again a negotiative depiction of education, a rhetorical, argumentative meeting of minds in which what is 'known' is merely what is claimed by somebody: it is open to scrutiny. And the scrutiny is a social process, not merely one of individual discovery but one of sharing, comparing, contrasting and arguing one's perspectives against those of others. We have commented on the difficulties that teachers may face in achieving such aims, against the easier demands of power and expedience, and supported by an ideology which encourages leaving children to discover things for themselves. But Bruner's statement offers other insights.

The notion of a metacognitive 'turning around on' one's own conceptions is surely a reference to that famous passage in Bartlett's classic *Remembering*, in which he ponders on the relation between memory and consciousness:

to go to that portion of the organized setting of past responses which is most relevant to the needs of the moment . . . an organism has somehow to acquire the capacity to turn around upon its own 'schemata' and to construct them afresh. . . . It is where consciousness comes in; it is what gives consciousness its most prominent function. I wish I knew exactly how this is done. (Bartlett 1932, p. 206)

As we have argued elsewhere (Edwards and Middleton 1986), the key to the process of remembering may well be the sort of discursive meeting of minds that Bruner writes of. The psychological study of cognition and of cognitive development has concentrated for several decades on how knowledge and thought are represented in the mind of a decontextualized 'lone organism', the individual experimental subject. We must surely now seek the essence of human thought in its cultural nature, its communicability, in our transactions with other people. The process of education, as Vygotsky and Bruner have always recognized, is at the heart of all that.

Let us pursue Bruner's statement about metacognition a little further. The phenomena that we have discussed in separate chapters, those of contextual embeddedness and of principle and ritual, may now be seen as closely related. In chapter 5 we contrasted our view of the inherent context-embeddedness of educated thought with various depictions of educated thought and talk as being particularly abstract, disembedded, universalistic or context-free. In chapter 6 we presented a distinction between kinds of knowledge characterized as 'ritual' or 'principled'. We are now in a position to take those analyses a step further. We can do this by redefining the notion of disembedded knowledge, which we have criticized, as being better conceived in terms of principled understanding. What distinguishes principled knowledge is not mere disembeddedness but reflectiveness. It is abstract not in the sense of being context-disembedded, but in the sense of being transcendent, applicable to many particular problems and contexts. It is a form of understanding that lends itself to reflective self-awareness, to 'metacognition'. Again, Bruner puts it well: 'Much of the process of education consists of being able to distance oneself in some way from what one knows by being able to reflect on one's own knowledge' (1986, p. 127).

This is not the same thing as abstractness, at least not in the sense that others following Piaget have defined it, exemplified best by the closed-system tautologies of mathematics and formal logic. Rather, it is a function of the development of self in relation to others, a process which George Mead (1934) also wrote of, in which we achieve higher-order perspectives on our own knowledge and position (or 'stance'), through interacting and talking with others. (Ironically, especially in earlier writings on the topic of egocentric thought and speech, Piaget himself advocated the importance of an argumentative meeting of minds in the development of objectivity and rational thought.) Bruner expresses in autobiographical terms something like the conception of reflective awareness that we are searching for:

> I do not think that my interest in theater and literature has made me more *abstract*. Instead, it has joined me to the possible worlds that provide the landscape for thinking about the human condition as it exists in the culture in which I live. (1986, p. 128)

Principled understanding is not so much disembedded as superordinate. It derives from and belongs to a rich cultural setting from which it cannot be divorced, a universe of educated thought and discourse (indeed, a 'forum', in Bruner's terms) in which the process of education, at its best, invites us to take part.

Some educational and psychological implications

So far as the educational implications of the research can be summarized, they fall into two categories. First, there are the benefits to be gained from observing and analysing the educational process as situated discourse – that is, applying the approach and methods we have used to examine classroom communication critically. Second, there are the consequences of questioning the adequacy of an accepted psychological model of cognitive development and learning, which legitimizes dominant educational ideologies and is used to justify particular educational practices. We shall consider each in turn.

By looking at education as situated discourse, as a process whereby teachers and children act and talk together to some supposed common purpose, the researcher (who may also be the teacher) can more easily identify ways in which, and occasions on which, this purpose is achieved or lost. Particular strategies for introducing topics, leading discussions, relating talk to action, consolidating shared experiences, resolving misunderstandings, and so on, may be developed with greater confidence. We have suggested elsewhere some ways in which practising teachers can begin to do this (Mercer 1985). But the acquisition of this kind of analytic technique by teachers would best be done through the specialized use of video and audio recordings of teaching practice as part of initial and in-service training. Simply 'sitting in' on other teachers' lessons, or having access only to transcripts, would not be enough. Suitable audio-visual equipment is now common in schools and colleges of education, and is even used in some institutions for analogous purposes (e.g. 'micro-teaching' analysis and social skills training), so technical matters should pose no intractable problems. There is, however, still much for us to do before feeling confident in detailing the form any such scheme should take.

It is difficult to summarize the educational implications of abandoning an individualistic perspective on the development of knowledge and understanding, and taking up instead a psychological viewpoint which gives primacy to culture and communication (a goal pursued notably by Michael Cole and his colleagues at the Laboratory of Comparative Human Cognition at San Diego). One implication would seem to be that 'learning failures' are not necessarily attributable to individual children or teachers, but to the inadequacies of the referential framework within which education takes place. In other words, they are failures of context. These might be locatable in particular events within the dynamics of discourse in a particular classroom over a given period of time, or attributable to inherent, permanent features of the process of teaching and learning, as tacitly defined by participants who must invoke their own conceptions of education to make sense of what they do. Good teaching will be reflexive, sensitive to the possibility of different kinds of understanding. It may be pursued through the careful creation of context, a framework for shared understanding with children based on joint knowledge and action which provides its own rationale for present activity and a strong foundation for future developments. This contextual edifice is the 'scaffolding' for children's mental explorations, a cognitive climbing-frame – built by children with their Vygotskyan teacher – which structures activity more systematically than the discovery sandpit of the Piagetian classroom. Talk between teachers and children helps build the scaffolding; children's activity, even 'discovery', in the absence of such a communicative framework may, in cognitive terms, lead nowhere. And if teachers insist on retaining tight control, dominating the agenda and discussion, determining in advance what should happen and what should be discovered, then even their more successful pupils will remain 'scaffolded' like some supported structure, unable to function independently or outside the precise context and content of what was 'done' in the classroom.

As far as implications for psychological research are concerned, it is hard to see how research that tried to address the issues set out above could be pursued by a researcher who equated empirical investigation in psychology with experimentation. As we have seen, the taproots of our approach lie in revelations about the ambiguities inherent in experimental tasks and the implications these have for the interpretation of experimental results (see, for example, Donaldson 1978; Labov 1972; Rogoff and Lave 1984; Cole and Means 1981; Neisser 1982). If we are interested in discourse and learning in real-life settings, we cannot expect to achieve much if we expressly remove the setting, or elicit from subjects only a limited set of predetermined responses. The research we are pursuing and advocating is probably neither easier nor harder to do than experimentation. It differs fundamentally by giving greater priority to relevance and less to control. At the time of writing, the kind of psychological research we would most like to be engaged in or read about would be studies of situated discourse in other social settings outside formal education, of people developing shared understanding in their pursuit of other purposes and in different cultural contexts.

We see our analysis as having implications for the study of cognitive development, and in particular for understanding the relations between discourse and learning and between knowledge and action. By looking at learning from a theoretical perspective which does not assume the overriding supremacy of action over talk, or which defines learning purely in terms of individual cognitions, one gains new insights into the inherently social, cultural and communicative basis of human cognition and learning. These insights – into how adults structure children's learning, how children interpret terms, tasks and activities, how teachers and pupils succeed or fail in establishing a mutuality, a shared universe of discourse – are valuable in themselves. But they can also be used to demonstrate the value of a general theoretical approach to cognitive development, to thought and language, which incorporates this more particular perspective on formal teaching and learning. We have argued that such an approach is more easily drawn from the work of Vygotsky and Bruner than from that of Piaget.

However, rather than simply recasting the process of classroom learning into Vygotskyan or Brunerian terms, we have sought to do so in a manner which raises the problematical nature of the process. If teachers and pupils are to engage fruitfully in scaffolded learning, then there are key features of the learning processes that we have observed which need to be emphasized and examined. These include the following:

1 There appears to be a fundamental dilemma for our teachers – that of balancing the conflicting demands of, on the one hand, a child-centred ideology of learning and, on the other hand, an essentially socializing role as the society's agents of cultural transmission in the context of a system of compulsory education. The pupils have to be seen to be learning the right sorts of things, but at the same time to be discovering them for themselves. The dilemma is resolved in ways that may make the educational process a more difficult one than the ideal of scaffolded learning would define as necessary. Pupils have to divine as best they can the unspoken and implicit ground-rules of the system, and must learn how to extract meaning from the teacher's hints and clues, how to play the classroom game. The child-centred ideology needs to be replaced with one that emphasizes the socio-cultural and discursive bases of knowledge and learning.

2 All of classroom education is conducted against a background of

implicit rules, assumptions and knowledge. To some extent this is natural and inevitable; the construction of context and continuity is, as we have emphasized, an intrinsic characteristic of education. But some things that could usefully be explicated remain unspoken. It appears to be a valued and common practice that teachers will conduct an entire lesson, or series of lessons, and never feel it appropriate to tell the pupils why they are doing particular activities, or where it all fits into what they have done and will do next. This appears to be no accidental state of affairs. The avoidance of explicit communication of the goals and contexts of class-room activity is a consequence of teachers' educational ideology – that pupils are essentially individuals in pursuit of a realization of their own individual potentials, that they are not to be 'told' things, that they should learn things for themselves.

3 The notion of experiential learning is clearly inadequate as a description of what actually happens in classrooms, and inadequate also as a pedagogic principle upon which to found pedagogic practice. The experiences and activities of the classroom are made meaningful by the sense made of those things by classroom talk. When teachers go out of their way to avoid offering to pupils overt help in making sense of their experiences, the consequences may be that the usefulness of those experiences is lost, or that teacher and pupils resort to more surreptitious means of communicating what is conventional sense. So we find teachers asking questions and miming the answers. For many pupils, learning from teachers must appear to be a mysterious and arbitrarily difficult process, the solution to which may be to concentrate on trying to do and say what appears to be expected – a basically 'ritual' solution. A greater emphasis on the importance of language and communication in creating a shared conceptual sense of the meaning and significance of experience and activity may help to make classroom education a more open and explicit business, and therefore a less mysterious and difficult process for pupils.

It seems to us that, despite practical constraints and resource limitations which must continually frustrate their intentions, the British primary school teachers we have observed try in good faith to carry out their interpretation of the progressive style of education advocated by the Plowden Report. This is their educational ideology, a set of beliefs about how children's cognitive development and learning are best assisted. They have good reasons for relying upon it, because it is an educational approach based on sensible criticisms of traditional didactic teaching methods, advocated by a high-status committee of educationists and legitimized by the most widely accepted theory of cognitive development. We believe along with other critics (e.g. Donaldson 1978; Walkerdine 1984), however, that the time is ripe for a reappraisal of this ideology, which remains dominant in British primary education. This is largely because the Piagetian theory upon which it stands has not withstood recent critical attacks; it no longer justifies educationists' trust. It encourages a pedagogy which overemphasizes the individual at the expense of the social, which undervalues talk as a tool for discovery, and which discourages teachers from making explicit to children the purposes of educational activities and the criteria for success. There is an alternative psychological approach which we believe offers more now to teachers and researchers, as we hope we have shown.

that their presence as observers must in some way influence what is observed. But, in the event, we felt that our recorded lessons were no less successful as examples of teaching and learning than those that took place normally in our absence. We were encouraged in this belief by the reflective judgements of the teachers concerned. Indeed, in terms of the teachers' preparedness and expertise in their chosen topics, the lessons were probably somewhat exemplary. Since we have concentrated as much on the problematics of the lessons as on their achievements, the possibility that the recorded lessons may have been idealizations of normal practice only strengthens the force of those analyses.

In order to build as complete a record as possible, we also collected copies of all reading materials used in the lessons, and of any pieces of writing done in connection with the work. Finally, we made audio recordings of interviews with the teachers and pupils after the lessons. These interviews were designed to provide us with additional information on how much mutual understanding had been reached between teachers and pupils, and to help highlight possible areas of misunderstanding.

Our fieldwork design for the main phase 2 data collection was strongly influenced by the more exploratory work of phase 1, as well as by the theoretical considerations which were developing along with the work, and which are the main themes of the book. We shall outline phases 1 and 2 in turn. The videotaped classroom sessions are referred to here and in the rest of the book as 'lessons'; in each case, the recordings began and ended with the teachers' own opening and closing of the session.

Fieldwork: phase 1

This was carried out in four ILEA schools where the ILEA Learning Materials Service Mobile Video Recording Section were making recordings of good teaching practice, for use in teacher training. We obtained permission from the schools concerned to 'sit in' on this activity, and to carry out follow-up interviews with teachers and pupils after the recordings had been made. Our pattern of activity in each of these schools was:

1 Preliminary visit to explain that we were studying classroom communication and wanted to interview, after the videotaped lesson, the teacher and five or six pupils who had been working together. During this visit we asked the teacher about her aims for the lesson which was to be recorded.
2 Second school visit to observe the lesson being videotaped by the ILEA crew. The recordings lasted between 40 and 60 minutes.
3 Viewing of the video material. We identified key points in the lesson about which we wanted to question the teacher and pupils.

Appendix:
Outline of the research project

JANET MAYBIN

The fieldwork on which this book is based was part of an ESRC-funded research project on 'The development of joint understanding in the classroom'. For that project, we carried out work in two distinct phases. Phase 1 involved three primary schools and one comprehensive school in the Inner London Education Authority (ILEA), and phase 2 was a more detailed study in four primary and middle schools in Buckinghamshire. The discussion in this book draws mainly on material from one of the phase 1 schools (the 'island' lesson) and three of the Buckinghamshire schools ('pendulums', 'computer graphics programming' and 'clay pots'). To protect the anonymity of the schools and pupils, fictitious names have been used throughout.

The aim of the fieldwork was to collect detailed information about the discourse and activity that constituted a number of classroom lessons. We wanted to make a qualitative analysis of this discourse, in the hope of uncovering clues to how knowledge is built and shared between teachers and pupils. We decided that video recording was essential to a close examination of the interrelatedness of talk and contextual activity. Inevitably, the presence of a video camera operator, sound recordist and the team's project officer would have been a distraction to pupils, and would have made teachers nervous, especially in the early stages of recording. Indeed, most social scientists have now resigned themselves to the fact

4 Third school visit to carry out the interviews. Pupils were withdrawn from class for this purpose, and teachers were interviewed during lunchtime or after school. Interviews with pupils lasted about 10–20 minutes, and those with the teachers 20–30 minutes.
5 Study of videotape transcripts provided by the ILEA recording team, and transcription and study of interview tapes.

The island lesson

The data discussed in chapter 4 came from one ILEA school. This school served an inner-city catchment area, and contained a wide ability range of pupils from varying social and racial backgrounds. A class of 9–10-year-olds were using curriculum materials developed in the ILEA along the authority's written guidelines for teaching social sciences in the primary school. The guidelines advised that children's learning in this area should be planned around certain key concepts, such as those of social control, conflict, co-operation, the division of labour and the distribution of power and authority. This learning, however, must also be experiential:

> Children will come to understand an abstract concept by approaching the practical application of it in their everyday experience. Concepts cannot be understood by being memorized like facts. The value of working in this way will be lost if children do not discover concepts and the relationships between them for themselves. It is not intended, therefore, that a teacher should tell children that there is a concept – like the division of labour – and begin to teach it from there. The abstract conceptual term may eventually be introduced by the teacher – but after the child has understood what it means by observing and investigating examples of it. (Social Sciences Curriculum Guidelines, ILEA, 1980)

The project on which pupils were working involved their being 'wrecked', in small groups on desert islands. Once on their island, each group was given a series of discussion cards (from the teaching kit *People Around Us: Friends* (London: A. and C. Black, 1979), produced in association with ILEA). The ensuing group oral work was supported by writing, art, craft, drama and whole-class discussion. For example, each group made a model of their camp on the island, and each pupil kept a detailed diary recording the outcome of group discussions, and the day's imaginary events. Before the videotaped lesson, the class had already spent some time on the project, and as a result each group had elected a captain, and made out a list of rules for their life together on the island.

The pupils stayed in their small discussion groups for about 45 minutes, and then for a further 15 minutes their teacher drew them together to compare the decisions that different groups had reached, and to try to encourage pupils to relate their island work to social issues back home.

She questioned them on how they thought that the English school attendance law might be altered, and whether they thought it was a good law. We conducted our follow-up interview with the teacher informally, using the following items as a checklist of issues to be covered:

What did you hope the children would get out of the lesson?
Were these aims realized?
  If not, why not?
  If so, how can you check?
What do you feel that the children learned in this lesson?
Do you ever discuss concepts explicitly with them?
Why the desert island simulation? Why not another setting, e.g. the playground at break?
Why 'bring the children home' at the end and ask the question about the school attendance law? What issues did you hope that the pupils would raise?
Do the children know what a law is?
Did any points arise from the lesson that you felt would be important to follow up later?

Four pupils from one of the subgroups (the Yellow Sands group) were also interviewed individually in a similar fashion, on the following points:

What they thought the lesson was about.
Whether they found any part of it confusing.
What they thought was the purpose of the lesson, and of the island work in general: what they thought the teacher wanted them to learn.
What they thought the teacher hoped they would learn from the lesson.
How they thought they might be able to use what they were learning in the island lessons in their everyday lives.
What is a law? Where does it come from? Can it be changed?
Which bit of the work they enjoyed most.
Which bit of the work they enjoyed least.
Which of the various island roles and tasks they would like to do now.

The following points concerning the design of phase 2 of the fieldwork emerged from the phase 1 study:

Age of subjects. The 8–11-year-olds appeared to provide the best focus for our investigation. Pupils in this age group engage in a wide range of classroom activities, and have had at least three years' experience of the primary school's ethos and procedures. On the other hand, they have not yet had to face the new set of expectations and procedures which will confront them on entry to secondary school.

Classroom observation. We decided that issues of content and continuity in classroom discourse could be examined more closely if we collected video recordings of three consecutive lessons where a teacher was working with one small group of pupils. These lessons should occur on three separate days, probably within one school week. This would give us more information about how teachers built on work from previous lessons, how children referred back to what they had already learnt, and how references to work yet to be tackled were followed up. The most fruitful classroom situation to explore in more depth, therefore, would be one where a teacher introduced a new concept or technique to the pupils in the first session we recorded. We could then study how the teacher and pupils moved towards shared understandings in the subsequent classroom work. It was a pattern of work in primary classrooms that we had already observed, where a teacher would start an activity with one group, leave them to get on with some follow-up work, and then talk with them a day or so later to check on their progress. Recording this process on videotape would inevitably mean collecting material with an above-normal proportion of teacher–pupil interaction, but, on the other hand, this was the very process in which we were most interested.

Interviews. In the phase 1 schools, we interviewed some pupils individually, some in pairs and some in groups. Pupils were most forthcoming and articulate when interviewed on their own, so we planned to carry out separate interviews with all pupils in phase 2 of the fieldwork.

Fieldwork: phase 2

The schools we used in Buckinghamshire had each had some earlier contact with the Open University, because a member of staff either had followed an OU course or had helped test out trial OU course materials. The three schools drawn on for this book took children from socially mixed catchment areas and contained a wide ability range of pupils, almost all of whom were white. The 'pendulums' and 'computer graphics' lessons came from relatively new schools which were built to service the rapidly growing city of Milton Keynes, and the 'clay pots' lessons came from a school on the outskirts of a small established town at one end of Milton Keynes city. Our procedure for each of these schools was as follows:

1 Initial contact via a letter to the headteacher, which explained that we wanted to videotape a teacher working with a group of children aged between 8 and 11 years, over three 20–30 minute sessions. We suggested that it would be most useful to us if the teacher was introducing a new topic or concept in the first session, then doing more work on it with the pupils in the next two sessions, but that we did not want teachers to embark on anything outside the range of their normal classroom work.

2 First school visit. Having secured the headteachers' agreement we visited each school and met the member of staff who had agreed to work with us. We explained to this teacher that we were interested in observing classroom talk, and discussed with her the work to be recorded. In every case this was planned round the teacher's current classroom concerns, and usually focused on a new topic which she (all phase 2 teachers happened to be women) had been planning to introduce to the class. At this first meeting, we also obtained the teacher's permission to interview her and each of the six pupils in the group with which she was working, after the three sessions had been recorded.

3 Video recording of first session.

4 Video recording of second session.

5 Video recording of third session.

6 Viewing of data, and drawing up of interview questions.

7 Audio recording of interviews with teacher and pupils. The teachers' interviews lasted 20–30 minutes, and those with the pupils 10–20 minutes.

8 Audio transcription of video and audio tapes.

9 Reviewing of video tapes and addition of context notes to transcripts. (The context notes to the right of the transcribed dialogue record physical props, movements, activities and gestures necessary to understanding the discourse.)

10 Further study of complete transcripts.

Table A.1 provides a brief summary of the content of each of the phase 2 lessons.

The pendulum lessons

As chapters 6 and 7 draw most heavily on these lessons, a more detailed description of the work on pendulums is chosen here as an example of the phase 2 research.

Pupils in a class of 10–11-year-olds had been working at their own pace through the school maths textbook (*Mathematics for Schools*, Level II, Book 8, second edition (London: Addison-Wesley, 1981). One pupil, Antony, had already passed the page with its exercise on pendulums, while several others were just about to reach it. The book explained how to construct a pendulum, how to measure and count periods of swing, and suggested using twenty swings and varying the length of the string and noting its effects. In conversation with the teacher before the recorded sessions, she explained why she wanted her pupils to do more than the rather mechanical exercise described in the textbook. She thought pupils should discover the properties of a pendulum for themselves, by testing out a number of different hypotheses. In this way they would 'learn the

Table A.1 Phase 2 schools: classroom topics

	Lesson 1	Lesson 2	Lesson 3
Pendulums	The teacher talked to the group about what a pendulum was, then split the 6 pupils into 3 pairs to investigate whether the angle of swing, the weight of the bob, or the length of the string, respectively, made any difference to the speed of the pendulum. Results were put into matrices, and their significance discussed.	The pupils had plotted the results of their investigations on graphs, using acetate paper. Teacher and pupils discussed these findings, using an overhead projector to study the graphs together.	In the class PE session, their teacher helped the pupils to test out the properties of a 'human pendulum', using the ropes and bars.
Clay pots	Pupils learned how to make a clay thumb-pot, modelling their own pots under the teacher's guidance and demonstration.	Children made a clay hedgehog or pig, with the teacher's guidance.	Children studied pictures of animals, and then made one of them in clay.
Computer graphics	Using the school's new microcomputer, the teacher showed 4 pupils how to instruct it to draw an F shape. Pupils then tried to write a program for a T shape, using forwards, backwards and angle-turning commands. They tried out and discussed these programs with the teacher, who then helped them write one for an equilateral triangle.	Pupils tried out and modified the programs for octagons, isosceles and equilateral triangles which they had written for homework. The teacher helped them write a program to draw a hexagon, and showed them how to use the 'pen off' and 'pen on' commands, and how to store a program.	The four children with their teacher introduced the work they had been doing to two other pupils from the class, and helped them to write and try out (run) programs for various shapes.

Note: Each lesson lasted for between 40 and 60 minutes.

concept' more effectively, increase their familiarity with experimental procedures, and gain practice in building equipment. The pupils had already had some experience of investigative science, and had worked with matrices and graphs. The teacher planned to set up a lesson with a small group of six, including Antony, and the others who had nearly reached that point in the book, so that they could generate and test out some hypotheses for themselves. She was able to state in advance what those hypotheses would be. As the analysis of the lesson in chapter 6 makes clear, these plans and preliminaries on the teacher's part had a telling influence on the problematical nature of the lesson and what was achieved in it.

Pendulum lesson 1. Before the first recorded lesson, the six pupils had constructed three pendulums, using the instructions in the textbook, but adding a strong wooden frame and base (see figure 6.1, page 100). The teacher drew these pupils together in one corner of the classroom, after she had set the rest of the class off on their work. She started by telling the group a story about Galileo, who felt bored during a church service and became interested in the motion of the censers that were being swung to and fro by the altar boys. She asked the pupils to suggest naturally occurring pendulums (e.g. a pendant necklace) and discussed with them what distinctive properties a pendulum must have. The pupils were then divided into three pairs, from each of which was elicited one of the three variables that would be altered, together with its associated hypothesis:

> Changing the mass of the pendulum bob affects the time of the swing.
> Changing the length of string affects the time of the swing.
> Changing the angle of the swing affects its time.

The teacher discussed with the group how these hypotheses might be tested, and it was decided that each pair of pupils would time how long their pendulum took to complete a swing (taking an average from twenty swings), while they varied the length of the string, the weight of the bob and the angle of swing, respectively. The teacher asked the pupils to plot the results of their investigations on a matrix, using acetate paper, so that they could study them together in the next session. Pupils spent the remainder of the first lesson carrying out the practical work and recording their results. The teacher moved between the pairs of pupils, talking with each of them about their actions and findings.

Pendulum lesson 2. The teacher and the six pupils spent the second lesson grouped around the overhead projector, to study the graphs they had made of their results. The first two graphs, from pupils investigating the effects of changing the weight of the bob and changing the angle of the swing, showed points plotted along two wavering, almost horizontal lines, while the third graph, from the pupils investigating the effects of changing the length of the string, showed the points plotted along a straight diagonal line. The teacher asked each pair of pupils to report back and comment on their findings. She pointed out the difficulty of making accurate recordings without sophisticated equipment; the first two graphs should, in fact, have shown points plotted along a straight horizontal line. The teacher then moved on to discuss notions of gravity and momentum and asked the children to speculate how their pendulum might behave if transported to the moon. She also referred pupils to a recent television programme they had watched together, where the crane operator lifting a chest from the wreckage of the Tudor vessel *Mary Rose* had lowered it back into the water to reduce the swing and thus prevent damage to the chest which was in danger of being smashed against the side of the ship. Finally, the teacher showed pupils a diagram of a simple clockwork mechanism, involving a rod, bob and interlocking sprockets. Asked to guess what this was, pupils suggested a brake, a bell and, finally, a clock. The teacher went on to discuss with the children how old-fashioned clocks used to lose time in summer, because the brass of which the rod and bob were made expanded, thus lengthening the time of the swing.

Pendulum lesson 3. The third lesson we recorded was in the school hall, where the whole class was having a physical education lesson. The teacher and PE instructor helped the pupils to time each other swinging on the end of ropes, simulating the action of a pendulum. They also tried swinging from a bar with legs straight and then with legs tucked up, and observed leg-swings involved in kicking a football.

The interviews

In all of our interviews with teachers and pupils our main aim was to gain supplementary contextual information to inform our analyses of the main data, the video recordings. We talked to participants in order to elicit their ideas about the content and purposes of the activities in which they had been engaged, and to help resolve for us any ambiguities in what had actually said. In our follow-up interview with the phase 2 teachers we again used an informal conversational style of interview, with a checklist of issues and topics to be covered. Although these were planned as a set order of questions, the teachers' responses were full and dis-cursive, so that in some cases the issues to be covered were dealt with spontaneously, without having to be overtly prompted by direct questioning. All the teachers were questioned on certain general issues:

How much had the pupils done on this topic in previous lessons?
Did she assume any knowledge or experience of the topic from outside the recorded lessons?
What did she want each lesson to achieve?
How much did she think the pupils had actually learned?

In what ways did or would she be able to check on their understanding?

How did she account for the fact that some pupils generally achieve more than others?

What did she think was the essence of good teaching? Did she try in her teaching to put into practice any particular pedagogic principles?

Would the lessons be followed up in later work and, if so, how?

How did she feel about being recorded, and how did it affect her teaching, and the talk, activity and involvement of the pupils?

These questions were readily adapted to the specific content of particular lessons and series of lessons, and were supplemented for each teacher by questions that arose from the investigators' preliminary viewing of the video recordings. So, for example, the pendulums teacher was asked why she thought it would be useful to introduce ideas additional to those found in the textbook, such as the testing of hypotheses which could be predicted to be false, and the story about Galileo in church. The computer graphics teacher was asked what she thought was the value of the comparisons and contrasts that she frequently made between computers and people, and why she got the pupils to draw and measure the angles of a regular hexagon with pencil and protractor, rather than calculating them mathematically. We shall not present detailed transcriptions of the interviews here because these would not be warranted by the essentially supplementary use that we have made of the interview data in the book, which concentrates mainly on the classroom discourse.

Interviews with pupils were conducted one-to-one by the project field officer who had met them all several times and had been present during the recording of the lessons. The interviews took place after the set of three lessons had been recorded and subjected to a preliminary viewing. Again, all pupils were asked a similar set of basic questions, supplemented by specific ones relating to issues arising from the recorded lessons. The checklist for the pendulums pupils included these:

General questions:

What did they think were the main things they had learnt?

What did they think the teacher wanted them to learn in the lesson?

Did they know anything about the lesson topic prior to the lesson, from other lessons or from outside school?

Did they find anything in the lesson confusing?

Did they think that the things they did in the lesson had any relation or relevance to their everyday lives?

Specific questions:

What exactly is a pendulum?

What did they understand by 'one complete swing'?

Why did they think that old clocks with brass pendulums went faster in winter than in summer?

What was the point of doing experiments (especially when some variables were found to have no effect)?

Why did they use twenty swings?

Why had the teacher suggested altering only one variable at a time?

What did they think the following words, used in the lessons, meant?

expand
contract
suspended
mass/bob/weight
average
period
interval
co-linear

Bibliography

Austin, J. L. (1962) *How to do Things with Words*. Oxford: Clarendon Press.

Bain, A. (1879) *Education as a Science*. London: Kegan Paul.

Banks, O. (1978) 'School and society'. In L. Barton and R. Meighan (eds), *Sociological Interpretations of Schooling and Classrooms: A Reappraisal*. Nafferton: Driffield.

Barnes, D. (1971) 'Language in the secondary classroom'. In D. Barnes, J. Britton and H. Rosen, *Language, the Learner and the School*. Harmondsworth: Penguin.

Barnes, D. (1976) *From Communication to Curriculum*. Harmondsworth: Penguin.

Barnes, D. (1982) *Practical Curriculum Study*. London: Routledge & Kegan Paul.

Barnes, D., Britton, J., and Rosen, H. (1971) *Language, the Learner and the School*. Harmondsworth: Penguin.

Barnes, D., and Todd, F. (1977) *Communication and Learning in Small Groups*. London: Routledge & Kegan Paul.

Bartlett, F. C. (1932) *Remembering: A Study in Experimental and Social Psychology*. Cambridge: Cambridge University Press.

Bennett, N. (1976) *Teaching Styles and Pupil Progress*. London: Open Books.

Bernstein, B. (1971) *Class, Codes and Control*. Vol. 1. London: Routledge & Kegan Paul.

Billig, M. (1987) *Arguing and Thinking: A Rhetorical Approach to Social Psychology*. Cambridge: Cambridge University Press.

Broadbent, D. (1975) 'Cognitive psychology and education', *British Journal of Educational Psychology*, 45, 162–76.

Brown, G., and Yule, G. (1983) *Discourse Analysis*. Cambridge: Cambridge University Press.

Bruner, J. S. (1964) 'The course of cognitive growth', *American Psychologist*, 19, 1–16.

Bruner, J. S. (1971) *The Relevance of Education*. Harmondsworth: Penguin.

Bruner, J. S. (1983a) *Child's Talk*. London: Oxford University Press.

Bruner, J. S. (1983b) *In Search of Mind: Essays in Autobiography*. New York: Harper & Row.

Bruner, J. S. (1985) 'Vygotsky: a historical and conceptual perspective'. In J. V. Wertsch (ed.), *Culture, Communication and Cognition: Vygotskian Perspectives*. Cambridge: Cambridge University Press.

Bruner, J. S. (1986) *Actual Minds, Possible Worlds*. London: Harvard University Press.

Bruner, J. S., Olver, R. R., and Greenfield, P. M. (1966) *Studies in Cognitive Growth*. New York: Wiley.

Chomsky, N. A. (1968) *Language and Mind*. New York: Harcourt, Brace & World.

Cole, M. (1985) 'The zone of proximal development: where culture and cognition create each other'. In J. V. Wertsch (ed.), *Culture, Communication and Cognition: Vygotskian Perspectives*. Cambridge: Cambridge University Press.

Cole, M., Gay, J., Glick, J., and Sharp, D. W. (1971) *The Cultural Context of Learning and Thinking*. New York: Basic Books.

Cole, M., and Means, B. (1981) *Comparative Studies of How People Think: An Introduction*, Cambridge, Mass.: Harvard University Press.

Cole, M., and Scribner, S. (1974) *Culture and Thought*. New York: Wiley.

Cooper, B. (1976) 'Bernstein's codes: a classroom study', *University of Sussex Education Area Occasional Paper 6*. (Also published as Supplementary Reading for *Language Development*, PE232, Block 4. Milton Keynes: Open University Press.)

Creber, P. (1972) *Lost for Words*. Harmondsworth: Penguin.

de Laguna, G. A. (1927) *Speech: Its Function and Development*. New Haven, Conn.: Yale University Press.

Denscombe, M. (1985) *Classroom Control: A Sociological Perspective*. London: Allen & Unwin.

Desforges, C. (1985) 'Training for the management of learning in the primary school'. In H. Francis (ed.), *Learning to Teach: Psychology in Teacher Training*, Lewes: The Falmer Press.

Dillon, J. T. (1982) 'The effect of questions in education and other enterprises', *Journal of Curriculum Studies*, 14, 2, 127–52.

Donaldson, M. (1978) *Children's Minds*. London: Fontana.

Driver, R. (1983) *The Pupil as Scientist?* Milton Keynes: Open University Press.

Edwards, A. D. (1980) 'Patterns of power and authority in classroom talk'. In P. Woods (ed.), *Teacher Strategies: Explorations in the Sociology of the School*. London: Croom Helm.

Edwards, A. D., and Furlong, V. J. (1978) *The Language of Teaching*. London: Heinemann.

Edwards, D., and Goodwin, R. Q. (1986) 'The language of shared attention and visual experience: a functional study of early nomination', *Journal of Pragmatics*, 9, 475–93.

Edwards, D., and Middleton, D. (1986) 'Joint remembering: constructing an account of shared experience', *Discourse Processes*, 9, 423–59.

Featherstone, J. (1967) 'Schools for children – what's happening in British classrooms', *New Republic*, 19 August, 17–21.

Feldman, C., and Wertsch, J. V. (1976) 'Context dependent properties of teachers' speech', *Youth and Society*, 8, 227–58.

Fisher, E. J. (1972) *Learning How to Learn*. New York: Harcourt Brace Jovanovich.

Flanders, N. A. (1970) *Analysing Teacher Behaviour*. Reading, Mass.: Addison-Wesley.

Fodor, J. A. (1975) *The Language of Thought*. New York: Thomas Y. Crowell.

Forman, E. A., and Cazden, C. B. (1985) 'Exploring Vygotskian perspectives in education: the cognitive value of peer interaction'. In J. V. Wertsch (ed.), *Culture, Communication and Cognition: Vygotskian Perspectives*. Cambridge: Cambridge University Press.

Gagné, R. (1965) *The Conditions of Learning*. New York: Holt, Rinehart & Winston.

Galton, M., Simon, B., and Croll, P. (1980) *Inside the Primary Classroom* (the ORACLE project). London: Routledge & Kegan Paul.

Garfinkel, H. (1967) *Studies in Ethnomethodology*. Englewood Cliffs, NJ: Prentice-Hall.

Goody, J., and Watt, I. (1968) 'The consequences of literacy'. In J. Goody (ed.), *Literacy in Traditional Societies*. London: Cambridge University Press.

Grice, H. P. (1975) 'Logic and conversation'. In P. Cole and J. Morgan (eds), *Syntax and Semantics, vol. 3: Speech Acts*. New York: Academic Press.

Griffin, P., and Cole, M. (1984) 'Current activity for the future: the zoped'. In B. Rogoff and J. V. Wertsch (eds), *Children's Learning in the Zone of Proximal Development*. New York: Jossey-Bass.

Griffin, P., and Mehan, H. (1981) 'Sense and ritual in classroom discourse'. In F. Coulmas (ed.), *Conversational Routine: Explorations in Standardized Communication Situations and Prepatterned Speech*. The Hague: Mouton.

Habermas, J. (1970) 'Toward a theory of communicative competence'. In H. P. Dreitzel (ed.) *Recent Sociology*. New York: Macmillan.

Halliday, M. A. K. (1967) 'Notes on transitivity and theme in English', parts 1, 2 and 3, *Journal of Linguistics*, 3, 1, 37–81; 3, 2, 199–244; 4, 3, 178–215.

Halliday, M. A. K., and Hasan, R. (1976) *Cohesion in English*. London: Longman.

Hammersley, M. (1977) 'School learning: the cultural resources required by pupils to answer a teacher's question'. In P. Woods and M. Hammersley (eds), *School Experience*. London: Croom Helm.

Hammersley, M. (1980) 'Classroom ethnography', *Educational Analysis*, 2, 2, 47–74.

Hammersley, M., and Woods, P. (1986) *Classroom Studies Module*, E812. Milton Keynes: Open University Press.

Heath, S. B. (1983) *Ways with Words*. Cambridge: Cambridge University Press.

Hockett, C., and Altmann, A. (1968) 'A note on design features'. In T. A. Sebeok (ed.), *Animal Communication*. Bloomington, Ind.: University of Indiana Press.

Holt, J. (1969) *Why Children Fail*. Harmondsworth: Penguin.

Hood, L., McDermott, R., and Cole, M. (1980) ' "Let's try to make it a good day" – some not so simple ways', *Discourse Processes*, 3, 155–68.

Howe, V. M. (1974) *Informal Teaching in the Open Classroom*. New York: Macmillan.

Hudson, L. (1972) *The Cult of the Fact*. London: Jonathan Cape.

Hull, R. (1985) *The Language Gap*. London: Methuen.

Hymes, D. H. (1979) 'Language in education: forward to fundamentals'. In O. K. Garnica and M. L. King (eds), *Language, Children and Society: The Effect of Social Factors on Children Learning to Communicate*. Oxford: Pergamon Press.

Itard, J. (1806) *The Wild Boy of Aveyron*. Trans. E. Fawcett, P. Ayrton and J. White. London: NLB, 1972.

James, W. (1899) *Talks to Teachers and to Students on Some of Life's Ideals*. London: Longmans.

Kagan, J., and Lang, C. (1978) *Psychology and Education: An Introduction*. New York: Harcourt Brace Jovanovich.

Keddie, N. (ed.) (1973) *Tinker, Tailor . . . : The Myth of Cultural Deprivation*. Harmondsworth: Penguin.

Kozulin, A. (1986) 'The concept of activity in Soviet psychology', *American Psychologist*, 41, 3, 264–74.

Kuhn, T. S. (1962) *The Structure of Scientific Revolutions*. Chicago, Ill.: University of Chicago Press.

Labov, W. (1970) 'The logic of nonstandard English'. In F. Williams (ed.), *Language and Poverty*. Chicago, Ill.: Markham.

Labov, W. (1972) 'Rules for ritual insults'. In D. Sudnow (ed.), *Studies in Social Interaction*. New York: Free Press.

Leese, J. (1973) 'Origins and antecedents'. In D. and L. Myers (eds), *Open Education Revisited*. Lexington, Mass., D. C. Heath.

Leontiev, A. N. (1981) 'The problem of activity in psychology'. In J. V. Wertsch (ed.), *The Concept of Activity in Soviet Psychology*. Armonk, NY: Sharpe.

Levinson, S. C. (1983) *Pragmatics*. Cambridge: Cambridge University Press.

Lock, A. J. (1979) *The Guided Reinvention of Language*. London: Academic Press.

Luria, A. R. (1979) *The Making of Mind: A Personal Account of Soviet Psychology*. Cambridge, Mass.: Harvard University Press.

McGarrigle, J., and Donaldson, M. (1974) 'Conservation accidents', *Cognition*, 3, 341–50.

MacLure, M., and French, P. (1980) 'Routes to right answers: on pupils' strategies for answering teachers' questions'. In P. Woods (ed.), *Pupil Strategies*. London: Croom Helm.

Mead, G. H. (1934) *Mind, Self and Society*. Chicago, Ill.: University of Chicago Press.

Mehan, H. (1979) *Learning Lessons: Social Organization in the Classroom*. Cambridge, Mass.: Harvard University Press.

Mercer, N. (1980) 'Making sense of school', *New Society*, 55, 953, 324–5.

Mercer, N. (1985) 'Communication in the classroom'. In *Every Child's Language: An In-Service Pack for Primary Teachers*, P534 (Book 1). Clevedon: Multilingual Matters/Open University.

Mercer, N., and Edwards, D. (1981) 'Ground rules for mutual understanding: towards a social psychological approach to classroom knowledge'. In N. Mercer (ed.), *Language in School and Community*. London: Edward Arnold.

Merrett, F., and Wheldall, K. (1978) 'Playing the game: a behavioural approach to classroom management in the junior school', *Educational Review*, 30, 1, 41–50.

Moffett, K. (1968) *Teaching the Universe of Discourse*, Boston, Mass.: Houghton Mifflin.

Neisser, U. (1976) 'General, academic and artificial intelligence'. In L. B. Resnick (ed.), *The Nature of Intelligence*. New York: Lawrence Erlbaum.

Neisser, U. (1982) *Memory Observed: Remembering in Natural Contexts*. Oxford: W. H. Freeman.

Nuffield Foundation (1967) *Nuffield Maths Project: I Do and I Understand*. London: W. and R. Chambers/ John Murray.

Olson, D. R. (1977) 'Oral and written language and the cognitive processes of children', *Journal of Communication*, 27, 3, 10–26.

Ong, W. J. (1967) *The Presence of the Word*. New Haven, Conn.: Yale University Press.

Philips, S. (1970) 'Acquisition of rules for appropriate speech usage'. In J. Alatis (ed.), *Bilingualism and Language Contact: Anthropological, Linguistic, Psychological and Sociological Approaches*. Washington, DC: Georgetown University Press.

Piaget, J. (1969) 'A genetic approach to the psychology of thought'. In J. de Cecco (ed.), *The Psychology of Language, Thought and Instruction*. London: Holt, Rinehart & Winston.

Piaget, J. (1970) 'Piaget's theory'. In P. H. Mussen (ed.), *Carmichael's Manual of Child Psychology*. New York: Wiley.

Piaget, J. (1971) *Science as Education and the Psychology of the Child*. London: Longmans.

Plowden Report (1967) *Children and their Primary Schools*. London: Central Advisory Council for Education.

Powell, H. (1976) Unpublished B.Ed. dissertation. North-East London Polytechnic.

Prince, E. F. (1981) 'Towards a taxonomy of given–new information'. In P. Cole (ed.), *Radical Pragmatics*. New York: Academic Press.

Rogers, V. R. (1970) *Teaching in the British Primary Schools*. New York: Macmillan.

Rogoff, B., and Lave, J. (1984) *Everyday Cognition: Its Development in Social Context*. Cambridge, Mass.: Harvard University Press.

Rose, S. A., and Blank, M. (1974) 'The potency of context in children's cognition: an illustration through conservation', *Child Development*, 45, 499–502.

Rutter, M., Maugham, B., Mortimore, P., and Ouston, J. (1979) *Fifteen Thousand Hours*. London: Open Books.

Scribner, S., and Cole, M. (1981) *The Psychology of Literacy*. London: Harvard University Press.

Searle, J. R. (1969) *Speech Acts*. Cambridge: Cambridge University Press.

Sinclair, H. (1969) 'Developmental psycholinguistics'. In D. Elkind and J. H. Flavell (eds), *Studies in Cognitive Development*. Oxford: Oxford University Press.

Sinclair, J. McH., and Coulthard, R. M. (1975) *Towards an Analysis of Discourse: The English used by Teachers and Pupils*. London: Oxford University Press.

Skinner, B. F. (1968) *The Technology of Learning*. Englewood Cliffs, NJ: Prentice-Hall.

Social Sciences Curriculum Guidelines (1980). London: ILEA.

Solomon, J. (1983) 'Learning about energy: how pupils think in two domains', *European Journal of Science Education*, 5, 1, 49–59.

Stephens, L. S. (1974) *The Teacher's Guide to Open Education*. New York: Holt, Rinehart & Winston.

Street, B. V. (1984) *Literacy in Theory and Practice*. Cambridge: Cambridge University Press.

Stubbs, M. (1976) *Language, Schools and Classrooms*. London: Methuen.

Stubbs, M. (1981) 'Scratching the surface: linguistic data in educational research'. In C. Adelman (ed.), *Uttering, Muttering: Collecting, Using and Reporting Talk for Social and Educational Research*. London: Grant McIntyre.

Stubbs, M., and Robinson, B. (1979) 'Analysing classroom language'. In *Language Development*, PE 232, Block 5. Milton Keynes: Open University Press.

Taba, H., and Elzey, F. (1964) 'Teaching strategies and thought processes', *Teachers College Record*, 65, 524–34.

Tizard, B., and Hughes, M. (1984) *Young Children Learning*. London: Fontana.

Tough, J. (1977) *The Development of Meaning*. London: Allen & Unwin.

Vygotsky, L. S. (1962) *Thought and Language*. Cambridge, Mass.: MIT Press.

Vygotsky, L. S. (1966) 'Development of the higher mental functions'. In A. Leontiev, A. Luria and A. Smirnov (eds), *Psychological Research in the USSR*, vol. 1. Moscow: Progress Publishing.

Vygotsky, L. S. (1978) *Mind in Society: The Development of Higher Psychological Processes*. London: Harvard University Press.

Walkerdine, V. (1982) 'From context to text: a psychosemiotic approach to abstract thought'. In M. Beveridge (ed.), *Children Thinking Through Language*. London: Edward Arnold.

Walkerdine, V. (1984) 'Developmental psychology and the child-centred pedagogy: the insertion of Piaget into early education'. In J. Henriques, W. Hollway, C. Urwin, C. Venn and V. Walkerdine, *Changing the Subject*. London: Methuen.

Wason, P. C., and Johnson-Laird, P. N. (1972) *Psychology of Reasoning: Structure and Content*. London: Batsford.

Wells, G. (1985) *Language at Home and at School*. Cambridge: Cambridge University Press.

Wertsch, J. V. (ed.) (1985) *Culture, Communication and Cognition: Vygotskian Perspectives*. Cambridge: Cambridge University Press.

Wertsch, J. V., and Stone, C. A. (1985) 'The concept of internalization in Vygotsky's account of the genesis of higher mental functions'. In J. V. Wertsch (ed.), *Culture, Communication and Cognition: Vygotskian Perspectives*. Cambridge: Cambridge University Press.

Willes, M. (1979) 'Early lessons learned too well'. In *Language Development*, PE 232, Block 5, Supplementary Readings. Milton Keynes: Open University Press.

Willes, M. (1983) *Children into Pupils: A Study of Language in Early Schooling*. London: Routledge & Kegan Paul.

Wood, D., Bruner, J. S., and Ross, G. (1976) 'The role of tutoring in problem solving', *Journal of Child Psychology and Child Psychiatry*, 17, 89–100.

Young, M. F. D. (1971) *Knowledge and Control: New Directions for the Sociology of Education*. London: Collier-Macmillan.

Index